DRIVING

MEXICO

PRENTICE
HALL
PRESS

New York • London • Toronto • Sydney • Tokyo • Singapore

CONTENTS

Written by Mona King

Original photography by Peter Wilson

Copy editor: Janet Tabinski

Edited, designed and produced by AA Publishing. Maps © The Automobile Association 1991.

The contents of this publication are believed correct at the time of printing. Nevertheless, the publishers cannot accept responsibility for errors or omissions, or for changes in details given.

ISBN 0-13-917659-4

Published in the United States by Prentice Hall Press. A division of Simon & Schuster Inc., 15 Columbus Circle, New York, New York 10023.

Typesetting: Servis Filmsetting Ltd, Manchester, England

Color Separation: Scantrans Pte Ltd, Singapore

Printed and bound in Italy by Printers SRL

Front cover: *Cathedral at Oaxaca*

Title page: *Round Pyramid at Calixtlahuaca*

Above: *Colorful sombreros in Mexico City*

Right: *Cactus landscape in Oaxaca*

INTRODUCTION

This book is not only a practical touring guide for the independent traveler, but is also invaluable for those who would like to know more about the country.

It is divided into 7 regions, each containing between 2 and 7 tours. The tours start and finish in major towns and cities which we consider to be the best centers for exploration. Each tour has details of the most interesting places to visit *en route*. Side panels cater for special interests and requirements and cover a range of categories – for those whose interest is in history, wildlife or walking, and those who have children. There are also panels which highlight scenic stretches of road and which give details of events, crafts and customs. The numbers link them to the appropriate main text.

The simple route directions are accompanied by an easy-to-use map of the tour, and there are addresses of local tourist information centers in some of the towns *en route* as well as in the start town.

Simple charts show how far it is from one town to the next in kilometers and miles. These can help you to decide where to take a break and stop overnight, for example. (All distances quoted are approximate.)

Before setting off it is advisable to check with the information center at the start of the tour for recommendations on where to break your journey and for additional information on what to see and do, and when best to visit.

MOTORING

Documents

Most foreign licenses are valid in Mexico but European ones may be unfamiliar so it is a good idea to carry an International Driving Permit.

Bringing a car into Mexico requires motorists to be issued with a different kind of tourist card from other visitors (see **ENTRY REGULATIONS**) which ensures they cannot leave without their car.

A market selling goods in a plaza in Querétaro. Colorful woolen articles are woven in the region

Breakdowns

To help motorists, Mexico has an effective 'Green Angel' (*Angeles Verdes*) service, a fleet of white-and-green radio-dispatched emergency vehicles which patrol the roads and highways. Labor is provided free, although a tip is appreciated. Spare parts are charged at cost. If you need assistance and are not spotted, call them on 250-8221.

Accidents

If you see an accident you should not go to help, but notify the first policeman or 'Green Angel' patrol that you can find. If you move an injured person you can be accused of *mal medicina*, and if the person dies, you can even be accused of causing the death.

Speed limits

The maximum speed limit is generally 80kph (50mph). In most towns and villages the limit is 40kph (25mph); in some cities 30kph (19mph).

Speed limits posted in accordance with local regulations take precedence over those listed above.

Driving conditions

Mexico's highway system is well-developed with tolls payable for use of freeways. Away from the large centers of population, roads are quite often narrow, winding and potholed.

Most road signs use international symbols; older signs are in Spanish. A sign saying *Bordos, Topes* or *Túmulos* means that sharp bumps are built into the road to force traffic to slow down, particularly before and after most villages.

Driving tips

It is not advisable to drive at night – hazards encountered during the day (livestock on the roads, potholes etc) become worse, and roads are not lighted.

Parking is not easy in cities and if you wish to avoid being towed away, use an *estacionamiento* (parking lot).

Car rental and fly/drive

Many visitors from overseas like to fly and rent a car. This can be easily arranged as many of the international car-rental firms have offices at airports, city centers and resorts. There are many local operations, but make sure you are well insured against accidents. There are rental cars in Mexico that would not be considered roadworthy back home.

If you rent a car in Mexico City, or at any point well above sea level, and drive to lower altitudes or to sea level, the engine may start to 'ping' during acceleration. A certain amount of this is normal, because the carburetor is adjusted for rarified air at the higher altitudes. Conversely, if the car is rented at a lower altitude and goes up to the levels of Mexico City or into the surrounding mountains, it will probably perform sluggishly on hills and during acceleration. This again is normal.

Route directions

Throughout the book the abbreviation **Mex** is used for the Mexico Federal roads.

Desert driving

Before you start check that the radiator is in good condition and filled to the correct level with the proper combination of water and coolant, and that the hoses are sound.

Check the oil when you stop for fuel.

If you are traveling during the summer or if there are young, elderly or infirm persons along, consider driving in the cooler hours of early morning and evening.

Stay on main roads.

Sandstorms and rainstorms can often suddenly occur. If one does and your vision is obscured, pull off the road until it is over, but don't stop in a low place that could become flooded.

ENTRY REGULATIONS

Passports are required by all visitors except nationals of the US and Canada holding proof of citizenship.

A tourist card (FMT in Spanish) is an entry-departure document (not a visa) which must be obtained before entry into Mexico. It is issued free of charge by Mexican embassies (or consulates), tourist offices, travel agencies and airlines serving Mexico. The areas of Mexico to be visited and the length of your stay (up to 90 days) must be specified.

A visa (replacing a tourist card) is required by nationals of Australia and New Zealand.

All persons under the age of 18 years, if not traveling with **both** parents, must contact their Mexican embassy before departure.

CUSTOMS REGULATIONS

Visitors over the age of 18 years can bring into Mexico the following goods duty-free: 400 cigarettes or 2 boxes of cigars or up to 250 grams of tobacco; 3 liters of spirits or wine; a reasonable quantity of perfume or eau-de-cologne; other goods up to the value of US$300, or equivalent; one photo, movie or video camera and up to 12 rolls of undeveloped film or video casettes.

You may bring into Mexico an unlimited amount of foreign currency, which must be declared to customs on arrival. You cannot take out more than the declared amount.

EMERGENCY TELEPHONE NUMBERS

Federal Police (Highway Patrol): 684-2142
Fire: 768-3700
Green Angels (Angeles Verdes) Tourist Patrol: 250-8221
Government Police: 06
Mexico City Emergency Number: 07
Red Cross (Cruz Roja) Ambulance: (5) 557-5758 or 557-4294
Ministry of Tourism (Secretaría de Turismo) 24-hour emergency hotline: (5) 250-0123

HEALTH

There are, at present, no inoculations required to enter Mexico unless you have visited a cholera-infected area within the two weeks prior to your entry to Mexico, in which case a cholera vaccination certificate is required.

The greatest threat to health in Mexico is water – it should be boiled or sterilized. Milk should also be boiled.

Some form of health insurance is essential. Public health care can be fairly rudimentary, but on the whole, medical facilities in privately run hospitals and clinics are good.

CURRENCY

The Mexican unit of currency is the *peso*, comprising 100 *centavos*. Coins are in denominations of 20 and 50 *centavos* and 1, 5, 10, 20, 50, 100 and 200 *pesos*. Paper currency comes in 500, 1,000, 2,000, 5,000, 10,000 and 20,000 *pesos*. The *peso* is written as $. So as not to confuse it with the American dollar ($US), it is sometimes written as $MN (for *Moneda Nacional*).

Currency rates can fluctuate daily due to the *peso's* weakness against other strong currencies. Banks generally give the best rate but exchange houses *(casas de cambio)* offer competitive rates.

CREDIT CARDS

Most international credit cards are widely accepted in the larger cities and resorts.

BANKS

Normal banking hours are from 9am to 1:30pm Monday to Friday, although some branches also open from 4 to 6pm.

POST OFFICES

Post offices in large cities open between 8am and 6pm Monday to Friday. It is advisable to check, however.

Mexican postal services (*correos*) can be very slow, though fairly dependable. Air mail to the US takes around a week, and two weeks to Europe and other destinations. If mail is important, take it to the post office rather than drop it in a mailbox.

You can also buy stamps and mail letters at your hotel desk.

TELEPHONES

Long-distance and international calls in Mexico are very expensive and it is advisable to place reversed-charge calls *(por cobrar)* when calling home.

Sayil's Palacio, built in AD730, with more than 50 chambers

PUBLIC HOLIDAYS

The main public holidays when virtually everything closes are:
1 January – New Year's Day
6 January – Epiphany
5 February – Constitution Day
21 March – Benito Juárez Day
March/April – Easter – Holy Thursday, Good Friday and Easter Sunday
1 May – Labor Day
5 May – Battle of Puebla
15/16 September – Independence Day
12 October – National Day
20 November – Anniversary of the Revolution
12 December – Festival of Our Lady of Guadalupe
25 December – Christmas Day
In addition, every town or village will take at least one day off a year for a fiesta.

TOURIST OFFICES

The *Secretaría de Turismo (SecTur)* has offices *(Turismo)* in Mexico City and throughout the country. Its main office is at: Presidente Masaryk 172, 11587 Mexico City (*tel:* (5) 250-8555).

In addition there are tourist offices run by state and municipal authorities and often you will find several rival operations in the same town.

The local telephone directory gives the address and phone number of both federal and local tourist offices.

Calls out of Mexico can be placed anywhere displaying the blue-and-white *Larga Distancia* sign. Most *Telefonos* offices also offer the service. Unless you wish to make a direct-dial call, the procedure is that you dial 09 for the English-speaking international operator who connects you and presents you with a bill afterwards (you can keep an eye on the cost which clicks up on a meter).

Local calls in Mexico, if not free, are very cheap. In Mexico City, local calls from old phone booths are usually free, while new ones take coins of one *peso* or more. To make long-distance calls within Mexico dial 02 for the long-distance operator: for the international long-distance operator (English speaking) dial 09.

To call Mexico from abroad dial the international access code, plus the code for Mexico (52), followed by the area code, then the number.

Sunset on Cancún's coral-sand beach: once home to Mayas and a haven for pirates, now a top resort

ELECTRICITY

The electricity supply is 110 volts AC, 60Hz, though fluctuations in the current can occur. Sockets accept simple two (flat) pin plugs. Most North American electrical appliances can be used, but appliances from Britain, Australia and New Zealand will need a voltage transformer, unless fitted with a dual-voltage switch. A plug adaptor is also necessary.

EMBASSIES

The main embassies are all in Mexico City, though some countries have consular representatives in other large towns.
Australia – Jaime Balmes 11-B-1002, Colon Losa Morales, 11510 Mexico City, DF (*tel:* (5) 395-98-69 and (5) 395-96-69).
Canada – Schiller 529, Colon Polanco, 11560 Mexico City, DF (*tel:* (5) 254-32-88).
New Zealand – Homero 229, Mexico City, DF (*tel:* (5) 566-10-10).
UK – Rio Lerma 71, Colon Cuauhtémoc, 06500 Mexico City 5, DF (*tel:* (5) 514-33-27 and (5) 514-38-86).
Consulado (Consulate): Río Usumacinta 30, Colon Cuauhtémoc, 06500 Mexico City, DF (*tel:* (5) 511-48-80).
US – Avenida Paseo de la Reforma 305, Colon Cuauhtémoc, 06500 Mexico City, DF (*tel:* (5) 211-00-42).

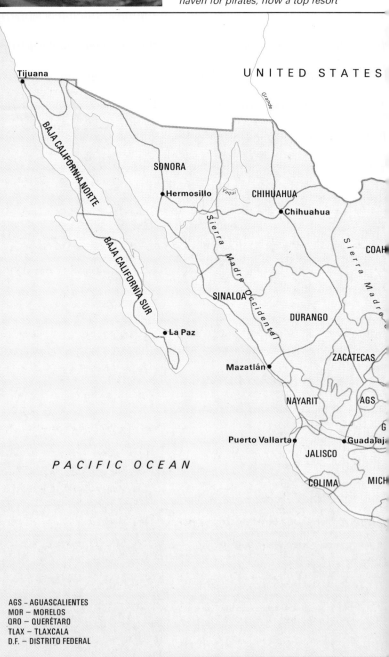

AGS – AGUASCALIENTES
MOR – MORELOS
QRO – QUERÉTARO
TLAX – TLAXCALA
D.F. – DISTRITO FEDERAL

TIME

Mexico spans three time zones. Expressed in relation to Greenwich Mean Time (GMT) these are:
Central Mexico time (GMT minus 6) – most areas in Mexico are on this time.
Mountain time (GMT minus 7) – Nayarit, Sinaloa, Sonora, and Baja California Sur.
Pacific Time (GMT minus 8) – Baja California Norte.
Daylight Saving comes into operation in some parts of Mexico during the summer, when clocks are put forward an hour. This affects the areas Coahuila, Durango, Nuevo León and Tamaulipas where local time becomes GMT minus 5, while time in Baja California Norte becomes GMT minus 7.

A small rural village, with its surrounding patchwork of pasture and cultivated land, is set amid the rugged, forest-clad terrain of the Sierra de Juárez

AMERICA

Gulf of Mexico

nterrey

NUEVO LEÓN

TAMAULIPAS

I LUIS TOSÍ

JUATO
QRO
HIDALGO
MÉXICO
CIUDAD TLAX
DE D.F
MEXICO MOR. PUEBLA VERACRUZ
PUEBLA
•Veracruz
GUERRERO
•Oaxaca
OAXACA
ulco•
CHIAPAS
TABASCO
Villahermosa
CAMPECHE
Mérida•
YUCATÁN
Cancún
QUINTANA ROO
BELIZE
GUATEMALA
HONDURAS
EL SALVADOR

USEFUL WORDS

The following words and phrases may be helpful.
Spanish English
azulejo decorative glazed tile, sometimes blue and white
caballeros gentlemen, on toilet doors
casa de cambio exchange house (money)
cenote large well for water storage
chac-mool sacrificial stone sculpture (pre-Hispanic)
damas ladies, sign on toilet door
DF Distrito Federal, often follows Mexico City
excusado toilet
ferrocarril railroad
hacienda estate
hombres men
iglesia church
malecón seafront promenade
mañana tomorrow
mariachi colorful musicians, typical of Mexico
mestizo people of mixed blood (Spanish and Indian)
palacio mansion, not necessarily royal
paseo broad avenue, walkway or pedestrian way
retablo carved decorative woodwork in churches
templo church, chapel, cathedral, convent
tianguis Náhuatl word for market
zócalo main plaza or square in any town
buenos días good morning/ good day
buenas tardes good afternoon
buenas noches good evening/good night
adios good-bye
hola hello
como está usted? how are you?
muy bien, gracias very well, thank you
buen viaje have a good journey
bien/esta muy bien good/ that's fine

CENTRAL MEXICO

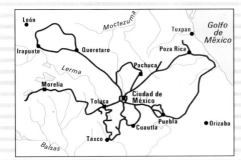

Central Mexico is one of the country's most beautiful and interesting regions, offering varying landscapes, climates and attractions. The states covered most extensively are México, Morelos, Puebla, Tlaxcala, Hidalgo and Querétaro, with the inclusion of Guanajuato, Michoacán, Guerrero and Veracruz a little further afield. The area enjoys a very favorable climate, with warm sunny days and cool evenings at the higher altitudes. The heartland of this region is a high plateau known as the Altiplano, or Mexican Highlands. Sweeping down either side are the mighty mountain ranges of the Sierra Madre Occidental and Oriental. Landscapes are constantly changing, with mountains, rolling hills and valleys, vast wooded areas, lakes and rivers, and a profusion of tropical flowers and greenery. The southern regions are dominated by spectacular volcanoes, of which the most famous are the snow-capped peaks of Popocatépetl and Iztaccíhuatl.

At the center of all this is the nation's capital, Mexico City. Back in the 14th century, the Aztec capital, known as Tenochtitlán, was built here on a lake. The city was destroyed when their powerful empire was crushed by Cortés and his soldiers in 1521. The new city built on the Aztec ruins became present-day Mexico City.

A number of relics from pre-Columbian civilizations can be seen in the area, ranging from grand ceremonial centers to small sites dotted about the countryside, although Aztec remains are minimal as so much was destroyed by the Spaniards. During 300 years of Colonial rule, new towns were constructed, with elegant buildings and beautiful churches. The central region has a rich Colonial heritage, and Mexico's loveliest cities are to be seen here. Some are real architectural jewels, with impressive mansions, squares and arcades. The region is known for the splendor of its Franciscan monasteries and numerous churches with rich baroque exteriors and exquisite gilded interiors.

The decade from 1810 to 1820 was one of bitter fighting for independence against the Spaniards. Two of the most historic centers in the region are the beautiful cities of Guanajuato and Querétaro, where important events took place during the War of Independence. Later, Querétaro was the scene of Emperor Maximilian's defeat and execution by Benito Juárez in 1867. At the outbreak of the 1910–20 Revolution, the state of Morelos saw much fighting. Many large estates were burned down by Emiliano Zapata, one of the great leaders of the movement, who rallied together the local peasants to press for land reforms.

This lovely part of Mexico caters to all tastes. Its archaeological and cultural interest combines with magnificent scenery, an agreeable climate and a delightful diversity of peoples, customs and traditions.

Mexico City:

Mexico City, the capital of Mexico, now ranks as the world's largest city, with about 18 million inhabitants. This giant metropolis spreads across the Valley of Mexico at an altitude of 2,240m (7,350 feet) encircled by high mountains. The joining of two cultures is reflected in the Mexico City of today, where old Colonial buildings are in sharp contrast to towering office blocks and hotels. The city is bursting with vitality – you feel it the minute you arrive. Streets are crowded with shops, kiosks, shoe-shine stands. Vendors might sell anything from lottery tickets to balloons. Traffic policemen trill their whistles amid chaotic traffic (pollution is a serious problem) and there is continuous activity and noise. Broad avenues and huge intersections, coupled with high sidewalks, often sorely in need of repair, discourage too much sightseeing on foot. There are some pleasant areas, however, for strolling. Mexico City's main avenue, **Paseo de la Reforma**, runs the length of the city and is one of its most attractive features. The boulevard, with a central pedestrian area, is lined with trees and flanked by modern office buildings, hotels and other structures.

A good place to start your visit is at the **Zócalo** (main square), considered the heart of the capital. Among the impressive Colonial buildings that front this vast square are the **Catedral Metropolitana** (Metropolitan Cathedral) and the **Palacio Nacional** (National Palace), which houses the Presidential offices. Inside are some outstanding murals by Diego Rivera, one of Mexico's most famous painters. Behind the Zócalo is a recently excavated zone called the **Templo Mayor** (Great Temple), showing the remains of an old Aztec temple.

The old part of town around the Zócalo is great to explore, with old narrow streets and shops crammed with silverware, jewelry and colorful Mexican goods. You can also enjoy strolling in the **Zona Rosa** (Pink Zone), just off Reforma, with its shops, boutiques and smart restaurants.

To the west of the city is beautiful **Bosque de Chapultepec** (Chapultepec Park), dominated by the **Castillo de Chapultepec** (Chapultepec Castle). Once the home of Emperor Maximilian and his wife Carlotta, it is now an interesting museum. No visitor should miss the famous **Museo de Antropología** (Museum of Anthropology), also in the park. It is considered one of the finest in the world for its unique collection of pre-Columbian art.

The city abounds with lively bars and restaurants, many of which offer some form of musical entertainment in the evenings. Take in the **Palacio de Bellas Artes** (Palace of Fine Arts) to see a performance of the colorful Ballet Folklorico or go down to Plaza Garibaldi to hear the mariachis play.

Mexico City, a city of 18 million, lies at an altitude of 2,240m (7,350 feet) in a great valley bounded by mountains on three sides. Its climate is spring-like all year round

4 days – 579km (357 miles)

COLONIAL GEMS & RELICS OF THE PAST

Ciudad de México (Mexico City) • Cuernavaca
Xochicalco • Laguna de Tequesquitengo • Taxco
Las Grutas de Cacahuamilpa • Ixtapan de la Sal
Tenancingo • Malinalco • Teotenango
Tianguistengo • Metepec • Toluca
Nevado de Toluca • Calixtlahuaca
Desierto de los Leones • Ciudad de México

This circular tour starts from Mexico City and takes you south and west of the capital, through the states of Morelos, Guerrero and Mexico. It is a particularly lovely route, passing over spectacular mountains and valleys, through rolling hills and pine forests. This temperate zone has a warm, pleasant climate and a profusion of flowers and semitropical vegetation. Included in the itinerary are beautiful Colonial towns, an old hacienda, a modern spa resort and typical little Mexican villages renowned for their handicrafts. You will get to explore some extraordinary caves and a number of fascinating pre-Columbian sites dotted about the region.

The cool, inviting gardens of the Hacienda Cortés offer respite for the weary, while a graceful St Anthony holds the Child Jesus

i Avenida Presidente Masaryk 172, Ciudad de México

*Take **toll highway 95** south for 85km (52 miles) to Cuernavaca.*

Cuernavaca, Morelos

1 The pleasant little resort town of Cuernavaca is the capital of Morelos. With its idyllic climate and abundance of flowers and foliage, it is often referred to as the 'City of Eternal Spring'. Many Mexicans from the capital have second homes here, with sumptuous gardens and swimming pools, usually concealed behind high walls. The town is dominated by the **Catedral de San Francisco** (Cathedral of St Francis), a massive fortress-like construction founded by the Spanish conquistador Hernán Cortés in 1529. At the rear of the cathedral is the **Capilla de la Tercera Order** (Chapel of the Third Order), with a lovely baroque façade. Nearby are the attractive **Jardines Borda** (Borda Gardens). Standing on one side of the **zócalo** (main square) is the former **Palacio Cortés** (Palace of Cortés), which now houses the **Museo Cuauhnácuac** (Museum of Cuauhnácuac). Of particular interest among its collection of paintings and sculptures is a mural by Diego Rivera, one of Mexico's most famous artists. Painted in 1929 and 1930, it depicts the Independence Wars, the Mexican Revolution and the history of Cuernavaca.

For a change of pace, spend some time sitting at one of the little cafés or restaurants on the main square. The

The interior of Cuernavaca's cathedral is unexpectedly modern

scene of much lively activity, it is always teeming with local vendors.

The town celebrates a number of special festivals, including Carnival (Mardi Gras) the week before Ash Wednesday, the Festival of Flowers on 2 May, Día de San Isidro Labrador on 15 May, and the Nativity of the Virgin Mary on 8 September.

ℹ️ Ignacio Comonfort 2 Altos Casa de las Campañas

*Continue south on **Mex 95** to Alpuyeca tollbooth. Turn northwest onto **Mex 421** and take turning to Xochicalco, 37km (22 miles).*

Xochicalco, Morelos

2 The pre-Columbian ruins of Xochicalco ('house of flowers' in Náhuatl, the ancient language of the Aztecs) lie on a hill overlooking a vast plain. Little is known of its early origins, but it is believed to date back to around AD500 and excavations indicate influences of various cultures. The major structure of this fortress-like site is the **Pirámide de las Serpientes Emplumadas** (Pyramid of the Feathered Serpents), suggesting influences of the Toltec, Mayan and Zapotec civilizations. The pyramid is decorated with carved reliefs of feathered serpents surrounding glyphs and seated figures. Other pyramids and structures can also be seen within the area. Down the hill is the entrance to a network of underground passages leading to a chamber with an orifice, believed to have been used by ancient priests for astrological purposes. Excavations have also revealed a ball court, possibly the earliest in Mexico.

*Return to Alpuyeca and take **Mex 8** southeast to Laguna de Tequesquitengo (Lake Tequesquitengo).*

Laguna de Tequesquitengo, Morelos

3 This small, pleasant resort attracts many Mexicans who come here at weekends to swim, sail and enjoy various water sports. The agreeable climate, pleasant surroundings and its proximity to the capital combine to make it a highly desirable vacation spot. Equipment for aquatic sports can be rented in the little town of Tequesquitengo, on the eastern shore of the lake. Horseback riding is also available. While you are in the vicinity, visit the **Hacienda Vista Hermosa**, an old sugar mill built some 400 years ago, and now a hotel. Have a look around the lovely old building, take a stroll in the gardens and, if time permits, relax with a drink by the large swimming pool, built under an ancient aqueduct.

*Return west to **Mex 95**, continue south, then branch off west to Taxco.*

Taxco, Guerrero

4 Taxco is considered by many to be the prettiest town in all of Mexico. A real Colonial gem, it has been designated a National Monument to preserve its character. Your first glimpse is of the town sprawling up the mountainside. With its whitewashed

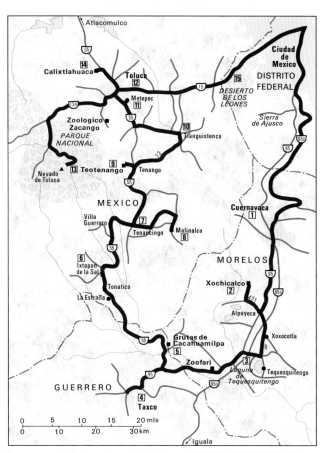

houses, red-tiled roofs and cobble-stoned streets winding their way up the hillside, it is a true delight. Famous for its silver industry, it is a shopper's paradise with a tremendous variety of attractive goods. Although known principally for its exquisite silverware, which is crafted locally and recognized for the originality of its designs, the choice of handicrafts is very tempting. Make sure you visit the local **market**, which starts off behind the cathedral and continues down several flights of steps, with colorful displays of goods all the way down. The **zócalo** (main square) is charming, with the typical Mexican bandstand in the middle, shady trees and benches around for relaxing. With its steep, narrow streets, Taxco is more suitable for walking than driving. The town is dominated by the beautiful **Iglesia de Santa Prisca** (St Prisca Church), which overlooks the main square. It was built by the 'Silver King', José de la Borda, as a token of gratitude for the fortune he made from the silver mining in Taxco. With its twin spires, lovely, local pink stone and richly decorated interior, it is considered one of the finest examples of baroque architecture to be found in Mexico.

Worth a visit, too, is the **Museo de Arqueología Guillermo Spratling** (William Spratling Museum), which houses a collection of pre-Columbian pieces, paintings and exhibits that depict the history of the Taxco area and its people.

ℹ️ Avenida John F Kennedy 28

*Return on **Mex 95** northeast, then join **Mex 55** heading northwest for 35km (19 miles) to Las Grutas de Cacahuamilpa (Caves of Cacahuamilpa).*

FOR CHILDREN

4 Two places will have a special appeal for children. About 33km (20 miles) east of Taxco is the **Zoofari Zoo**. Its 70 hectares (173 acres) reproduces natural habitats for a large collection of mammals, birds and amphibians.

12 Southwest of Toluca is the **Zoológico Zacango** (Zacango Zoo) set in the gardens of an old hacienda. A great variety of animals roam around freely, and others are housed in separate areas. A cinema, originally the chapel of the old hacienda, has continuous film shows on animals, ecology and nature and there is a large area set aside with games and amusements.

FOR HISTORY BUFFS

4 The original settlement of Tlachco ('where the ball game is played') was a center of the Tlahuícas and was situated a few miles from present-day Taxco. This was later taken over by the Aztecs, destroyed by the Spaniards after the Conquest and rebuilt. The town's real development started when a Frenchman, José de la Borda, came here in 1716 and founded the San Ignacio silver mine – so began the business for which Taxco became famous. De la Borda amassed a fortune and built the beautiful Santa Prisca Cathedral as a token of gratitude.

4 Some very colorful and attractive festivals are celebrated in Taxco. On Palm Sunday, processions re-enact the arrival of Jesus on a donkey, followed by a crowd of 'penitents'. Celebrations follow during Holy Week. On 1 December is the annual Silver Fair when the best pieces of silver from all over the country are exhibited, and from 16 December to Christmas the streets are full of people carrying candles from one church to another, with images of Joseph and Mary, ending up with parties in each other's homes.

Las Grutas de Cacahuamilpa, Guerrero

5 Las Grutas de Cacahuamilpa are the largest caves in central Mexico and can only be described as spectacular. Lighting effects in different hues bring out the fascinating forms of the stalactites, stalagmites and boulders, many of which are named according to the shapes created. Tours depart at intervals and it is best to join one. The full visit normally takes a little under two hours. Be sure to wear comfortable shoes, as there is quite a bit of scrambling about involved.

*Continue northwest on **Mex 55** to Ixtapan de la Sal.*

Ixtapan de la Sal, Mexico

6 Ixtapan de la Sal is a popular spa resort of attractive hotels, swimming pools and thermal springs, built in classical Greek and Roman styles. Cascading fountains, fresh green lawns and flowers give the complex a cool, refreshing appearance. About 11km (7 miles) south off **Mex 55** are the **Grutas de la Estrella** (Star Grottoes). They are at their most dramatic during July to September when waterfalls cascade among spectacular rock formations.

*Continue on **Mex 55** north for 33km (20 miles) to Tenancingo.*

Tenancingo, Mexico

7 Tenancingo ('place of little walls' in Náhuatl) is renowned for its *rebozos* (long scarves) and wooden furniture. Make a brief stop to have a look around. It is best to visit on a Thursday or Sunday, when there is an open-air *tianguis* (market). Take a look at the 18th-century **Convento del Santo Desierto de Tenancingo** (Carmelite

Reaching heavenwards, Taxco's parish church dominates the town. Its style is Churrigueresque, a florid extension of baroque

convent), where many of the *rebozos* are produced. It is located just outside the town on a plateau of the Nixcongo mountains and is surrounded by a thick wall. In one of the chapels is a statue called **El Cristo de las Siete Suertes** (Christ of the Seven Lucks).

Take the road 17km (10 miles) east to Malinalco.

Malinalco, Mexico

8 Wander around the little village of Malinalco, with its whitewashed houses, tiny narrow streets and 16th-century Augustinian **Convento de Santa Monica**, before proceeding to the ruins. You can park your car a mile or two from the center of the village. From here it is quite a steep climb up to **Cerro de los Idolos** (Hill of Idols) to the pre-Columbian site of Malinalco, set among forests and rugged rocks. Excavation indicates the area was inhabited by various tribes before it was taken over by the Aztecs, who started building new structures of importance in the early 1500s. Of special interest is the impressive circular **Temple of the Eagles and Jaguar**, one of the few pre-Hispanic structures hewn from the rock. A stairway flanked by a number of interesting sculptures leads to the entrance of the temple, which is shaped in the form of an open-mouthed serpent.

*Return to Tenancingo and continue on **Mex 55** north. Near Tenango, on the west side of the road, stop at Teotenango.*

Teotenango, Mexico

9 The pre-Columbian site of Teotenango ('place of the divine wall') dates back to around the 7th century AD and probably reached its peak between the 10th and 12th centuries. It is believed to have been an important ceremonial center of the Matlatzinca tribe, although evidence suggests there were influences of previous civilizations. The site has been well preserved and its pyramids, palaces and various structures cover a large area. The **museum** has an interesting collection of archaeological finds from the region, including two notable exhibits; the statue of Ehécatl (god of the wind) from Calixtlahuaca and a carved wooden drum found in Malinalco.

*Take the connecting road, **Mex 13**, northeast to Tianguistengo.*

Tianguistengo, Mexico

10 This charming village is renowned for its handicrafts and has an interesting market on Tuesdays that offers a wide choice of products from throughout the Toluca Valley. Buildings of note include the 18th-century parish **Church of Nuestra Señora del Buen Seco**, with an extravagantly baroque façade, and the handsome **Palacio Municipal** (Town Hall). Tianguistengo is surrounded by lovely countryside and is a good center for excursions into the interior.

*Return west. Join **Mex 55** and continue northwest. Turn off to Metepec, about 2km (1 mile).*

Metepec, Mexico

11 Metepec is famous for the production of its gaily colored clay figures, in particular the imaginative sculptures known as the **Arbol de la Vida** (the 'Tree of Life'). The idea was originally brought to Mexico by the Spaniards (influenced by the Moors) and developed by the potters in Metepec. The village is picturesque, with a small main square flanked by a Franciscan convent dedicated to **San Juan Bautista** (St John the Baptist) and the **Templo del Calvario** (Temple of Calvary).

*Continue on **Mex 55** northwest to Toluca, 7km (4 miles).*

Toluca, Mexico

12 Toluca is the capital of the state of Mexico and the highest-altitude city in the country. It lies in the Valley of Mexico, which is dominated by the majestic, snowcapped Nevado de Toluca volcano, also known as Xinantécatl. Although mainly a busy commercial center, the town is pleasant, with attractive gardens and squares. Its main attraction is the famous Friday **market**, considered one of the largest and most colorful in Mexico. Indians from all over the region gather here by the hundreds to buy and sell. There is a tremendous variety of goods on show and the scene is lively, noisy and highly enjoyable, so try to arrange your arrival for a Friday. It has a pleasant zócalo (main square), surrounded by arcades, overlooked by the **cathedral**, built in the 19th century in neoclassical style. On the north side stands the **Palacio de Gobierno** (Government Palace), which was built in 1872. Take a look at the **Museo de Bellas Artes** (Museum of Fine Arts) and the **Casa de las Artesanías** with handicrafts from the region.

i Avenida Vicente Villada 123, Col Centro

*Take roads southwest onto **Mex 134**. Turn south after 18km (11 miles) to Nevado de Toluca.*

SCENIC ROUTES

The stretch of road on the first part of the tour becomes very scenic once you leave Mexico City behind. There are beautiful views of two volcanoes, Popocatépetl and Iztaccíhuatl, as you ascend the slopes of the Ajusco mountains. After the Tres Cumbres Pass, fine views of the valley unfold below you. The drive in the Nevado de Toluca National Park up to the top of the volcano leads through pine and fir forests to the volcanic landscapes around the rim of the crater. From Toluca back to Mexico City there are excellent views of the snowcapped Nevado de Toluca.

The Caves of Cacahuamilpa – warm, humid and vast – have yet to be fully explored

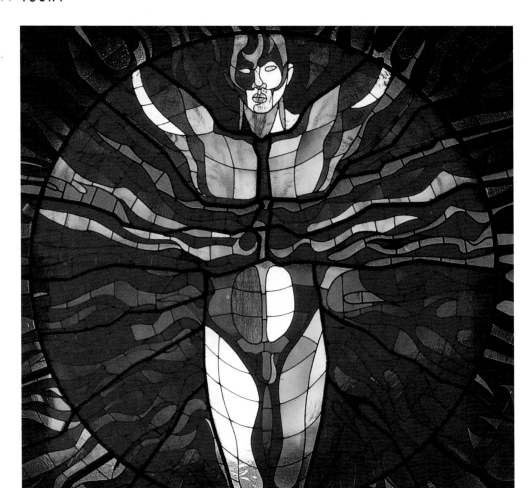

RECOMMENDED WALKS

13 The itinerary offers a number of places where you can stretch your legs in lovely surroundings. But for a unique experience, leave your car behind at the rim of the crater of the Nevado de Toluca and walk down to the two crater lakes, **Laguna del Sol** (Lake of the Sun) and **Laguna de la Luna** (Lake of the Moon). If you are in top physical condition, you can also walk up to the highest point, the Pico del Fraile, where you will have a magnificent view of the surroundings.

BACK TO NATURE

15 The Desierto de los Leones National Park is a spectacular and extensive area of forest comprising largely fir trees, harboring a wide variety of birdlife. Among the foliage, look for Steller's jays, western flycatchers and American robins as well as more active species such as Hutton's vireos, golden-crowned kinglets and white-eared hummingbirds. The area is prone to thefts from cars so try to stay within sight of your vehicle if possible.

Toluca's botanical gardens boast a churchlike stained-glass window

Nevado de Toluca, Mexico

13 This is a beautiful drive through the Nevado de Toluca National Park. Following a winding mountain track through pine forests, you come up to the crater of the magnificent volcanic Nevado de Toluca, Mexico's fourth highest summit with an altitude of 4,680m (15,355 feet). In the crater are the Lakes of the Sun and Moon.

*Return to Toluca, take **Mex 55** northwest, and branch off left to Calixtlahuaca.*

Calixtlahuaca, Mexico

14 The archaeological site of Calixtlahuaca ('place with houses on the plain') has a commanding position over the Toluca Valley. Believed to have been an important center of the Matlatzinca people, it later fell under the domination of the Aztecs. The site consists of several pyramids and temples which have been only partly excavated. The most notable structure here is the four-story **Temple of Quetzalcóatl**, with a shrine dedicated to Ehécatl. Other buildings of interest are the **Temple of Tláloc**, the **Tzompantlí** (House of Skulls) and the **Temple of Huitzilopochtli**.

*Return to Toluca. Take **Mex 15** towards Ciudad de México turning off to the Desierto de los Leones.*

Desierto de los Leones, Mexico

15 The name Desierto de los Leones, which means 'Desert of Lions', is a bit misleading, since it is not a desert and there are no lions to be seen. The Leones apparently refers to the name of a family who lived here in the past. Desierto de los Leones is, in fact, a National Park of coniferous forests and a pleasant, refreshing place in which to take a stroll among the firs and pine trees. The 17th-century Carmelite monastery in the grounds, **Desierto de Santa Fé** (Desert of Santa Fé), is well worth a visit.

*Return to Ciudad de México, driving east on **Mex 15** for 24km (15 miles).*

Ciudad de México – Cuernavaca **85 (52)**
Cuernavaca – Xochicalco **37 (22)**
Xochicalco – Laguna de Tequesquitengo **29 (18)**
Laguna de Tequesquitengo – Taxco **58 (36)**
Taxco – Las Grutas de Cacahuamilpa **30 (19)**
Las Grutas de Cacahuamilpa – Ixtapan de la Sal **36 (22)**
Ixtapan de la Sal – Tenancingo **33 (20)**
Tenancingo – Malinalco **17 (10)**
Malinalco – Teotenango **41 (25)**
Teotenango – Tianguistengo **19 (12)**
Tianguistengo – Metepec **22 (14)**
Metepec – Toluca **7 (4)**
Toluca – Nevado de Toluca **45 (28)**
Nevado de Toluca – Calixtlahuaca **54 (34)**
Calixtlahuaca – Desierto de los Leones **42 (26)**
Desierto de los Leones – Ciudad de México **24 (15)**

The Sunday market at Amecameca is sure to have something for everyone – a pot for Juanita, perhaps?

i Avenida Presidente Masaryk 172, Ciudad de México

*From Mexico City take **Mex 190** southeast for some 29km (18 miles) to Tlapacoya. From the village center follow the signs to the archaeological zone.*

Tlapacoya, Mexico

1 The archaeological site of Tlapacoya is significant as the earliest traces of civilization in Mexico were found here. Explorations are helping to gain fresh knowledge about the country's early history. The six-story **pyramid** is believed to belong to the period between the 6th and 4th centuries BC. There are also a number of tombs to be seen, with figurines, placed at around 1200BC.

*Return to the village and continue southeast on **Mex 190**, then south on **Mex 115** for 10km (6 miles) to Chalco.*

Chalco, Mexico

2 This old Indian town played an important role in Mexico's history. Its original inhabitants, the Chalca people who were an important Nahua tribe, fell under the yoke of the Aztecs in 1485. When Cortés passed here in 1519 on his way to the Aztec capital, Tenochtitlán, the Chalcas allied themselves to him and helped him fight against the Aztecs. The town's main feature is the 16th-century **Franciscan friary** and **church**, whose façade was rebuilt in the 18th century. Take a little time to explore the local **market**.

*Take **Mex 115** southeast for 10km (6 miles) to Tlalmanalco.*

Tlalmanalco, Mexico

3 The name Tlalmanalco means 'on the plain' in Náhuatl. Stop off here to look at the **Franciscan friary** dedicated to San Luis Obispo (Bishop St Louis), built between 1585 and 1591, where remains of frescos can be seen in the cloisters. The **church**, built in the late 16th century, has a Renaissance-style façade. Inside you can see the baroque altar and some fine paintings. Five richly carved arches stand in the open chapel, representing a fine example of the Indian Plateresque style.

*Continue on **Mex 115** for 10km (6 miles) to Amecameca.*

Amecameca, Mexico

4 Much of this little town's charm lies in the magnificence of its setting, as it nestles at the foot of the famous twin volcanoes, Popocatépetl and Iztaccíhuatl, known respectively as the 'Smoking Mountain' and the 'Sleeping Woman'. Cortés and his soldiers passed through here on their march to Tenochtitlán. The 16th-century **Convento Dominico de la Asunción** (Dominican Church of the Assumption) on the main square has richly decorated altars in the baroque style and a well-preserved cloister. On Sundays there is a colorful **market**, when Indians gather from the sur-

OFF THE BEATEN TRACK

Ciudad de México (Mexico City) ● Tlapacoya ● Chalco
Tlalmanalco ● Amecameca ● Ozumba ● Cuautla
Oaxtepec ● Yautepec ● Tepoztlán ● Ciudad de México

This itinerary from Mexico City takes you on a round trip to the east and southeast of the capital, passing through the states of Mexico and Morelos. You will get to visit some fascinating places on this trip which, being a bit off the beaten track, are perhaps not so familiar to the majority of visitors to Mexico. The journey will take you through some spectacular scenery, with magnificent views of snowcapped volcanoes and dramatic rock formations. Along the way, too, charming little rural towns and splendid examples of Colonial churches contrast with modern vacation centers and places of archaeological interest.

FOR HISTORY BUFFS

6 Those interested in events connected with the Revolution of 1910 to 1920 might be interested in paying a visit to the little town of Anencuilco, some 6km (4 miles) south of Cuautla. This was the birthplace of Emiliano Zapata, one of the great heroes of the Revolution. His former home now houses a museum with artifacts and items relating to his life.

RECOMMENDED WALKS

4 The volcanoes Popocatépetl and Iztaccíhuatl can be climbed from bases past the Paso de Cortés, though only experienced climbers should attempt these climbs and professional guides should be used. Tlamacas is the starting point for Popo (as it is called for short) and the climb can be done in six to eight hours (one way), with a view into the crater that is a fitting reward. The base for Iztaccíhuatl is La Joya, a little further along. This climb is much more difficult and dangerous, normally taking about two days to reach the summit.

rounding areas to buy and sell their wares. The town is a good base for excursions to the surrounding mountains and climbing trips up the volcanoes. A short distance to the south, a turn to the left leads to the **Paso de Cortés** (Pass of Cortés). A monument marks the spot where he passed on 3 November, 1519, on the long march to the capital Tenochtitlán. A little further on is Tlamacas Pass, a base for climbing trips. There are excellent views from here of the valley of Puebla and the Pico de Orizaba and La Malinche volcanoes.

*Continue south on **Mex 115** for 12km (7 miles) to Ozumba.*

Ozumba, Mexico

5 The original settlement of Ozumba was founded by the Aztecs in 1382. Of special note is the 16th-century **monastery**. Inside are some interesting frescos depicting the Spanish ruler Cortés receiving the first 12 Franciscan friars in New Spain, as Mexico was called after the Conquest. The church was rebuilt in the 18th century and has a fine baroque altar. For a couple of pleasant side trips, visit the **Salto de Chimal** waterfall and the charming little town of Chimalhuacán.

*Continue southwest on **Mex 115** to Cuautla.*

Cuautla, Morelos

6 Cuautla lies in a fertile valley of lush vegetation and enjoys a mild, sub-tropical climate. With its mineral springs the town was a favorite resort of the Aztecs, and it became a fashionable Spanish spa in the 17th century. Cuautla was the scene of a fierce battle during the Independence War against Spain (1810–20). The main buildings of interest are the 17th-century **convents of Santo Domingo** and of **San Diego** and the **Museo Casa de Morelos** (museum), which displays relics of the Independence War. While in the vicinity you should visit Zacualpan de Amilpas, a pretty little village north of Cuautla with a fine Augustinian **convent**; the **Church of San Mateo** in the village of Chalcatzingo; and **Cerro de la Cantera**, a pre-Columbian site with some interesting reliefs carved from the rock, believed to date back to the early period of the Olmecs, between 1100 and 500BC.

*Take the connecting road to **Mex 26** and head north for some 10km (6 miles), then turn right and continue for 3km (2 miles) to Oaxtepec.*

The serene cloisters of the Church of the Assumption in Amecameca calm the too-busy traveler

Oaxtepec, Morelos

7 The pleasant town of Oaxtepec, with its springs, gardens and attractive 16th-century **Dominican convent**, now housing a school and archaeological finds from Morelos state, was once a favorite retreat of the Aztec ruler Moctezuma, and you can see the remains of large botanical gardens thought to have been laid out by him. Cortés also visited the resort during his time in Mexico. It is now a popular vacation center, with hot springs, campgrounds, swimming pools and recreation facilities.

*Take the road south to join **Mex 160**. Continue west to Yautepec, about 13km (8 miles).*

Yautepec, Morelos

8 Yautepec is an old town with a lot of rural charm. Movie fans might be interested to know this was the setting for *Veracruz*, starring Burt Lancaster. During the Revolution of 1910 to 1920 the town was used by Revolutionary hero Emiliano Zapata as his barracks, and the **parish church** is referred to as Zapata's Church. Worth a look is the 16th-century **Dominican monastery**, with a well-preserved open chapel, and the **Convento de la Asunción** (Convent of the Assumption), also from the 16th century, with a semicircle of arches in the chapel.

*Take the road northeast, then join **toll road 115** northwest for 15km (9 miles) to Tepoztlán.*

The view over Tepoztlán

Tepoztlán, Morelos

9 The centuries-old village of Tepoztlán ('place of the axe') is perched dramatically on craggy cliff tops among strange rock formations. The natives still speak Náhuatl, the ancient tongue of the Aztecs, which is unusual in Mexico. Narrow, cobble-stoned streets wind their way up the steep hillside, but its main feature is the massive **Convento de la Navidad de la Virgen María** (Dominican monastery), which Zapata used in 1910 to house his rebel troops. Built between 1559 and 1588, its doorway is a fine example of Plateresque design, an elaborately decorative architectural style, of intricate workmanship carved on stone. From the building's upper floor you will have a superb view of the surrounding mountains. Behind the monastery is the small **Museo Arqueológico** (museum) with a collection of archaeological artifacts.

*Continue north on **Mex 115**, then join **toll road 95** back to Ciudad de México.*

Ciudad de México – Tlapacoya **29 (18)**
Tlapacoya – Chalco **10 (6)**
Chalco – Tlalmanalco **10 (6)**
Tlalmanalco – Amecameca **10 (6)**
Amecameca – Ozumba **12 (7)**
Ozumba – Cuautla **29 (18)**
Cuautla – Oaxtepec **13 (8)**
Oaxtepec – Yautepec **13 (8)**
Yautepec – Tepoztlán **15 (9)**
Tepoztlán – Ciudad de México **74 (46)**

2/3 days – 288km (180 miles)

GRAND PYRAMIDS & CHURCHES

Ciudad de México (Mexico City) • Tenayuca
Santa Cecilia Acatitlán • Tepotzotlán • Tula
Actopán • Pachuca • Teotihuacán • Acolman
Basílica de Guadalupe • Ciudad de México

This itinerary leaves Mexico City to take you north and northeast, passing through the states of Mexico and Hidalgo. The emphasis here is on archaeological sites, churches and monasteries – some of them outstanding examples – rather than on scenery. Among the pre-Columbian sites included is Teotihuacán, one of Mexico's most famous and impressive archaeological centers and a highlight of this trip. The rest of the tour combines pleasant little towns, a lovely monastery, one of Mexico's most magnificent churches and a visit to the most venerated shrine in the land.

FOR HISTORY BUFFS

9 According to tradition, it was in Guadalupe in December 1531 that a simple Indian boy, Juan Diego, had a vision of the Virgin Mary. She asked that a church be built on the spot. When the boy relayed this to the local bishop, he was asked to provide proof of his story. Juan Diego returned to the hillside, nearby Tepeyác Hill, and saw the Virgin again. She asked him to gather some roses, which he did, returning to show them to the bishop. Upon unfolding his cloak the image of the Virgin, with the dark features of an Indian, was found imprinted there. The **Capilla del Tepeyác**, a small chapel, was built on the spot and became a place of veneration. There are fine frescos by Fernando Leal portraying the miraculous story. No one has been able to explain the mystery of the image on the cloak, which is in the Basílica of Guadalupe for everyone to view.

i Avenida Presidente Masaryk 172, Ciudad de México

Take the Calle Vallejo road north for 11km (7 miles) towards Tlalnepantla. Just outside, take the road to the Tenayuca site.

Tenayuca, Mexico

1 Tenayuca, which means 'walled site', is a pre-Columbian location of some importance. It formed part of the Chichimec empire in the 12th century and fell under the domination of the Aztecs in the 15th century. The remaining structure, the **Serpent Pyramid**, adorned by a number of feathered serpents, is considered one of the finest examples of Aztec architecture discovered to date. A frieze of skulls stares out from the foot of the stairway on one side. It is thought that the pyramid may have been used for astronomical purposes.

Take the road north for 3km (2 miles) to Santa Cecilia Acatitlán.

Santa Cecilia Acatitlán, Mexico

2 It is a delightful surprise to come upon this small, well-preserved **temple pyramid** standing in its neat garden setting. The pyramid is Aztec and has a shrine dedicated to the god of war, Huitzilopochtli. The ruin of a second shrine, dedicated to Tláloc, the Toltec rain god, stands next to it. A small **museum** in the grounds has a collection of pre-Columbian artifacts.

Like grim-faced sentinels guarding the past, the Atlantes of Tula survived a 13th-century sacking. The site was discovered in 1938

*Join **toll road 57** north, then follow a minor road for about 3km (2 miles) to Tepotzotlán.*

Tepotzotlán, Mexico

3 The Colonial village of Tepotzotlán has a charm all of its own, but the big attraction is the magnificent convent **Church of San Francisco Xavier**, facing the main square. Originally, Tepotzotlán was an Otomi settlement. In 1584 the Jesuit **Colegio de San Martín** (College of St Martin) was founded and it became an important center of religious education. Over the years the convent was enlarged, and the restored church of today is a jewel of Mexican baroque architecture. The façade, which is the work of a number of different artists, is richly decorated with hand-carved sculptures. The highly ornate interior is considered one of Mexico's most magnificent examples of the Churrigueresque style, a highly elaborate form of decorative baroque architecture. There are seven richly gilded altars, and the high altar has a statue of St Francis Xavier in the center. The old Jesuit college is now the **Museo Nacional del Virreinato** (National Museum of the Viceroyalty) and houses exhibits of Colonial and religious art. About 27km (17 miles) to the west is **Los Arcos del Sitio**, the highest aqueduct in Mexico, with arches reaching up to 60m (196 feet) high. It was built by the Jesuits in the 18th century to supply water to Tepotzotlán.

*Return to **toll road 57** and continue northwest. Turn off at Tepejí de Río. Continue for about 20km (12 miles), then turn right just before the bridge to the archaeological site of Tula.*

Tula, Hidalgo

4 Tula (Tollan, as it was formerly called) was the capital and ceremonial center of the Toltec people from the 8th century until 1168, when it was sacked by the Chichimeca tribe. Tula is characterized by several gigantic figures, the **Atlantes of Tula**, which stand atop a flat plateau, forming a dramatic silhouette on top of a platform. Once they supported the roof of a temple, long since gone. The great statues stand 4.5m (15 feet) high and are decorated with feathered crowns and breastplates. The warriors, each with a spear, stand on the **Templo de Tlahuizcalpantecuhtli** (the Temple of the Morning Star), also called the Pyramid of Quetzalcoatl. Behind the pyramid is the **Serpent Wall** with spiral and geometric carvings. You can also see the remains of a large ball court and **Palacio Quemado** (the Burnt Palace). Two *Chac-mool* statues stand in the main courtyard. These recumbent stone figures hold a vessel, supposedly for the purpose of receiving the hearts torn out from victims during sacrificial ceremonies in pre-Hispanic times. The small **Museo Jorge R Acosta** (museum) on the site displays interesting finds from the area. On the

RECOMMENDED WALKS

9 When you visit the Basilica of Guadalupe, take a walk up Tepeyác Hill to the **Capilla del Tepeyác**, the chapel built in the 18th century on the spot where the Virgin is said to have appeared before the Indian boy Juan Diego. There are also pleasant walks around the Monastery of Acolman, which is in a very peaceful setting of trees and greenery.

SPECIAL TO …

9 One of Mexico's grandest festivals is **Día de Nuestra Señora de Guadalupe** (the Festival of Our Lady of Guadalupe), on 12 December. Processions begin many days before, and continue for days after. The celebrations start with the singing of *Las Mañanitas* (a special birthday song) by artistic groups. Then there are performances of different kinds of dances from all over Mexico which go on all day – a very colorful and lively event not to be missed if possible.

other side of the river, in the little town of Tula de Allende, is a fortified **Franciscan church** from the 16th century with an attractive façade and fine interior vaulting.

Take the road northeast for some 56km (35 miles) through Tlahuelilpa, Mixquiahuala and Progreso, to Actopán.

Actopán, Hidalgo

5 Actopán ('in rich and fertile soil') lies in the Valley of Mezquital, a farming region in the mountainous state of Hidalgo. The town is mostly inhabited by Otomí Indians. Its major attraction is the **Templo y Convento de San Nicolás** (St Nicholas' Church and Monastery). Founded in 1548 and dedicated to St Nicholas of Tolentino, it is a fine example of the architecture of this period. Features worth noting are its Renaissance doorway, frescos and Gothic arches. The large square bell tower suggests a Moorish influence. A **museum**, reached through the garden, has a small display of Otomí folk art.

The town celebrates the Festival of St Nicholas of Tolentino (Día de San Nicolas Tolentino) on 10 September. Before continuing the main tour, you might like to venture 45km (28 miles) northwest to the little town of Ixmiquilpan, where there is a colorful Otomí market on Mondays. Once the capital of the Otomí Indians, the town boasts the 16th-century

Carved with consummate skill, countless figures of saints and angels adorn the façade of Tepotzotlán's church, named for Jesuit missionary Francis Xavier

Augustinian **Church of San Miguel**, with a lovely Plateresque façade in pink-colored stone and some interesting frescos inside.

*Take **R 85** southeast to Pachuca, some 36km (22 miles) from Actopán.*

Pachuca, Hidalgo

6 Pachuca is the capital of the state of Hidalgo and the center of a rich mining area. The original settlement of Patlachiuhcán is thought to have been established by the Aztecs in the mid-15th century. In 1527 the Spanish town of Pachuca ('confined space') was founded. The town has a number of interesting buildings. The 17th-century **Ex-Convento de San Francisco** (former convent) has a fine altar in Churrigueresque style. Within the convent are the Casasola Archives, a collection of photographs depicting historical events from the late 19th century and early 20th century, including the Mexican Revolution. On the main square stands the **Torre del Reloj** (the tall clock tower) in neoclassical style. While you are in Pachuca, you might want to sample *pulque*, a mild alcoholic drink produced here from the maguey cactus.

BACK TO NATURE

6 Lovers of nature will enjoy a stop-off at **Parque Nacional El Chico** (El Chico National Park), located north of Pachuca on the route to the Mineral del Chico, where there are beautiful pine forests and huge rock formations. Look for American robins which feed both on the ground and among the branches, northern flickers, pygmy nuthatches, eastern bluebirds, Hutton's vireos and chipping sparrows.

From the top of Teotihuacán's pyramids, you can make out the plan of the ancient city. At a time when most European capitals were little more than villages, about 1,500 years ago, Teotihuacán may have been the biggest city in the world. To the Aztecs it was sacred

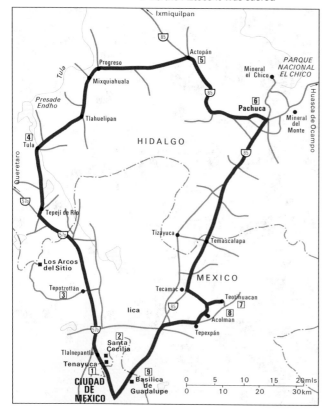

Before proceeding along the main route, you can make one or more side trips. The old mining town of Mineral del Monte, some 12km (7 miles) east, overlooks the town of Pachuca. With its steep, cobblestoned streets, it is renowned for having had one of the richest silver mines in the world. About 24km (15 miles) north of Pachuca is another old mining town, Mineral del Chico, reached by passing through **Parque Nacional El Chico** (El Chico National Park).

i Plaza de la Independencia No 110

*From Pachuca take **Mex 85** south to Tecamac and turn southeast to Teotihuacán.*

Teotihuacán, Mexico

7 Teotihuacán is the largest pre-Columbian site in Central America and one of the most impressive. Little is known of its origins, but it was thought to have been built by a people called the Teotihuacanos and used as a ceremonial center. The major structures were probably erected between about 100BC and AD600, and during its peak period (AD450–650) the city was estimated to have a population of over 200,000. In the 8th century the city went into decline; with much of it being destroyed by fire, it became virtually deserted. Later the city fell under the domination of the Toltecs, until the 14th century when the Aztecs came to the Valley of Mexico. They gave it the name Teotihuacán ('the place where men became gods') and regarded it as a sacred place. The **Calle de los Muertos** (Avenue of the Dead) runs the length of the site, to the south of the **Pirámide de la Luna** (Pyramid of the Moon). From the top of its broad stairway (a relatively easy climb), you will have a good view of the site and of the magnificent **Pirámide del Sol** (Pyramid of the Sun). Located further down the Avenue, this majestic building dominates the entire site. Built in five levels, it rises to a height of approximately 63m (206 feet). A stairway on its west side leads to the top, where again there is a superb view of the surroundings. Just remember when attempting these climbs, you are already over 2,130m (7,000 feet) above sea-level and the air is thin, so go easy.

There are many other interesting temples and buildings to visit in the area. The **Palacio de Quetzalpapálotl** (Palace of the Quetzal Butterfly) near the Pyramid of the Moon, has columns covered by bas-reliefs of mythological figures of the Quetzal butterfly and other fascinating decorations. The **Templo de la Agricultura** (Temple of Agriculture) has a number of frescos. At the south of the site is **La Ciudadela** (the Citadel), a huge area enclosing several temples. Among the various notable structures is the **Templo de Quetzalcóatl** (the Temple of Quetzalcóatl – the Feathered Serpent) with huge serpent heads decorating some of the walls. Facing the Citadel is the **Unidad Cultural Museum**, with a collection of archaeological and historical exhibits. Take something warm to wear, as the temperature can get distinctly chilly at night.

Take the road southwest for 10km (6 miles) to Acolman.

Acolman, Mexico

8 El Convento de San Agústin de Acolman (the Monastery of St Augustine of Acolman) was built between 1539 and 1560 and is considered a very fine example of the Plateresque style. Its name means 'surrounded by water'. The fine façade has two sets of columns flanking the entrance and a statue of a saint between each. An impressive bell tower rises above the battlements which top the façade, while inside are some fine paintings. The lovely stone cross in the atrium depicts the figure of Christ as the Man of Sorrows. Not far away, in the village of Tepexpan to the southwest, is a small **museum** boasting the remains of a mammoth found nearby, believed to be around 11,000 years old.

*Return to **Mex 85** and head towards Mexico City, to the Basilica of Guadalupe (located on the outskirts of the capital).*

Basílica de Guadalupe, Federal District

9 Mexico's most revered shrine is the **Basílica de la Virgen de Guadalupe** (Basilica of the Virgin of Guadalupe). Every year countless pilgrims from all over the country, indeed the world, come to pay homage to the patron saint of Mexico, the Virgin of Guadalupe, whose image is in the church. An earlier Basilica de Nuestra Señora de Guadalupe was built in 1707 on the site of a still earlier

At the monastery in Acolman, orange trees grow in a shady courtyard

church. Gradually the church began to sink into the subsoil (Mexico City had been built on a lake bed). When that became too dangerous, the present basilica was built next to it. This building, a strikingly modern structure of concrete and marble, was designed by top Mexican architect Pedro Ramírez Vázquez. It was consecrated in 1976 and can accommodate up to 20,000. The image of the Virgin, high above the altar, can be viewed from a moving passage without disturbing those who wish to pray. Among the thousands of visitors who come here all year round, Indian pilgrims can usually be seen in the large courtyard surrounding the basilica completing the last stage of their journey of faith upon their knees.

Nearby is the 18th-century **Capilla del Pocito** (Chapel of the Spring). A spring trickling from a rock inside is believed by the Indians to have healing powers, and they come to fill their bottles with the water.

*Return to the center of Mexico City via **Mex 85**.*

Ciudad de México – Tenayuca **11 (7)**
Tenayuca – Santa Cecilia **3 (2)**
Santa Cecilia – Tepotzotlán **22 (14)**
Tepotzotlán – Tula **48 (30)**
Tula – Actopán **56 (35)**
Actopán – Pachuca **36 (22)**
Pachuca – Teotihuacán **64 (40)**
Teotihuacán – Acolman **10 (6)**
Acolman – Basílica de Guadalupe **32 (20)**
Basílica de Guadalupe – Ciudad de México **6 (4)**

SCENIC ROUTES

Much of this route takes you through rolling hills and plains, with pleasant, if not spectacular scenery. Some of the most attractive stretches of road are to be found around Pachuca, where there is a particularly scenic stretch between Actopán and Pachuca.

FOR CHILDREN

This is one tour where it is probably a good idea not to take younger children as, basically, it is mainly archaeological and does not really cater for them.

3 days – 310km (193 miles)

COLONIAL TOWNS & VOLCANOES

Ciudad de México (Mexico City) • Cacaxtla
Tlaxcala • Puebla • Acatepec • Tonantzintla
Cholula • Huejotzingo • San Andrés de Calpan
Ciudad de México

This tour takes you to the east and southeast of the capital, traveling through the states of Tlaxcala and Puebla. This very interesting and beautiful region of Mexico combines places of historic importance and cultural value. One of Mexico's most attractive Colonial towns, Puebla, is included in the itinerary, together with beautiful old monasteries and churches. There are also some pre-Columbian sites to be seen during the course of your journey, which will take you through spectacular scenery, with superb views of the snowcapped volcanoes – some extinct, some only dormant – that characterize the area.

Straw crucifixes make a humble contrast to the dazzling beauty of the Rosary Chapel in Puebla

i Avenida Presidente Masaryk 172, Ciudad de México

*From Mexico City take **toll road 150** east towards Puebla. At San Martín Texmelucan, some 94km (58 miles) further on, join **Mex 119** toward Navitas and Tepeyanco. Turn off to Cacaxtla.*

Cacaxtla, Tlaxcala

1 A short walk up a path from the parking lot leads to the pre-Columbian site of Cacaxtla, on a hill overlooking the Valley of Puebla. Little is known of its origins, but evidence suggests the center may have been inhabited at one time by small groups from the Maya region, with its peak period between AD700 and 900. The site consists of several pyramids and temples, discovered as recently as 1975 when tomb robbers stumbled upon the remains of some frescos. Wall paintings of particular interest are in the **Edificio de las Pinturas** (the Building of the Painters), otherwise known as Building A. There are representations of Quetzalcóatl (the Feathered Serpent) and the rain god Tláloc, which suggest Mayan influences. Also of interest is the large fresco in Building B. This painting, thought to date back to AD75, depicts a fierce battle between two opposing tribes, the Jaguars and the Bird Men. There is still much to be excavated in the area.

*Return to **Mex 119**. Turn left and continue for 16km (10 miles) to Tlaxcala.*

Tlaxcala, Tlaxcala

2 Tlaxcala, capital of the smallest state in Mexico, is situated in the Highlands, surrounded by woodlands. The town was formerly inhabited by a group of the Chichimec tribe, known as the Tlaxcalans. Having always bitterly opposed the dominance of the Aztecs, the Tlaxcalans joined forces with Cortés and his soldiers when they passed through the area and proved an important ally of the Spaniards in their fight against the Aztecs.

Today, Tlaxcala is an attractive Colonial-style town with an Indian flavor that is especially evident in the colorful woolen *serapes* (shawls) and clothes produced here. Around the main square are some lovely churches and attractive buildings. The **parish church** has an attractive façade of the typical tiles from Puebla. Take a look at the **Palacio Municipal** (Town Hall) with its fine window arches combining Indian and Moorish styles. Frescos in the **Palacio de Gobierno** (Government Palace) trace the events of Tlaxcala's history. The **Ex-Convento de San Francisco** (Convent of St Francis), with its church, was founded in 1525, making it one of the earliest convents in Mexico. See the interesting Moorish-style ceiling studded with stars and

The brilliant white portal of Tlaxcala's basilica is offset by twin towers of plain red tiles

fine Gothic open chapel at a lower level. There are also some fine paintings in the church. About 1.5km (1 mile) away is one of Mexico's loveliest churches, the **Basílica de la Virgen de Ocotlán** (Basilica of the Virgin of Ocotlán) ('place of the pine trees'), situated above the town. Built in the mid-18th century by an Indian architect, Francisco Miguel, the church is a striking combination of red-tiled towers on either side of its ornate white stucco portal and magnificent white twin towers. Note the high altar, decorated in many colors, and the image of the Virgin in the small chapel behind it. The church is a place of pilgrimage and many people make their way to Ocotlán from all over the country.

ⓘ Blvd Mariano Sánchez 11B, 1st floor

*From Tlaxcala take **Mex 119** south to Puebla.*

Puebla, Puebla

3 Puebla is the state capital and the fourth largest city in Mexico. With its Colonial architecture, quiet dignity and charm, it is possibly the most characteristically Spanish town in the land. Lying 2,160m (7,000 feet) above sea level in a fertile valley surrounded by four of Mexico's most famous volcanoes – Popocatépetl, Iztaccíhuatl, Malinche and Citlaltépetl (Orizaba) – Puebla offers magnificent views of their snowy peaks.

The town was neatly laid out by the Spaniards, with lavish use of tiles to adorn the churches, houses, fountains and official buildings. These Talavera tiles were first introduced by tilemakers from the town of Talavera, near Toledo in Spain.

Puebla is a pleasing combination of pretty squares, flowers, Spanish-style wrought-iron balconies and many splendid churches. As with most Mexican towns, life centers on the zócalo (main square), with its fountains and trees, set off by arcades. **La Catedral de Nuestra Señora de la Inmaculada Concepción** (the Cathedral of the Immaculate Conception), on the south side of the square, is considered one of Mexico's greatest churches. Built between 1575 and 1649 of a grey-blue stone, it is remarkable for its carved façade, vast doors and impressive bell towers.

The **Iglesia de Santo Domingo** (Church of St Dominic), two blocks north of the zócalo, dates from the 16th century and is a fine example of the Mexican style. Don't miss the **Capilla del Rosario** (Chapel of the Rosary) which is richly decorated with gold leaf, tiles, sculptures and carvings. Near by is the colorful market, where onyx, ceramics and baskets are among the wares for sale.

To the east of the main square is the Jesuit **Templo de la Compañía** (Church of la Compañía). The façade is Churrigueresque and the dome sparkles with blue and white tiles.

Take a look, too, at the **Museo Regional de Puebla** (Regional Museum of Puebla), which is housed in the **Casa del Alfeñique** (Almond-cake House), a handsome 17th-century mansion. There are displays of archaeological artifacts and historical relics on the first floor, while the second floor is furnished as an old Colonial residence.

A short drive up the hill northeast of town takes you to the ruins of two old forts – the **Fuerte de Guadalupe** (Fort Guadalupe) and **Fuerte de Loreto** (Fort Loreto) – which mark the spot of a battle fought in 1862 between French troops and Mexico's General Zaragoza. The museum here has relics of historical events and offers a good view of the city.

Places of interest include Atlixco, a popular weekend resort, and Tochimilco, which is set in a dramatic volcanic landscape with a magnificent view of the towering Popocatépetl and Huaquechula.

ⓘ Calle 13 Sur 1303

*Take **Mex 190** southwest for 10km (6 miles) to Acatepec.*

Acatepec, Puebla

4 The stop-off at Acatepec is to visit the splendid **Templo de San Francisco Acatepec** (Church of St Francis of Acatepec). Built in the 18th century, it is considered one of the finest examples of high baroque architecture in the region. The beautiful façade of colorful tiles and red bricks is the work of local Indian artists under Spanish guidance. Inside it is decorated with stucco ornaments and wood carvings.

Take the road west for about 2km (1 mile) to Tonantzintla.

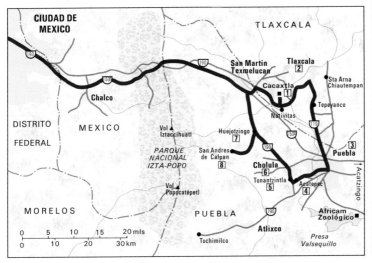

The mind-boggling detail of the interior of Tonantzintla's Church of Santa Maria, encrusted with every conceivable decorative medium, reflecting the glory of God

Tonantzintla, Puebla

5 Again, the main feature of this town is a church – **Santa María de Tonantzintla**, another fine example of high baroque architecture. The interior is a mass of color, decorated with fruits, flowers, birds and some Christmas themes, the combined effort of European and local Indian artists.

Continue northeast to Cholula.

Cholula, Puebla

6 Cholula is derived from its earlier name, Atchollán, 'place from which the water flows'. It was formerly a ceremonial center, thought to have been inhabited from as early as 400BC by a number of different tribes, including Olmecs, Toltecs, Mixtecs and, later, the Aztecs. In 1519 the city was destroyed by the Spaniards, who then built churches on the old temples which, according to reports, numbered around 365, one for each day of the year. Although nothing like this number exists today, there are still many churches. **El Convento de San Gabriel** (the Convent of St Gabriel), built by the Franciscans in the mid-16th century, is an impressive example, with seven aisles, 49 small domes and a large atrium and doorway in Plateresque style. Cholula is also the site of the renowned **Universidad de las Americas** (University of the Americas), originally in Mexico City and moved to its present site in 1970.

A major attraction of Cholula, however, is the **Tepanapa Pyramid**, located near the zócalo (main square). Overgrown with vegetation and looking much like a small hill, it is in fact the largest structure of its kind in the world. Excavations have revealed the remains of a number of platforms, walls and courtyards, suggesting the pyramid was built seven times over. Frescos depict butterflies and grasshoppers, and a long, colorful painting portrays large figures in drinking sessions. The pyramid was dedicated to the Feathered Serpent, Quetzalcóatl. Parts of the tunnel are lit up and guides are available to show you around. A small **museum** near the entrance has a model of the original pyramid as it was in pre-Hispanic times and a collection of interesting artifacts. Built right on top of the pyramid is the **Santuario de Nuestra Señora de los Remedios** (Sanctuary of Our Lady of Perpetual Succor).

*Take **Mex 190** northwest for 14km (9 miles) to Huejotzingo.*

SPECIAL TO . . .

3 Puebla is a city renowned for its cuisine and its most famous dish is *mole poblano*. A rich sauce made up of countless ingredients, including cocoa, it is used as an accompaniment to turkey, chicken or pork and is traditionally prepared on feast days and special occasions. The dish is said to have been concocted by the nuns of the Santa Rosa Convent.

6 Several festivals are celebrated in Cholula every year. **Día de la Virgen de los Remedios** (the Festival of Our Lady of Perpetual Succor) is celebrated with colorful dances from 1 to 8 September in the atrium of the **Santuario de Nuestra Señora de los Remedios**, on top of the Tepanapa pyramid.

Cholula, a city of churches: with missionary zeal the Spaniards built churches over many pagan temples which, in this ancient ceremonial center, numbered about 365

Huejotzingo, Puebla

7 Huejotzingo lies at the foot of the beautiful snowcapped volcano Iztaccíhuatl, in a region of fruit plantations. The town played a significant role in the Spanish Conquest by allying itself to the neighboring town of Tlaxcala and joining up with the Spaniards against the Aztecs. Its most notable feature is the **Convento de San Francisco** (Convent of St Francis of Huejotzingo), situated opposite the main square. Built between 1525 and 1570, it was one of the first churches to be founded in Mexico by the Spaniards. The fortified church is well preserved. Its façade is decorated in Spanish-Plateresque style, with columns and decorations typical of that elaborate style. In the nave is an impressive *retablo* (religious painting), with 14 statues. Some fine oil panels and remains of frescos can also be seen. Have a look also at the 16th-century **Iglesia de San Diego** (Church of St James) with its richly decorated façade and ornate roof.

The area of Huejotzingo is noted for its colorful *serapes* (woolen shawls) and rugs and is a center for the production of cider (the annual Apple Juice Festival begins on 23 September and goes on for nine days). Market days are on Tuesdays and Saturdays.

Take an unsurfaced road southwest for 10km (6 miles) to San Andrés de Calpan.

San Andrés de Calpan, Puebla

8 Another fine monastery is to be seen in San Andrés de Calpan. Founded in 1548, its façade is sculpted with ornate decorations in the Plateresque style. Notice the triumphal arch inside and the atrium with four splendid chapels, considered to be among the finest in Mexico. These are beautifully adorned with sculptures of flowers and angels, geometric patterns and religious events.

Return to Huejotzingo and to Mexico City northwest on **Mex 190***.*

Ciudad de México – Cacaxtla **99 (62)**
Cacaxtla – Tlaxcala **21 (13)**
Tlaxcala – Puebla **27 (17)**
Puebla – Acatepec **10 (6)**
Acatepec – Tonantzintla **2 (1)**
Tonantzintla – Cholula **3 (2)**
Cholula – Huejotzingo **14 (9)**
Huejotzingo – San Andrés de Calpan **10 (6)**
San Andrés de Calpan – Ciudad de México **124 (77)**

BACK TO NATURE

3 The parks and gardens to the south and east of Puebla provide some excellent opportunities for the birdwatcher while outside the city itself, fields and cultivated areas provide contrast. Black vultures are ever-present both in the skies and often beside the roads, while smaller species include chipping sparrows, house finches, vermilion flycatchers and yellow warblers. Boat-tailed grackles, with their long, fan-shaped tails, perch beside the road often along with barn swallows and violet-green swallows.

4 days – 724km (450 miles)

THE HISTORIC ROUTE OF INDEPENDENCE

Ciudad de México (Mexico City) • Querétaro
San Miguel de Allende • Atotonilco
Dolores Hidalgo • Guanajuato • Irapuato
Salamanca • Celaya • Ciudad de México

This tour from Mexico City takes you to the northwest of the capital, through the states of Querétaro and Guanajuato, the very heartland of Mexico. The interesting and historic itinerary is along the Route of Independence, so-called because of the role this part of the country played during the struggle for independence against the Spaniards. Along the way are several of Mexico's most beautiful Colonial towns, where you can admire the finest examples of period architecture and enjoy the individual appeal of each place. Fine churches and a famous pilgrimage center are also seen on this tour, considered one of the most attractive in Mexico.

> *i* Avenida Presidente Masaryk 172, Ciudad de México
>
> *From Mexico City take* **toll road 57D** *north for 219km (137 miles) to Querétaro.*

Off many big streets in Querétaro you will find a little plaza, cobblestoned byways and fountains

Querétaro, Querétaro

1 Querétaro is the state capital and one of Mexico's most historic cities. Nowadays it is a busy manufacturing town with important industries on the outskirts. Don't be discouraged by the industrial aspect as you approach: the heart of the city is very attractive and well kept, with elegant buildings, shaded parks and gardens. It has a distinctive Spanish flavor, offering quiet elegance and style, and you can happily spend a lot of time just strolling around its pleasant streets and squares. Querétaro is renowned for its opals and other gems, which are well displayed in its many shops and boutiques.

The town was taken over by the Spanish in 1531 and declared a city in 1699. Since then, various events of historical significance have taken place here. There are numerous churches, palaces and buildings worth seeing. The **Convento de la Cruz** (Church and Convent of the Cross) is one of the largest monasteries in Mexico (originally from the 16th century and rebuilt later). Emperor Maximilian made his headquarters here in 1867, and was later detained as a prisoner after his defeat by Benito Juárez. Another notable church is the **Convento de San Antonio** (Convent of St Anthony), originally 16th-century, with a museum displaying Colonial-era relics.

The **Templo de Santa Clara** (Church of St Clare) has a magnificent interior, richly decorated with carved and gilded *retablos*. The elegant **Fuente de Neptuno** (Fountain of Neptune) stands in front. **El Ex-Convento de Santa Rosa de Viterbo** (the Church of St Rose), mid-18th-century, has an

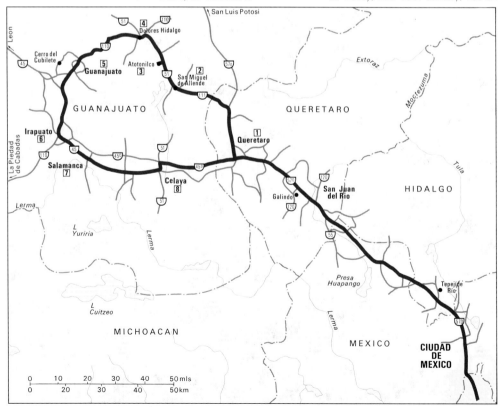

San Miguel, with its palaces and ornate mansions, was once a fashionable center for the wealthy

Most of this route passes through pleasant landscapes of rolling hills and plains, with mountain ranges in the distance. The mountainous area around Guanajuato is exceptional, and the panoramic route that circles the town offers good views of the city nestling below, with a colossal statue of El Pipila, Guanajuato's great hero of the Independence War, along it.

FOR HISTORY BUFFS

5 Outside the town of Guanajuato is the old **Valenciana Mine**. Discovered in 1766, it was once one of the greatest silver mines in the world. It has recently been opened and visitors can see the pyramid-shaped walls over which the Indian workers used to haul the baskets of ore.

Oriental look, with flying buttresses and dragon faces and a richly carved interior.

Among the secular buildings, take a look at the old **Palacio Municipal** (City Hall) and the **Palacio Federal**, a handsome building with a baroque façade and elegant pillars.

The **Museo Règional de Querétaro** (Regional Museum) houses material relating to Colonial history. Among the many items of interest here is the desk of the council which pronounced the death sentence on Emperor Maximilian. An elegant fountain, dedicated to Hebe, the Greek goddess of youth, graces the **Plaza Obregón**, where evening band concerts are sometimes held.

Another feature of the town is the impressive aqueduct. Built between 1726 and 1738, with a length of some 9km (6 miles) and 74 arches, it is still in operation today.

Drive up to the **Cerro de las Campanas** (Hill of Bells), where a chapel built by the Austrian government marks the spot of Maximilian's execution by Juárez's troops in 1867. An enormous statue of Benito Juárez overlooks it, rather grimly.

ℹ️ Escokedo 22, 5 de Mayo 61

*Take **toll road 57D** northwest for 28km (17 miles), then turn off west on **Mex 111** to San Miguel de Allende.*

San Miguel de Allende, Guanajuato

2 San Miguel de Allende is one of Mexico's Colonial gems, set in a valley against a background of rolling hills and plains. Narrow cobblestoned streets wind their way down to this little town of arcades, courtyards and Colonial buildings.

The place has long attracted writers and painters, many of whom have made their home here. San Miguel has many galleries, boutiques and shops crammed with colorful handicrafts. One of the great heroes of the Independence Wars, General Ignacio de Allende, was born here.

The small main square, shaded by trees and surrounded by arcades, is the focal point of the town. Overlooking the square is San Miguel's dominant feature, **La Parroqua** (parish church), a vast structure built in neo-Gothic style around 1880. In the chapel of Señor de la Conquista is a much revered statue of Christ, made by local Indians of corn paste and crushed flowers.

There are a number of interesting buildings to visit. The **Casa del Mayorazgo de Canal** (literally 'the house of the eldest son of Canal') combines baroque and neoclassic styles and has a lovely inner courtyard. Also worth a visit are the **Capilla de San Rafael** (Chapel of St Raphael), and the 18th-century **Iglesia de la Concepción** (Church and Convent of the Conception). The **Instituto Allende** (Allende Institute), an important art center founded in the

SPECIAL TO...

5 The Cervantes Festival, which takes place in Guanajuato from mid-October to early November is a great event that attracts artists from all over the world. There are concerts, plays, opera and films, and the works of Cervantes, author of *Don Quixote*, are performed against the superb background of the city. The *estudiantinos* perform their music throughout and are a colorful feature of the festival. Check the exact dates well in advance, as this is a very popular event.

FOR CHILDREN

Even the younger children should enjoy visiting some of the enchanting towns on this tour, such as Querétaro, San Miguel and Guanajuato, but there are no real attractions specifically aimed at children.

RECOMMENDED WALKS

5 Take the road to Silao from the **Panteón Municipal** (Municipal Cemetery) which houses the Mummy Museum. After about 16km (10 miles), a turning takes you to the Cerro del Cubilete where you will come upon the statue of **El Cristo Rey** (Christ the King). Here you can take a short stroll in the vicinity, which offers a magnificent panorama of the forests and mountains of the surrounding area.

1930s, has students from all over the Americas. It also has a center specializing in writing and language and is renowned for its equestrian school.

The town changes totally on market days (Tuesdays and Sundays) when Indians arrive from all over bringing much color and hustle and bustle.

ⓘ corner of the *zócalo (main square)*

*Take **Mex 51** north for about 14km (9 miles). Turn west and continue for 2km (1 mile) to Atotonilco.*

Atotonilco, Guanajuato

3 Atotonilco is famous for its Santuario de Jesús Nazareno (Sanctuary of Jesus of Nazareth), a famous pilgrimage center for Indians who have been coming here from the surrounding area for centuries. The convent was established in 1740 and has a much venerated statue of Christ the Redeemer. The church has fine frescos based on folk themes.

*Return to **Mex 51** and continue north for 28km (17 miles) to Dolores Hidalgo.*

Dolores Hidalgo, Guanajuato

4 Dolores Hidalgo is known as the 'Cradle of National Independence' on account of its historic role during the War of Independence against the Spanish. Here on 15 September, 1810, the parish priest, Father Miguel Hidalgo, rang the bell of his church uttering the famous 'Grito de Dolores' (Call of Dolores) to summon his followers. So began the struggle for independence, which was finally gained in 1821. The celebrated **Parroquía** (parish church), built between 1712 and 1728, has a façade in the Churrigueresque style. Of note are the two *retablos*, with a gilded image of the famous Virgin in the one on the left. The **Museo Casa de**

Dolores Hidalgo, where the church bells rang out for revolution

Hidalgo (house of Father Hidalgo) contains paintings, books and furnishings relating to his life, and on the main square is a statue of him. The town is also renowned for its colored tiles (*azulejos*).

ⓘ Plaza Principal

*Take **Mex 110** southwest for 54km (32 miles) to Guanajuato.*

Guanajuato, Guanajuato

5 This lovely Colonial city lies in a narrow canyon surrounded by a ring of mountains and is one of the country's best-preserved cities, declared a national historic monument. With its houses painted in different colors, the town has many churches, squares, grand steps and little narrow streets, and a network of underground streets for cars. Guanajuato was formerly inhabited in its time by the Tarascans, who called it 'Cuanax-huato', meaning 'hill of frogs'. The area was settled by the Spaniards after the Conquest of 1521 and, soon after, the first silver mines were worked. The city prospered and, by the 1700s, became one of the largest silver producers in the world.

A feature of Guanajuato is the impressive **Teatro Juárez** (Juárez Theater) which stands on the main square, Plaza de la Unión. Built in 1903 with fine Doric columns, it is the opera house of Guanajuato and the main site of the famous Cervantes Festival. Guanajuato has one of the most important universities in Mexico. An impressive flight of steps leads up to the building, which is of white stone and shows Moorish influences. The town is known for the *estudiantinos*, student musicians who stroll around in colorful minstrel costumes, serenading and giving performances on special occasions. Take a look at the baroque **Basílica Nuestra Señora de Guanajuato** (Basilica of Our Lady of Guanajuato). Dating from the 17th century, it has a

Once the richest town in the land, Guanajuato has seven plazas opening off the Avenida Juárez

statue of the Virgin of Guanajuato, supposedly a gift from Philip II of Spain in 1557. **Alhóndiga de Granaditas**, the site of a major rebel victory, is now an important art museum. The **Museo de Diego Rivera** (Diego Rivera Museum), birthplace of Mexico's celebrated painter, houses a number of his works. The **Museo de las Momias** (Mummy Museum), located just outside the town, is something unique to Guanajuato and worth a visit. In its vaults are a hundred or so well-preserved mummies. They apparently owe their good condition to the mineral salts in the soil of the local cemetery.

Further along **Mex 110** you can turn north to reach **Cerro del Cubilete** (Cubilete Mountain), a prominent hill on which stands an impressive statue of Christ the King. From here there are magnificent views of the area. Considered the geographical center of Mexico, the spot is much visited by pilgrims.

ℹ️ Calle de Insurgencia No 6

*Take **Mex 45** southeast for 46km (28 miles) to Irapuato.*

Irapuato, Guanajuato

6 The town of Irapuato is one of the largest producers of strawberries. It has a few buildings worth visiting, namely the **Palacio Municipal** (Town Hall) built in a neoclassical style and with the largest open courtyard in the country, the **Templo de Guadalupe**, and the **Templo de San Francisco**, which has two notable paintings by the well-known Mexican artists Miguel Cabrera and Francisco Eduardo Tresguerras.

*Take **Mex 45** southwest for another 22km (14 miles) to Salamanca.*

Salamanca, Guanajuato

7 The city of Salamanca lies on the northern banks of the Rio Lerma (Lerma River) in a fertile plain. Its main feature is the 17th-century **Templo de San Agustín** (Church of St Augustine), renowned for its rich interior which is almost completely covered with paneling, painted and gilded with ornate decorations. Moorish influences can be seen in the carved and gilded dome. Its two altars, dedicated to St Joseph and St Anne, are outstanding examples of the elaborate Churrigueresque style.

*Take **Mex 45** southeast to Celaya.*

Celaya, Guanajuato

8 Celaya lies in a valley basin known as El Bajío. The town has attractive squares and gardens and a few buildings of note. Take a look at the **Palacio Municipal** (Town Hall) and the neoclassical **Templo de Carmen** (Church of Our Lady of Carmen), which has an impressive dome. Celaya was the home of artist Francisco Eduardo Tresguerras (1759–1833), and some of his work can be seen in the church. Of special interest is his wall painting in the **Capilla del Juicio** (Chapel of the Last Judgement). The bridge over the Río Laja is an unusual neoclassical-style construction, and is also the work of Tresguerras.

*Return to Mexico City via **toll road 45D** to Querétaro and then **toll road 57D**.*

Ciudad de México – Querétaro **219 (137)**
Querétaro – San Miguel de Allende **58 (36)**
San Miguel de Allende – Atotonilco **16 (10)**
Atotonilco – Dolores Hidalgo **28 (17)**
Dolores Hidalgo – Guanajuato **54 (32)**
Guanajuato – Irapuato **46 (28)**
Irapuato – Salamanca **22 (14)**
Salamanca – Celaya **38 (24)**
Celaya – Ciudad de México **243 (152)**

BACK TO NATURE

5 Even in the heart of Guanajuato there is plenty for the birdwatcher to see. House finches, brown towhees and lesser goldfinches can be found in the parks and gardens while vermilion flycatchers, Inca doves and canyon wrens prefer the more open scrub further away from the center. Oak and manzanita woodland away from the city is home to white-eared hummingbirds, American robins, northern flickers and rufous-crowned sparrows, the numbers of these resident species being swollen by winter visitors from North America such as orange-crowned warblers, Townsend's warblers and hermit warblers.

4 days – 774km (480 miles)

THE LAND OF THE TARASCANS

Ciudad de México (Mexico City) • Valle de Bravo
San José Purúa • Mil Cumbres • Morelia
Tzintzuntzan • Pátzcuaro • Santa Clara del Cobre
Ciudad de México

This tour sets out from Mexico City, taking you west through the states of Mexico and Michoacán, one of the loveliest regions in the country. This is a route of great scenic beauty, passing through long stretches of fir and pine forests, reminiscent of alpine landscapes. There are magnificent panoramas of mountains, deep gorges and subtropical valleys, with lakes, rivers and waterfalls. You will visit one of Mexico's most elegant Colonial cities and a quaint little Indian lakeside town. Also included are typical Mexican villages renowned for their colorful handicrafts. The climate in this region is generally pleasantly mild, with cool evenings.

Watching the world go by at a donkey's pace: a resident of Janitzio, in Lake Pátzcuaro

ⓘ Avenida Presidente Masaryk 172, Ciudad de México

*From Mexico City take **Mex 15** southwest to Toluca. From Toluca take **Mex 134** for some 42km (26 miles), then branch off to Valle de Bravo.*

Valle de Bravo, Mexico

1 Valle de Bravo is a quaint little town overlooking the Laguna de Avandaro (Lake Avandaro). Its little houses, with whitewashed walls, thatched roofs and stone chimneys, give it a distinctive charm. In the **Iglesia de Santa María** (Church of St Mary) is a much venerated black Christ figure. The town is renowned for its pottery and the cultivation of exotic plants. It also forms part of the monarch butterfly sanctuary.

The lake, which was formed by the large Alemán Dam, is surrounded by pine forests, hidden creeks and streams. The scenery here is magnificent and the region is often referred to as 'Little Switzerland'. It is a popular weekend resort for Mexican families, many of whom have second homes here. There are facilities for golfing, boating, windsurfing, water skiing and all types of water sports. Camping facilities are also available.

*Take the road northeast. Join **Mex 15** heading for Toluca–Morelia and continue to San José Purúa.*

San José Purúa, Michoacán

2 On the way to San José Purúa make a short stop in the little town of Zitácuaro, which is renowned for its fine woodcarvings and silver jewelry.

In the village of San José is the **spa**

A view of the aptly named Mil Cumbres ('a thousand peaks')

Overlooking the main square in Morelia is its cathedral, said to be one of the loveliest in the country. The shoeshine boy is wearing a boldly designed poncho, a blanket-like woven garment

hotel of San José Purúa, a long-time favorite with Mexicans from the capital and for visitors worldwide, who come to benefit from its thermal waters. It is worth taking a look around the lovely old building, set in attractive gardens, and you can admire the magnificent view of the canyons that stretch out before you. The region is a profusion of tropical flowers, royal palms, pines and groves of bananas and mangoes.

Continue on **Mex 15** *to Mil Cumbres.*

Mil Cumbres, Michoacán

3 Although this is only a stop *en route* to Morelia, it is not to be missed on any account. Mil Cumbres means 'a thousand peaks' in Spanish and this is what awaits you at this lookout point, which is well marked. The extraordinary view is unforgettable, as you gaze at the thickly wooded Sierra Madre mountain range that seems to go on forever.

Continue on **Mex 15** *for Morelia.*

Morelia, Michoacán

4 Morelia is one of Mexico's loveliest Colonial cities. Characterized by the soft pinkish-beige color of its elegant buildings, the city exudes an air of elegance and tranquillity. It is the capital of the state of Michoacán and has a fine university. Broad avenues are flanked by lovely arcades, typical of the Spanish architecture. The Plaza de los Mártires (the main square) is lined with laurels and overlooked by one of the most beautiful **cathedrals** in Mexico. Built between 1640 and 1744, it has a lovely rose-colored façade, twin towers and a tile-covered dome. Inside are some fine *retablos* and an impressive German organ, reputed to be one of the largest in the world. There are a number of interesting buildings to visit. The Templo de San Francisco Xavier, now a public library, is a fine example of the baroque style. In the cloister is the Casa de las Artesanías (the House of Handicrafts), with displays from all over the region, and you can watch the artisans at work.

The **Palacio de Gobierno** (Government Palace) is a handsome Colonial building with some interesting murals adorning the courtyard, and the **Museo Regional Michoacno** (Michoacán Museum) has a collection of artifacts from every period.

Many shops display attractive handicrafts and local products and

FOR THE CHILDREN

4 Children will enjoy a visit to **Juárez Park**, on the outskirts of Morelia, 3km (2 miles) south of the *zócalo*. The zoological gardens have a good collection of animals and birds in beautifully laid-out grounds, and it is a pleasant spot for a picnic.

RECOMMENDED WALKS

1 The area in and around Valle de Bravo will appeal to those who enjoy walking through cool forests of firs and pines. You will stumble upon all sorts of delightful little streams and inlets, and there are a number of pretty waterfalls in the area.

7 If you take the side trip to Uruapan from Santa Clara del Cobre, the **Parque Nacional Eduardo Ruíz** in Uruapan is a lovely place for a stroll, with its cascading waters, rocks and springs, set among lush tropical vegetation.

BACK TO NATURE

2 There are a number of butterfly refuges in the central highlands of Michoacán. One of the best-known is **El Refugio de las Mariposas Monarca** (El Rosario Monarch Butterfly Sanctuary), located 42km (36 miles) northeast of San José Purúa near the town of Angangueo. Each winter millions of monarch butterflies arrive here from southern Canada and the northern US. They can be seen from early November to late March. In spring, the butterflies depart and head northwards. There are several broods each year – the caterpillars feed on milkweeds – and successive generations spread up to and beyond the Canadian border by the end of the summer.

The Fountain of the Tarascans, *a handsome and unusual sculpture in a city known for its elegance*

One of the major attractions of this itinerary is the beauty of the regions through which you will travel. Varied landscapes of pine forests, endless mountain ranges, deep gorges and valleys will continuously unfold before you, not to mention the lakes, rivers and waterfalls. There are particularly beautiful stretches of road, however, in the area surrounding Valle de Bravo, where you will pass through heavily wooded regions, and the scenery is spectacular as you continue through San José Purúa and Mil Cumbres to Morelia.

6 The island of Janitzio on Lake Pátzcuaro is renowned for its unique **Día de los Muertos** (Festival of the Day of the Dead) which takes place on 1 and 2 November (All Saints and All Souls days). On the night of 1 November, the villagers gather to decorate the graves of their departed ones with offerings of flowers and food. They hold an all-night candlelit vigil, with Mass, prayers and music. Large crowds of tourists arrive every year to witness this fascinating event.

the local market is certainly worth a visit. On Sundays there is a band concert in the main square and weekly open-air concerts in the **Garden of Roses**. A famous landmark of this lovely city is **El Acueducto** (the aqueduct), built 1785 to 1789. With its 253 arches, it is about 1.5km (1 mile) in length. A short drive up the hillside offers an outstanding view of the city and its surroundings. For an enjoyable side trip, take **Mex 43** north for about 35km (22 miles) to Cuitzeo, on the shores of Lake Cuitzeo. This quaint fishing village is distinguished by its low white buildings with red bases and portals. The 16th-century Augustinian **Convento de Santa María Magdalena** (Convent of St Mary Magdalene) has an ornate façade in the Plateresque style and remains of old frescos in the cloisters.

Take **Mex 15***, then turn southwest at Guiroga on* **Mex 41** *to Tzintzuntzan.*

Tzintzuntzan, Michoacán

5 This curious-sounding name means 'the place of the hummingbirds' in Tarascan. Once an important center for the Tarascan Indians, it is believed to have been founded in the 11th century. It is now a sleepy little village lying on the shores of Lake Pátzcuaro. The local Indians produce attractive hand-painted pottery and woven

baskets and the **market** has a good selection of handicrafts and other regional products. A short drive up the hill leads to the ruins of an ancient Tarascan **pyramid**. This unusual structure consists of a large platform with the remains of five low temples, called *yácatas* in Náhuatl. Originally the platforms were probably tombs and the *yácatas* were cult centers, dedicated to Curicaveri, the god of fire. The place offers a fine view of **Lago de Pátzcuaro** (Lake Pátzcuaro).

Take the road south along the lakeshore to Pátzcuaro.

Pátzcuaro, Michoacán

6 Pátzcuaro is an enchanting little town of red-tiled roofs and narrow cobblestoned streets. With donkeys and carts ambling by, the place has managed to retain much of its Tarascan past. The pace of life is slow and cars are not much in evidence here. Pátzcuaro was once a center of the Tarascan Indians, or Purepechas as they called themselves. After the Spanish Conquest the Indians were badly oppressed until the arrival of Vasco de Quiroga, the Bishop of Michoacán from 1539 to 1565. The Bishop devoted himself to helping the Indians by founding new settlements and teaching them how to develop and promote their traditional crafts. Known affectionately as 'Tata Vasco', he was greatly loved by the local people. Today, the Indians live mainly by fishing and farming, and continue to produce attractive pottery, basketware and lacquerware, much as before.

The main square is small and delightful, lined by neatly trimmed trees and flanked by attractive Colonial-style buildings. Several are worth a visit. The **Casa de los Once Patios** (House of the Eleven Patios) has been made into studios and you can watch artists at their work. The **Basílica de Nuestra Señora de la Salud** (Church of Our Lady of Health), founded by Bishop Quiroga in 1540, contains a much venerated statue of the **Virgen de la Salud** (Virgin of Health), who is attributed with healing powers. An interesting mural by Juan O'Gorman, one of Mexico's leading artists, can be seen in the **Biblioteca** (library).

The **Casa del Gigante** (the House of the Giant) features a huge carving of a warrior on one of its pillars. The Friday **market** is a very colorful event in Pátzcuaro, when Tarascans gather from all over the region to buy and sell their goods.

Its houses clinging to its steep contours, the island of Janitzio sits prettily in Lake Pátzcuaro

A short drive takes you to the shores of Lake Pátzcuaro. This pretty little lake is renowned for its butterfly-net style of fishing, although unfortunately it is less in use these days and tends to come out just for the benefit of photographers. The fish caught here, known simply as white fish (*pescado blanco*), are considered a delicacy. Several small islands in the lake can be reached by launches hired from the quayside. The most striking is the island of Janitzio, which rises up sharply from the middle of the lake. Gaily colored houses cling to the steep hill, which is crowned by a colossal statue of Morelos, one of the great heroes of the struggle for independence. A staircase inside the statue is lined with frescos showing scenes of Morelos's life, and there is a fine panoramic view of the lake from the head.

i Plaza Quiroga

*Take **Mex 120** south for 16km (10 miles) to Santa Clara del Cobre.*

Santa Clara del Cobre, Michoacán

7 The old Tarascan town of Santa Clara del Cobre (now officially known as Villa Escalante) is a coppersmithing center. The town has a long tradition of this craft, and many beautiful objects of finely beaten copper are sold in shops under the arcades around the main square. You can watch artisans at work and visit the small copper

museum at the entrance of the town. A Copper Fair (Feria del Cobre) is held in mid-August.

Before returning to Mexico City, take a detour to Uruapan via Pátzcuaro, on the road southwest. This attractive Colonial town of beautiful parks and tropical vegetation is renowned for its distinctive lacquerwork. About 10km (6 miles) south of town is the spectacular waterfall of Tzaráracua, set in beautiful woodlands. Follow **Mex 37** north for 16km (10 miles), then turn west onto a gravel road for about 19km (12 miles) to the Paricutín volcano. In 1943 a local farmer was astonished to witness an unexpected eruption right in his own cornfield. In a few days the volcano had risen to 30m (98 feet) and continued to erupt, causing much destruction to the villages in the vicinity and forcing thousands to flee their homes. There has been no further volcanic activity since 1952. The half-buried **Church of San Juan Parangaricutiro** can be seen rising forlornly from the lava. To reach the crater you must leave your car in the village of Angahuan and continue on horseback (or on foot) for a few miles.

Return to Mexico City via Morelia.

Ciudad de México – Valle de Bravo	118 (74)
Valle de Bravo – San José Purúa	83 (52)
San José Purúa – Mil Cumbres	48 (30)
Mil Cumbres – Morelia	64 (40)
Morelia – Tzintzuntzan	45 (28)
Tzintzuntzan – Pátzcuaro	13 (8)
Pátzcuaro – Santa Clara del Cobre	16 (10)
Santa Clara deCobre – Ciudad de México	387 (238)

FOR HISTORY BUFFS

4 Morelia was originally inhabited by a tribe called the Matlazincas and was later taken over by the Tarascans. The town was established by the Spaniards in 1541 and called Valladolid. In 1582 it became the capital of Michoacán. After independence was won from the Spaniards, its name was changed to Morelia (1828) in honor of the priest José María Morelos y Pavón, one of the great heroes of the war. You can visit his birthplace, the **Casa Natal de Morelos**, which has documents and relics relating to that period of history. Eight rooms have been turned into a museum and there is an eternal flame in the coach entrance on the side to mark the place where he was born in 1765.

4/5 days – 818km (510 miles)

THE TRAIL OF
THE TOTONACA

Ciudad de México (Mexico City) • Tulancingo
Pahuatlán • Castillo de Teayo • El Tajín • Papantla
Tecolutla • Nautla • Perote • Acatzingo
Ciudad de México

This tour from Mexico City takes you northeast of the capital through the states of Hidalgo, Puebla and Veracruz right to the Gulf of Mexico. The scenery is greatly varied, combining rugged mountain ranges with coffee plantations and lush vegetation, hot and humid tropical forests, and the sweeping beaches of the eastern shores. A highlight of your journey is a visit to one of Mexico's more unusual and remote pre-Columbian religious centers, buried deep in the jungle and still largely unexcavated. There is also a chance to explore fascinating Indian villages and visit some of the area's lovely churches and monasteries.

BACK TO NATURE

Mexico is an excellent country in which to see hummingbirds: numerous species occur, each with its own special habitat requirements, with the result that individuals of one kind or another can be seen almost anywhere. Hummingbirds feed on nectar and are especially attracted to red flowers. With this in mind, many hotels and private residences put out hummingbird feeders which comprise a bottle of sugar water with a red nozzle. Among the more regularly seen species are the rufous hummingbird, the broad-tailed hummingbird and the white-eared hummingbird.

i Avenida Presidente Masaryk 172, Ciudad de México

*From Mexico City take **Mex 132** northeast, then join **Mex 130** to Tulancingo.*

Tulancingo, Hidalgo

1 On the way to Tulancingo you might like to stop at Singuilucán. The 16th-century Augustinian con-vent here has a doorway in the Plateresque style and fine cloisters and some interesting *retablos* can be seen in the baroque-style **church**.
Tulancingo itself, once a Toltec city of some importance, is now a flour-ishing industrial center. Cider, *serapes* (colorful woolen shawls) and textiles are among its specialties. Worth a visit is the neoclassical-style **cathedral**, founded in the 18th century and adjoining an Augustinian **convent**. North of the town are the sparse ruins of Huapalcalco, an old Toltec center.

*Continue northeast on **Mex 130**. Turn left onto a road in poor condition for some 27km (17 miles) to Pahuatlán.*

As if transported through time from Mexico's proud and glorious past, this dancer decked out in Aztec costume displays the bold colors and dramatic design that have been favored by Mexicans down the ages

Pahuatlán, Puebla

2 Pahuatlán lies in the heart of an agricultural area and is a center for the production of fruits, maize, tobacco, sugarcane and vanilla, among others. It also makes a good base for visiting other interesting Indian villages, such as nearby San Pablito, a village of Otomí Indians who still follow strange, ancient customs involving witchcraft and magic. The local women can be seen in their colorful costumes sitting in front of their dwellings flattening out the bark for the famous *papel amates*, brightly painted Indian bark paintings found all over Mexico.

*Return to **Mex 130**. Continue northeast for 82km (51 miles) to Poza Rica. Take **Mex 180** north for 18km (11 miles), then turn left to Castillo de Teayo, about 19km (12 miles).*

Castillo de Teayo, Veracruz

3 On the way to Teayo there are a few places worth a stop-off. The town of Huauchinango is renowned for its magnificent flower market, with a permanent exhibition of countless varieties of azaleas. Its annual flower festival takes place at the end of February and lasts for a week. Build-ings of note are the **templo parroquial** (parish church), with its impressive cupola, and handsome **Palacio Municipal** (Town Hall). About 22km (16 miles) from Huauchinango is the immense hydroelectric dam of Necaxa, set amidst luxuriant vege-tation. About 11km (7 miles) north of the dam is the lovely Necaxa waterfall, with a drop of over 160m (525 feet). Continuing along **Mex 130** you might also like to stop briefly at the coffee-growing center of Xicotepec, set in tropical surroundings.
Right in the heart of the village of Teayo, on the main square, is a well-preserved pyramid called the **Castillo de Teayo** (Castle of Teayo). The remains of a temple stand on top of a three-tiered structure, with a staircase leading up to the top platform. The pyramid's architectural style suggests it was built by the Aztecs, but recent evidence has led experts to believe the site may well date back several hundred years earlier, to the time of the Toltecs. Pieces of pre-Hispanic sculpture found in the vicinity are displayed around the pyramid. The little village of Teayo is only about a hundred years old and was built by the local Indians, who used materials from previous Indian dwellings.
The road northeast of Tihuatlán leads to Tuxpan, situated about 11km (7 miles) north of the mouth of the Tuxpan River. The place is popular for its freshwater and deep-sea fishing. Fishing competitions are held at the end of June and beginning of July, attracting many competitors. The **Museo Regional de Antropología e Historia** (museum) here has an attractive collection of pottery and artifacts of the Huastec culture.

[i] Corregidora Parque Reforma

*Return to Tihualtán. Take **Mex 180** south to Poza Rica. Continue southeast for 20km (12 miles) on **Mex 127** to El Tajín.*

El Tajín, Veracruz

4 El Tajín (which means 'lightning' in Totonac) is one of Mexico's most interesting and unusual archaeological sites, set in a region of lush green hills and vanilla plantations. Although the site extends over a large area, only a small part has been excavated. Once the religious center of a Gulf Coast culture, its earliest structures are thought to date back to the 4th and 5th centuries AD (early Classic period). There are signs of Toltec influences at the time of its cultural peak, from AD100 to 900. The city was dedicated to the cult of Tajín, the god of lightning.

El Tajín's Pyramid of the Niches, with its precarious-looking steps ascending six steep tiers

RECOMMENDED WALKS

Two areas that offer pleasant surroundings in which to take a leisurely stroll are the **Necaxa Dam (3)**, where you can wander surrounded by tropical vegetation, and the **Cofre de Perote National Park (8)**, with its dramatic landscape of trees and boulders amidst bizarre rock formations.

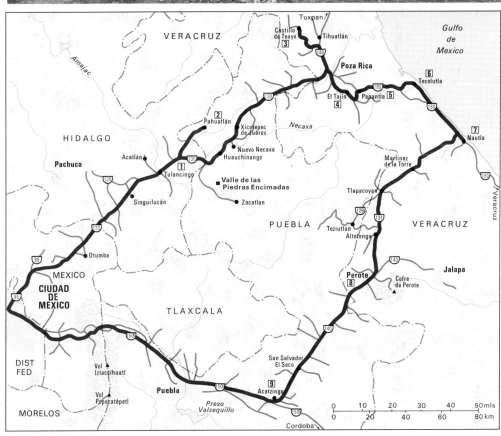

SCENIC ROUTES

This route combines mountainous areas, lush tropical regions and coastal drives. The first part of the drive offers magnificent views as you cross the Sierra Madre Oriental mountains. Just before Castillo de Teayo this will gradually give way to the exciting jungle terrain of verdant foliage and hot, humid tropical forests. There are some particularly scenic stretches around Perote, with dramatic views of the volcanoes and mountainous landscapes. The return journey from Puebla back to Mexico City also affords excellent views of the two volcanoes, Popocatépetl and Iztaccíhuatl.

The Sierra Madre Oriental, a formidable barrier between the Central Plateau and the east coast

The most striking structure is the famous **Pirámide de los Nichos** (Pyramid of the Niches). Set on a large, square base, it stands 25m (82 feet) high. The building consists of six stories, with a temple on top. Running up one side is a wide staircase flanked by carved mosaics and broken up by five small platforms on the way up. Its distinctive feature, however, is the effect of the 365 shallow niches carved into the tiers around the pyramid, symbolizing the days of the year and apparently used merely for decorative purposes. Although the original colors have long since faded, the effects created by light and shadow give the massive structure its unique appearance.

Other remains can be seen dotted around the area on various levels. Several **ball courts** have been found, suggesting this may have been a center for *pelota*. The walls of the two restored ball courts bear reliefs depicting scenes from the sport. A road runs north to another part of the site from a later period, where there is a small square, called **Plaza el Tajín Chico**, and some groups of buildings. Standing on a mound is the impressive **Edificio de las Columnas** (Building of the Columns). Its niches are decorated, and the massive columns at the base of the structure have relief carvings depicting various scenes and personages. A climb to the top will give an impressive view of the entire site and its surroundings. Another structure of interest in the group is known as the **Edificio de los Tuneles** (Tunnel Building), from which two underground passageways lead onto a large courtyard.

Take the road northeast for 16km (10 miles) to Papantla.

Papantla, Veracruz

5 Papantla, Mexico's most important producer of vanilla, lies among large vanilla plantations amid hills of tropical vegetation. The place was once

the capital of the Totonac kingdom, and its descendants live here today. The little town is very attractive and produces a variety of handicrafts, in particular textiles, embroidery, pottery and jewelry. Its main claim to fame, however, are the dramatic **Voladores de Papantla** (Flying Men of Papantla).

i Palacio Municipal

Continue on **Mex 180** *east for 41km (25 miles) to Tecolutla.*

Tecolutla, Veracruz

6 This picturesque fishing village is situated on the Gulf Coast at the mouth of the River Tecolutla. The long, flat beach is shaded with palms and set against a background of lush tropical foliage. This resort is the one closest to Mexico City and is a relaxing spot for swimming, fishing or sailing.

Take the southeast coast road to join **Mex 180** *to Nautla.*

Nautla, Veracruz

7 Situated further down the Gulf of Mexico is the quaint fishing village of Nautla, which offers good fishing and water sports. There are some old Totonac ruins which you can visit in the vicinity.

Take **Mex 129** *and* **131** *southwest to Perote.*

Paseo de la Reforma by night: Mexico City's grand boulevard of smart shops, restaurants, hotels and office towers is 30 blocks long

Perote, Veracruz

8 Perote lies at the foot of the impressive **Cofre de Perote** volcano (also called Nauhcampatépetl). The main attraction here is the **Cofre de Perote National Park**, an area of extraordinary rock formations. These were formed by eruptions in the past and give the impression of a trunk or chest (cofre). On the outskirts of town is **El Fuerte de San Carlos** (fort), which was built towards the end of the 18th century and later used as a prison.

Take **Mex 140** *southwest to Acatzingo.*

Acatzingo, Puebla

9 Acatzingo is noted mainly for its splendid Franciscan **Convento de San Juan Evangelista** (Monastery of St John the Evangelist), dating from the early 16th century. The church has impressive Gothic vaults and an exceptional stone baptismal font.

Attractive handicrafts can be bought here, and on Tuesdays there is a lively market.

Return to Ciudad de México via Puebla on **toll road 150D** *west.*

Ciudad de México – Tulancingo **115 (72)**
Tulancingo – Pahuatlán **35 (22)**
Pahuatlán – Castillo de Teayo **163 (102)**
Castillo de Teayo – El Tajín **54 (34)**
El Tajín – Papantla **16 (10)**
Papantla – Tecolutla **35 (22)**
Tecolutla – Nautla **41 (25)**
Nautla – Perote **102 (64)**
Perote – Acatzingo **91 (55)**
Acatzingo – Ciudad de México **166 (104)**

SPECIAL TO ...

5 The ritual of the **Voladores de Papantla** (Flying Men of Papantla) goes back to pre-Hispanic times and is thought to be related to agriculture and fertility. Five men, dressed in traditional costumes, climb up a tall pole onto a tiny platform on top. One stays playing a tune on his pipe while doing a little dance. The other four, secured by ropes entwined around their bodies, jump off head first and twirl down slowly to the ground in ever widening circles. Just before touching down, they do a somersault and land on their feet. Aspects of the dance are apparently related to the old Mesoamerican calendar: each of the four flyers circles the pole 13 times, making a total of 52, representing the number of months in the Aztec calendar and the number of years in their 'century'. Performances occur on special festivals, particularly during the week-long fiesta of Corpus Christi.

FOR HISTORY BUFFS

4 After the Spanish Conquest nothing was heard of El Tajín until the site was visited by Diego Ruiz in 1785, who wrote an account of it. In 1811 it was visited by the famous explorer Alexander von Humboldt and in 1836 by the Austrian traveler W Dupaix. Excavations commenced in 1934 under the direction of Mexican archaeologist José García Payon, and continued by others. Much, however, is still to be done.

FOR CHILDREN

Although the main appeal of this tour is its cultural aspect, children would certainly enjoy the colorful festivals that could be encountered *en route* during certain times of the year.

6 Tecolutla is a pleasant little seaside resort with a fine palm-fringed beach and is a welcome place to stop and let them enjoy the water.

THE SOUTH & SOUTHEAST

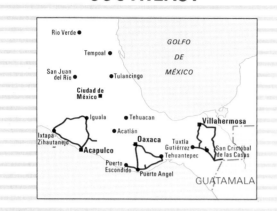

T his is a large area covering the states of Guerrero, Oaxaca, Tabasco and Chiapas. The region is fascinating, with great changes of climate, scenery and cultures. The mighty mountain ranges of the Sierra Madre del Sur (Southern Sierra Madre) dominate the states of Guerrero and Oaxaca, diminishing finally into the jungle highlands of Chiapas to the east. The Pacific coastline to the south is magnificent, with hundreds of miles of palm-fringed beaches, wide bays, rocky outcrops and inlets. Mexico's most famous resort, Acapulco, is located in Guerrero. Among the resorts dotted about the southern coast is the brand-new development of Huatulco, south of Oaxaca. Much of the coast, however, is still untouched and retains its original wild beauty. Chiapas, Mexico's southernmost state, is a region of tropical rain forests, with rivers, waterfalls and lagoons. There are areas of stunning beauty, and the region is rich in flora and fauna.

The states of Oaxaca and Chiapas have an important archaeological past. During the Classic period of the Mayan civilization, between the 7th and 10th centuries, great cities were built all over southeastern Mexico and parts of Central America. Thousands of sites in the region have yet to be explored. Among those that have been restored are the ruins of Palenque. Set deep in the jungles of Chiapas, they are perhaps the most magnificent of all the Mayan remains in Mexico. The beautiful ruins of Monte Alban and Mitla, near the city of Oaxaca, are relics of the Zapotec and Mixtec civilizations, which inhabited the region long before the Spaniards arrived in the mid-16th century. The Conquistadores encountered fierce resistance in this part of Mexico, and it was some time before the area was settled. Oaxaca and Chiapas are still essentially Indian. Many different tribes continue to live here and speak their own language, practicing old ways and traditions with little evidence of modern influences. Chiapas is more remote and inaccessible than many other parts of Mexico, and will appeal to the more adventurous type of traveler.

Lovely towns and churches were built during the 300 years of Spanish rule, and some fine examples in the area combine Colonial architecture with a strong Indian flavor. Oaxaca and San Cristóbal, in particular, demonstrate the blend of Indian and Hispanic cultures.

The range of attractions in these four states is immense, from pre-Columbian ruins, fascinating Indian towns and Colonial architecture to glittering beach resorts. Handicrafts and colorful markets are also a delight. And the beauty of nature – the scenery, exotic birds and brilliant flowers – is unbeatable.

Oaxaca:

Known as the 'Jade City', the state capital is one of the most charming cities in Mexico. Lying in the Valley of Oaxaca and ringed by beautiful mountains, the town is Colonial in architecture but Indian in flavor. The main square is always lively, with street vendors, concerts, marimba music and mariachis. Among the portals are cafés, restaurants and shops. At night the scene becomes even more active, as the whole town seems to converge on the square.

The glory of Oaxaca is the 17th-century **Iglesia Santo Domingo** (Church of St Dominic) with a magnificent interior, richly inlaid with gold. The **cathedral** on the zócalo (main square) and the **Church of La Soledad** are other buildings of note. The **Museo Regional de Oaxaca** (Regional Museum) has a priceless collection of Zapotec and Mixtec treasures. The town is renowned for its pottery and handicrafts, and its Saturday market is famed throughout Mexico.

In the high, semitropical valley near Oaxaca, many cacti flourish

Acapulco:

Acapulco has long been Mexico's most famous resort. Acapulco Bay is a dazzling sight, with its gorgeous sweep of beach set against a backdrop of mountains. White sands are shaded by luscious palms and surrounded by rich, colorful vegetation. High-rise hotels and condominiums with swimming pools and tropical gardens line the shores. Acapulco is essentially a fun place, with water skiing, parasailing, boating, bay cruises and constant activity around the beach, which is lined with restaurants. Acapulco by night has a special pulse. As the beautiful sunsets fade and the resort becomes a mass of twinkling lights, everyone sets off to invade the bars and restaurants and dance the night away.

A unique attraction in the vicinity is **La Quebrada**, where daring clifftop divers do a swan dive into the swirling waters of the Pacific far below. The scene is most dramatic at night, when the descent is lit by flares.

Acapulco's green foothills dip down to the hospitable waters of its bay

Villahermosa:

Villahermosa, capital of the state of Tabasco, lies on the banks of the Grijalva River amid steamy jungle terrain. A somewhat brash oil boom town, it is useful as a base for visiting Palenque and the surrounding region, but the town has two of its own major attractions. At **Parque La Venta**, a wonderful open-air museum, a collection of monolithic heads and sculptures from the Olmec civilization is displayed in a jungle setting. Deer, monkeys, tapirs and racoons roam freely, while caged jaguars and croco- diles can also be seen. Another place of interest is the **Museo Regional de Antropología** (Museum of Anthro- pology of the State of Tabasco), which has an excellent collection of artifacts from the Olmec, Mayan and other pre-Hispanic cultures.

Villahermosa's downtown area has an attractive pedestrian zone with shops, and the *malecón* along the river is pleasant for walking. Boat trips along the Grijalva are available.

4/5 days – 853km (531 miles)

THE ZAPOTEC & MIXTEC CULTURES

Oaxaca • Santa María del Tule • Dainzú
Lambityeco • Yagul • Mitla • Tehuantepec
Huatulco • Puerto Angel • Puerto Escondido
Monte Albán • Oaxaca

This tour from Oaxaca explores the eastern and southern parts of the state. This is a fascinating trip through rugged, mountainous landscapes, woods and valleys, and arid regions of scrub and cacti. You will visit two of Mexico's major pre-Columbian sites, boasting the finest examples of the ancient Zapotec and Mixtec cultures. The route passes through little Indian towns with gaily colored churches and fine examples of local handicrafts. As a contrast, you can relax in some of the beach resorts along the southern coastline, with their beautiful sandy beaches, rocky inlets and abundant tropical vegetation.

i Matamoros 105, Esq García Vigil, Oaxaca

*Take **Mex 190** east for 10km (6 miles) to Santa María del Tule.*

Markets and shops are a showcase of skill in old traditions like lacemaking, crochet and weaving

Santa María del Tule, Oaxaca

1 The main attraction in the tiny village of Santa María del Tule is the famed **Arbol del Tule** (Tule Tree). This giant ahuehuete tree, in the cypress family, is really a group of trees springing from the same roots and merging together. It is said to have the largest girth in the world, some 42m (140 feet), a measurement equal to its own height. Believed to be over 2,000 years old, it may be the oldest living thing in Mexico. Truly a unique sight, it stands in the grounds of a charming little white church with painted decorations on its façade, typical of the local style.

*Continue on **Mex 190** east for another 19km (12 miles) with a brief detour to Tlacochahuaya, then turn right to Dainzú, a short distance from the main road.*

Dainzú, Oaxaca

2 Before Dainzú, make a brief detour to the village of Tlacochahuaya. The 16th-century **Church of San Jerónimo** has an exquisite interior, baroque altar and Indian wall paintings. The pre-Columbian site of Dainzú is in a beautiful setting. Evidence suggests the old settlement was inhabited from about 800BC till the 15th century. At one time an important Zapotec cult center, it probably reached its peak around 800 to 300BC. Only part of the site has been excavated so far, but work is continuing. One of the largest structures has interesting carvings of ball players, priests and figures that suggest influences of the Olmec culture. A small ball court that has been uncovered probably dates from the 10th or 11th century.

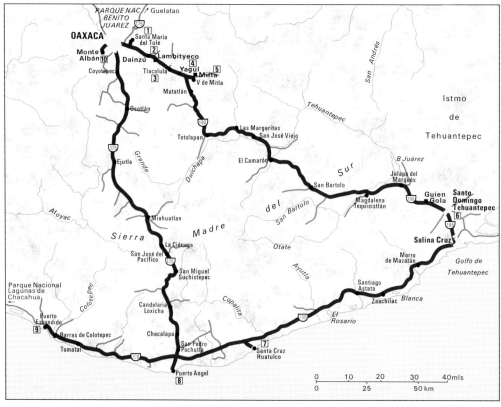

*Continue on **Mex 190** for a few miles further to Lambityeco, close to the main road.*

Lambityeco, Oaxaca

3 Lambityeco was also a center of the Zapotec civilization and is believed to have been inhabited between the 7th and 9th centuries AD, corresponding to the time of the decline of the great city of Monte Albán. Beneath a small pyramid a house was uncovered and several tombs were found. Of special interest is **Tomb 5**, on which are carved two faces with names, most probably those of the owner and his wife.

*Continue on **Mex 190** for 5km (3 miles). Turn left for a short distance to the Yagul ruins.*

Yagul, Oaxaca

4 This ancient Zapotec site lies on a flat mountaintop surrounded by clusters of the cacti typical of this region. The place dates back to around 800BC and reached its peak between AD900 and 1200. Groups of temples and palaces stand on three levels; on the second level a large ball court was uncovered. A number of tombs have been found here, carved with geometric patterns, and are similar to those found at the ancient site of Mitla. Perhaps the most interesting building is the **Palacio de los Seis Patios** (Palace of the Six Court-yards) with its six inner courts. The climb to the top of the building is steep but it offers a rewarding view of the whole valley below.

Before proceeding with the main itinerary, take a little side trip to the Zapotec village of Tlacolula, located nearby to the right of **Mex 190**. The **parish church**, in baroque style, is noted for its lavishly decorated **Capilla del Santo Cristo** (Chapel of Christ). The impressive cast-iron gate is a fine example of Colonial art. Tlacolula is

The ruins of Yagul, among the most interesting and spectacular in Oaxaca. The large ball court is beautifully restored

famed for its colorful Sunday market, when the place teems with Indians from all over the region and a great variety of goods are displayed.

*Return to **Mex 190** and continue southeast to Mitla.*

Mitla, Oaxaca

5 On the edge of the tiny village of Mitla stand the ruins of Mitla, which rate among Mexico's major pre-Columbian centers. At the entrance to the site is a local market selling brightly colored woven shawls and blankets, as well as many other handicrafts. The tourist is a target here, and you will immediately be surrounded by the local vendors, so be prepared.

The name Mitla means 'place of the dead' in Náhuatl, the ancient tongue of the Aztecs. The site is relatively small in area. A row of cacti forms a tall fence along one side, and a gaily painted church in the background completes the setting. The site was inhabited by the Zapotec people long before the Christian era. By the 1st century AD it had grown into an important religious center. Around the 10th century a tribe called the Mixtecs arrived in the area and built the city as it stands today. As well as being gifted builders, the Mixtecs were brilliant jewelers and potters. When the Spaniards arrived after the Conquest in 1521, the city was still inhabited and the buildings in good condition. Little restoration has been necessary.

The most attractive feature of Mitla is the beauty of the intricate stone mosaics covering many of the buildings. These form thousands of geometric patterns, so finely done that they give the impression of lacework.

FOR HISTORY BUFFS

Those interested in people and events of the last century might like to take a trip to Guelatao, located about 63km (37 miles) north of Oaxaca on **Mex 175**. It is the birthplace of Benito Juárez, one of Mexico's greatest leaders. Born a Zapotec Indian of humble origin, he twice became Mexico's president, the second time in 1867 when he defeated the Hapsburg Emperor Maximilian, whom he had executed. He is remembered for his efforts to improve the plight of the poor, for his land reform, and for curtailing the privileges of the church. A monument to Juárez stands in the main square of the village. Take a look at the museum, which houses a collection of documents and relics relating to his life.

BACK TO NATURE

9 To the west of Puerto Escondido is **Parque Nacional Lagunas de Chacahua** (Chacahua Lakes National Park) – as the name implies, an area of lagoons, a river, and mangrove and bamboo swamps. Here you can see crocodiles and alligators, iguanas, crabs and many species of migratory birds.

Great egrets and snowy egrets wade elegantly in the water, sometimes joined by wood storks and green herons. Waders such as solitary sandpipers, least sandpipers, willets and lesser yellowlegs spend the winter here before returning north in spring to breed.

RECOMMENDED WALKS

6 A drive of 15km (9 miles) west of Tehuantepec leads to a track which runs for about 6km (4 miles) to a path. Here you must leave the car and continue on foot up a rocky hillside (about an hour or so) to reach the imposing pre-Columbian site called **Guien Gola**. The climb is quite steep and takes you through an attractive terrain of rocks and greenery. Here, a ceremonial center is laid out on a platform, and there are temples and the remains of a palace constructed like a labyrinth, with a number of rooms.

Beneath Mitla's palace ruins, the ground is honeycombed with cruciform tombs and other chambers

Five groups of structures are spread out over the complex. The most important of these is the **Grupo de las Columnas** (Group of Columns), built around two courtyards surrounded by three large halls. The **Salón de las Columnas** (Hall of Columns) has six large columns, each made from a single stone, and walls covered by countless mosaic patterns. A narrow passageway with a low roof leads into a small chamber called the **Patio de las Grecas**. You can't help marveling at the magnificent workmanship involved in the creation of the mosaics. The various patterns, including a Greek-key-type motif, are thought to relate to religious concepts. Note the fine pillared doorway of another building on one side of the **Patio de las Cruces** (Patio of the Crosses), characteristic of the architecture in Mitla. In front is the entrance to an underground tomb, also decorated with mosaic patterns; clamber down and have a look around. A single column at the north side of the tomb is known as **La Columna de la Vida** (the Column of Life) and visitors can measure their life expectancy by stretching their arms around the pillar. The structures that form part of the **Grupo de las Iglesias** (Churches Group) are also decorated by fine mosaics and contain some remains of frescos. On the other side of the stream which runs through the site are other buildings, not yet fully restored.

In the village of Mitla itself, near the main square, the **Museo Frissell de Arte Zapoteca** (Frissell Museum) has an excellent collection of artifacts from the Zapotec and Mixtec cultures.

*Continue on **Mex 190** east, stopping off at Tequesistlán, then continue to Tehuantepec, for a total of about 212km (132 miles).*

Tehuantepec, Oaxaca

6 *En route* to Tehuantepec, make a stop at Tequesistlán, an attractive little oasis of palm trees situated on the river of the same name. A variety of handicrafts are produced here. Take a look at **El Templo de Santa María Magdalena** (the Temple of St Mary Magdalene), which was constructed in the last century, then proceed to Tehuantepec.

The town of Tehuantepec lies on the Istmo de Tehuantepec (Isthmus of Tehuantepec), the narrowest part of land in Mexico. Here the Gulf of Mexico and the Pacific Ocean are separated by only 225km (140 miles). Plans for a canal to link the two bodies of water have not yet been realized. The town, with its tropical setting, has a hot and humid climate. Its inhabitants are mainly descendants of the Zapotec Indians and *mestizos,* (mixed Indian and Spanish blood). Tehuantepec is known for its fiestas and the beauty of its women, who are famed for their statuesque bearing. The traditional costume, donned for special occasions, is particularly lovely, with elaborate embroidery and flowers. Heavy gold necklaces are worn, and a headdress of stiff white lace. The women play a dominant role in many aspects of daily life, and Tehuantepec is close to having a matriarchal society. Take a look at the lively local market, which is run mostly by women. Two buildings of note are the **cathedral**, founded as a Dominican church in 1544, and the **Palacio Municipal** (Town Hall), an impressive building of light-colored stone built on columns.

*Take **Mex 185** to Salina Cruz. Continue on **Mex 200** southwest to Huatulco.*

Huatulco, Oaxaca

7 Huatulco is Mexico's most recent resort development, and it is expected to become a huge complex within the next few years. The setting is certainly beautiful. A series of nine interlocking bays with white sand beaches, stretching on either side of the little fishing village of Santa Cruz Huatulco, is broken up by boulders and rocks and set against a background of the dense jungles of Oaxaca. Small islands are dotted about in the gulf, and there is a large nature reserve in the area. It is a marvelous place for swimming, sailing, fishing and enjoying all types of aquatic sports, with facilities readily available, and you can take boat trips to beautiful secluded beaches.

Continue on **Mex 200** *south for 35km (21 miles). At Pochutla, turn south to Puerto Angel.*

Puerto Angel, Oaxaca

8 On the way to Puerto Angel, you might like to make a short stop in the little village of Pochutla. It has a pretty main square and attractive local handicrafts.

The small fishing village of Puerto Angel has long been a favorite hideout for those seeking a quiet relaxed existence. The resort has a lovely bay with sandy beaches and clear blue waters, set against the luxuriant tropical vegetation of the south. Little open-air restaurants on the beachfront offer freshly caught fish. Facili-

---

The market at Ocotlán: specialties include reed baskets and embroidery

ties are available for a variety of water sports and the atmosphere here is casual and tends to appeal to the younger set.

Return to **Mex 200** *and continue west to Puerto Escondido.*

Puerto Escondido, Oaxaca

9 Puerto Escondido, meaning 'hidden port' in Spanish, is aptly named. This sleepy little fishing village was indeed a hidden spot until recent years, when the building of a new airport made it more accessible. The resort lies in an inlet, with a backdrop of densely wooded cliffs. A number of small shops, restaurants and hotels line the seashore. The atmosphere is very relaxed, with daily life centering on beach activities – swimming, sailing, fishing and the usual water sports. Some beaches have big, rolling waves and offer good surfing. The **lighthouse** at one end of the resort offers a good view of the little town and its surroundings.

i Avenida Oaxaca at Avenida Hidalgo 120

Return on **Mex 200** *east to Pochutla. Take* **Mex 175** *north to Oaxaca, about 238km (148 miles). A few miles from Oaxaca, take the road southwest to Monte Albán, about 9km (6 miles).*

SPECIAL TO ...

6 Tehuantepec celebrates a number of festivals during the year. The **Día de San Sebastián** (the Festival of St Sebastian) is a particularly colorful event, starting on 22 January and continuing for six days. Important local women lead a procession through the old part of the town, followed by unmarried women and new brides, carrying standards and dressed in fine costumes and jewelry. Following a ceremony called the **Tirada de Frutas** (the throwing of the fruit), there is a gathering to choose the new headwoman for the following year. Lively marimba music and torchlit processions are featured each evening.

This drive passes through greatly varying scenery, with stretches of bare and arid terrain, contrasting with dramatic mountain scenery and lush tropical growth. There is a very scenic stretch after Mitla as you pass over the Sierra Madre del Sur mountains. This gradually gives way to the abundant green of the tropics as you approach Tehuantepec. The return journey from Puerto Escondido takes you through soaring mountain peaks, tropical forests, cascades, and around many hairpin bends.

Children will probably most enjoy themselves at the beach resorts of Puerto Escondido and Puerto Angel on the south coast, where they can swim, take boat trips, see the fish and generally let loose.

Monte Albán was once a major religious city. Tomb 7 has yielded Mexico's most important caches of gold and jewelry

Monte Albán, Oaxaca

10 On the way to Monte Albán, some miles before the turnoff, make a stop at the little Indian village of Ocotlán. The **Palacio Municipal** (Town Hall), a lovely building, is made of pink stone, while the **Templo de Santo Domingo** (Temple of St Dominic) is adorned by two golden lions in the neoclassical style. Its Friday market is a match for others in the region in its liveliness and color when local Indians in traditional costumes congregate here from all over. Red clay figurines are a village specialty.

The pre-Columbian site of Monte Albán ('white mountain') is without doubt one of Mexico's most impressive archaeological sites. The setting of its Acropolis-like buildings is magnificent, as they sit on top of a plateau surrounded by a ring of mountains. A visit at dawn or sunset is positively magical.

As with so many of Mexico's pre-Columbian centers, its origins are obscure. It is thought that the place may have been inhabited as early as 1000BC, possibly by the Zapotecs. The settlement grew into a sizeable city and flourished until about AD900, when it gradually went into a decline. When the Mixtec invaders arrived in the area in the 13th century, Monte Albán was used only as a burial place. The site comprises an enormous central area, called the **Gran Plaza** (Grand Plaza), surrounded by a number of buildings, platforms and stairways. During excavations many artifacts were found, and tombs yielded dazzling treasures of gold, quartz and turquoise (these can be seen in Oaxaca's excellent Regional Museum). As you enter the area you will notice the **Juego de Pelota** (Ball Court). The most prominent buildings are the **Pirámide** (Pyramid) and the **Palacio** (Palace). Other important groups of structures are the Central Group, the South Platform and the North Platform. An easy climb to the top of some of the platforms will give panoramic views of the surrounding terrain. Although a fair bit of clambering up and down stairways and terraces is involved, it is all relatively easy going.

Perhaps the most interesting monument on the site, however, is the **Edificio de los Danzantes** (Building of the Dancers). Here you will see stone slabs, originally part of a high wall, with relief carvings of figures depicted in strange positions, some of them showing deformities. Experts still puzzle over their significance, which they consider could relate to medical studies, torture or other activities. Some of the faces have strong Negroid features, suggesting a link between the Zapotecs and the Olmecs. Stelae (upright pillars) dotted about the area are carved with number hieroglyphs. The small archaeological exhibition near the parking lot is worth a visit before you leave.

*Return to Oaxaca, 9km (6 miles) north on **Mex 175**.*

Oaxaca – Santa María del Tule **10 (6)**
Santa María del Tule – Dainzú **19 (12)**
Dainzú – Lambityeco **5 (3)**
Lambityeco – Yagul **5 (3)**
Yagul – Mitla **3 (2)**
Mitla – Tehuantepec **212 (132)**
Tehuantepec – Huatulco **148 (92)**
Huatulco – Puerto Angel **44 (27)**
Puerto Angel – Puerto Escondido **80 (50)**
Puerto Escondido – Monte Albán **318 (199)**
Monte Albán – Oaxaca **9 (5)**

Souvenirs from Acapulco's market are better bargains than those sold in hotels and on the beaches

ⓘ Costera Miguel Alemán 187, Acapulco

From Acapulco take Mex 95 north, briefly stopping at Mochitlán near Petaquillas. Turn off east at Petaquillas to Colotlipa for 37km (23 miles). Continue for about 8km (5 miles) to Grutas de Juxtlahuaca.

Grutas de Juxtlahuaca, Guerrero

1 After Petaquillas, you can make a brief stop at the little village of Mochitlán, renowned for its local festivities and *charreadas* (Mexican rodeos). Then proceed to the national park, where you will find the caves of Juxtlahuaca, which cover a vast area and contain beautiful stalactites and crystal formations. Rock paintings dating back 3000 years show signs of Olmec influence. The full tour takes about three hours and should be accompanied by a guide.

Return to Mex 95 and continue north for 11km (7 miles) to Chilpancingo.

Chilpancingo, Guerrero

2 Chilpancingo ('place of wasps' in Náhuatl) is the state capital. Originally inhabited by the Otomís, it was settled by the Spanish in 1591. Mexico's first National Congress met here in 1813. Places of interest include the **Palacio de Gobierno** (Government Palace), which contains murals depicting Mexican history, **la Casa del Primer Congreso Revolucionario** (the House of the First Revolutionary Congress), **Iglesia de la Asunción** and a 16th-century bridge. Pottery, leather goods and hunting knives are produced here and are readily on sale.

ⓘ Ayuntamiento, Juárez 1

Continue north for 100km (62 miles) on Mex 95 to Iguala.

Iguala, Guerrero

3 Iguala played an important role in Mexican history, when the Plan de Iguala (or Three Guarantees) was issued here on 24 February, 1921. It marked Mexico's Declaration of Independence against the Spaniards, and a plaque in the City Hall commemorates the event. The first national flag was produced by a local tailor: in nearby **Parque de la Bandera** (Flag Park) stands a monument to the national banner, surrounded by tamarind trees planted in 1832. Take a look also at the painting that adorns the front of the 19th-century **Church of San Francisco**.

Take Mex 51 west to Ciudad Altamirano. Continue southwest on Mex 134 to Ixtapa on the Pacific Coast.

Ixtapa, Guerrero

4 *En route* to Ixtapa stop off at Almoyola to see the little 18th-century Augustinian **church**, which features a notable baroque altarpiece. In the vicinity are some ruins known

BEACHES & JUNGLES OF THE SOUTH

Acapulco • Grutas de Juxtlahuaca • Chilpancingo
Iguala • Ixtapa • Zihuatanejo • Laguna de Coyuca
Pie de la Cuesta • Acapulco

This tour from Acapulco takes you to the north and the west of the state of Guerrero. Being a bit off the beaten track, it is something of a venture into the unknown. A major attraction is the drive into the interior of this tropical region. You will travel over the rugged mountain ranges of the Sierra Madre Occidental and through areas of lush, green vegetation, flowers and cacti. You will also get to visit a couple of towns of historical interest and some fascinating caves. And, to round off the itinerary, there is the chance to spend some time in two beach resorts offering a total contrast to Acapulco.

as **Los Monos** (the monkeys), probably from the 7th or 8th century AD. Then drive on to Ixtapa, a modern tourist complex that has developed into a popular vacation resort over recent years. With its wide sandy beaches, palm trees and choice of hotels, set against a dense tropical background, it has become a firm favorite with Mexican families. Tiny islands can be seen in the distance, while dramatic rock formations at Punta Ixtapa and Punta Carrizo add to the attraction of Ixtapa. Tasty seafood is served in the casual, open-air restaurants along the beach, which is alive with all sorts of aquatic activities. Swimmers should beware of strong waves and currents at certain times – check for signs.

Take Mex 200 for 10km (6 miles) to Zihuatanejo.

Zihuatanejo, Guerrero

5 Although just a short distance away, Zihuatanejo offers a total contrast to Ixtapa. This quaint fishing village nestles in a wide, curved bay ringed by mountains covered with dense green foliage. This tropical paradise still remains a favorite with its many regulars. The atmosphere is totally informal, and the swimming is excellent. Do not miss a trip to the delightful **Playa las Gatas** (Beach of the Cats), reached by a launch trip across the bay. This is a great place for swimming and snorkeling. Hundreds of brilliantly colored tropical fish can be seen in a cove of crystal-clear waters. Succulent seafood is the

FOR CHILDREN

2 There is little on this tour specifically aimed at children, but there is a small **zoo** and an **amusement park** at Chilpancingo which are worth a visit.

BACK TO NATURE

6 Large concentrations of waterbirds can be seen on the Laguna de Coyuca. The more prominent include neotropic cormorants, snowy egrets, great egrets, tricolored herons, wood ibises and roseate spoonbills. American avocets, black-necked stilts and willets sometimes put in an appearance; overhead look for royal terns, ring-billed gulls and ever-present magnificent frigatebirds.

SCENIC ROUTES

Most of this drive offers exotic jungle scenery with luxuriant vegetation, combined with stretches along the Pacific Coast. Note the superb view of Acapulco Bay as you ascend on the first lap of the journey. The section from Acapulco to Chilpancingo and Iguala is particularly attractive, with its variety of tropical foliage and brightly colored flowers. Further north, past the village of Río Balsas, note the huge organ cacti scattered all over the hillside.

RECOMMENDED WALKS

Many of the little towns on this tour are in jungle surroundings and walking is not recommended on the outskirts. The long stretch of beach at Pie de la Cuesta (7) is a wonderful place for walking and watching the relentless surf pounding the sand with a tremendous roar. Hammocks slung along the beaches provide relaxation.

SPECIAL TO . . .

3 The **Día de la Virgen de Guadalupe** (Festival of Our Lady of Guadalupe) is celebrated in Ciudad Altamirano, on 12 December, with floats, military bands and bullfights. Pilgrims arrive from all over the region to worship at the shrine of the **Virgen Morena** (Brown Virgin). Celebrations start at dawn with music and dances.

FOR HISTORY BUFFS

Acapulco's history can be traced back to the 1530s, when a Spanish settlement was established here to build ships for exploration. It became the main port on the west coast for ships from the Orient. Cargos of ivory, silk and spices would arrive here and be transported by mule to Mexico City and Veracruz, where they were shipped on to Spain. When pirates began raiding these precious cargos, the **Fuerte de San Diego** (Fort of St James) was built as a protection. Rebuilt after an earthquake destroyed it in 1776, it remains one of the oldest buildings in Acapulco.

The crescent beaches of Acapulco offer almost every activity on, under or above the water

specialty at the open-air restaurants lining the idyllic beach.

i Paseo del Pescador 20

*Take **Mex 200** along the coast for some 210km (131 miles) to Laguna de Coyuca.*

Laguna de Coyuca, Guerrero

6 This beauty spot is known for its large freshwater lagoon bird sanctuary and the small islets which can be visited by boat or canoe. Mango, coconut and banana groves fringe the shoreline and tropical fish abound in its waters. There is good swimming, and facilities for aquatic sports are available.

Cross the road to Pie de la Cuesta.

Pie de la Cuesta, Guerrero

7 Pie de la Cuesta is famous for its spectacular sunsets, when sky and sea blend together in an artist's palette of vivid red and orange. Even if you miss this terrific spectacle, it is worth a visit to see the gigantic rollers crashing onto the shore. There are many little restaurants and bars along this wild beach, and water skiing and horseback riding are available.

*Return to Acapulco along **Mex 299**.*

Acapulco – Grutas de Juxtlahuaca **181 (113)**
Grutas de Juxtlahuaca – Chilpancingo **56 (35)**
Chilpancingo – Iguala **100 (62)**
Iguala — Ixtapa **363 (227)**
Ixtapa – Zihuatanejo **10 (6)**
Zihuatanejo – Laguna de Coyuca **210 (131)**
Laguna de Coyuca – Pie de la Cuesta **across road**
Pie de la Cuesta – Acapulco **17 (11)**

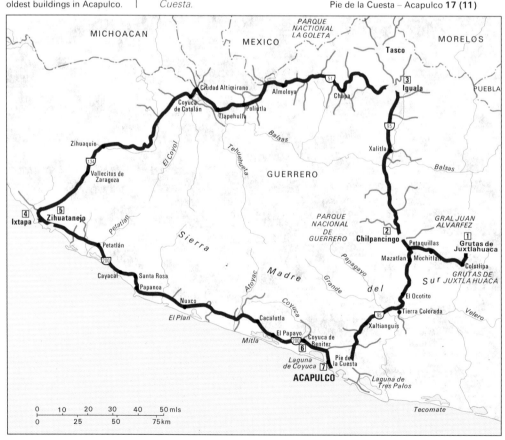

A colossal stone head, a legacy of Olmec culture, at the open-air La Venta Museum, Villahermosa

ⓘ Lerdo 101, 1st Floor, Esq Malecón y Lic Carlos A Madrazo, Villahermosa

*From Villahermosa take **Mex 186** east for 115km (72 miles) to Catazajá, then take **Mex 199** for 28km (17 miles) to the village of Palenque. Turn off to the archaeological site of Palenque, some 8km (5 miles) further on.*

Palenque, Chiapas

1 The Mayan ruins at Palenque are considered by many to be the most sensational of all the pre-Columbian sites in Mexico. Set deep in the jungle at the foot of a chain of hills, and with its air of brooding mystery, Palenque suggests one of those ancient 'lost cities' stumbled upon by chance. Wear comfortable clothing, as the visit involves quite a lot of clambering up and down rocky paths and slopes.

Palenque (which means 'palisade' in Spanish) is one of the great Mayan cities. It was abandoned in the 9th century and, as with other Mayan cities, the reasons have yet to be discovered. The city soon fell into ruin and was swallowed up by the jungle. The Spaniards discovered it in 1786 and found it to be one of the most highly developed ceremonial centers of the classic Mayan era.

The **Templo de las Inscripciones** (Temple of the Inscriptions) is the focal point of the site (see **FOR HISTORY BUFFS**).

5 days – 995km (622 miles)

CITIES & CULTURES OF THE RAIN FORESTS

Villahermosa • Palenque • Agua Azul • Comitán
Lagunas de Montebello • San Cristóbal de las Casas
Chamula • Chiapa de Corzo • Cañón del Sumidero
Villahermosa

This is an exciting itinerary that starts out from Villahermosa and takes you through the steamy jungles of Chiapas in southeastern Mexico. This is a region of rain forests, green hills, canyons, waterfalls, rivers and lakes. A major highlight will no doubt be the visit to Mexico's fabulous Mayan ruins, set deep in the jungles of Chiapas. Among the many other fascinating places on the journey are picturesque little Indian towns, beautiful lagoons, dramatic canyons and breathtaking waterfalls. Of equal interest, on the human side, are the local Indians who still adhere proudly to many of their traditional ways, some of which predate the Spanish Conquest.

FOR HISTORY BUFFS

1 The **Templo de las Inscripciones** (Temple of the Inscriptions) is one of the most interesting buildings at Palenque. It stands on top of a large pyramid, with a broad stairway up one side. You can reach the top of the structure by climbing up a rough path of boulders and bushes at the rear, and descend by the stairway running down the front of the temple. A staircase in the pyramid's interior leads to a crypt where a sarcophagus containing a male skeleton covered with a jade mask and ornaments was found, the first evidence of Mesoamerican pyramids having been used as funeral monuments, but because of the steep and slippery nature of the descent, it does not appeal to everyone.

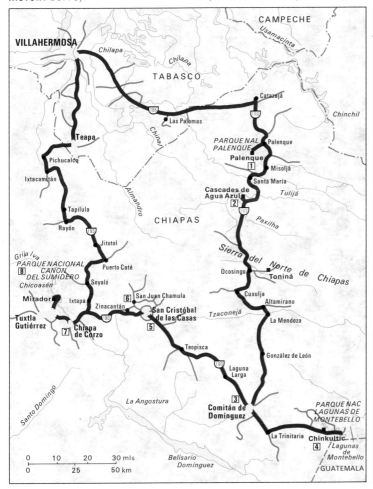

RECOMMENDED WALKS

4 The Parque Nacional Lagunas de Montebello (Montebello Lakes National Park) offers some lovely walks around the beautiful lakes, pine forests and lush, tropical vegetation. Among the 60 or so lagoons in this extensive park, there is a group of five lakes by the road leading to the entrance of the area. These are joined by pathways, where you can stroll around the differently colored lakes in quiet surroundings.

The Temple of the Inscriptions, Palenque: its crypt has stalactites on ceilings and walls

The **Palacio** (Palace) is a building of some importance. Dominated by a square tower, the complex is made up of a group of structures set on a huge platform around four courtyards. There are underground passages, and broad stairways run up two sides of the pyramid. Stucco reliefs can be seen on the pillars at the entrance, and many of the walls are decorated with carvings and glyphs.

Also of interest are the **Templo del Sol** (Temple of the Sun), the **Templo de la Cruz** (Temple of the Cross), the **Templo de la Cruz Foliada** (Temple of the Foliated Cross) and a smaller one known as **Temple XIV**.

The **Templo del Conde** (Temple of the Count) was named after the Austrian writer Jean Frederick von Waldeck, who lived in it in 1832. This is the oldest building excavated so far

on the site, dating back to around AD650. Near the set of temples known as the **Northern Group** is a small museum with a collection of artifacts from the region. A short walk beyond this takes you to a lovely spot among plants and trees, where a waterfall cascades down far below. If you are feeling adventurous, you can make a brief excursion into the jungle by following a path, not far from the **Templo de las Inscripciones**, which leads into the interior. Here, the gigantic trees and magnificent plants, combined with the exotic sounds of the wildlife, will really give you the feel of the jungle. (It is unwise to stray from defined paths.)

i Palacio Municipal

*Return to **Mex 199** and continue south for 70km (43 miles). Turn right and continue for 4km (2½ miles) to the Agua Azul Waterfalls.*

Agua Azul, Chiapas

2 Agua Azul (meaning 'blue water') is a series of waterfalls cascading down over a number of limestone terraces into basins of water far below. The water is sparkling clear and an intense shade of blue, created by the effect of the limestone beneath. The waterfalls are set in luxuriant vegetation. This is a good place for picnics and camping, and you can also have a swim in the natural rock pools beyond the rapids.

*Return to **Mex 199** and continue south and southwest to Ocosingo. Take the road south to Altamirano, then on to Comitán.*

Comitán, Chiapas

3 On the way to Comitán there are a number of interesting little Indian villages in the surrounding hills and some Mayan ruins at Toniná, about 14km (9 miles) east of Ocosingo. A series of structures fortified by a wall are built on several levels on the slopes of a hill. There are sweeping views of the valley from the temple tops. Of special interest are a large flat disc carved with glyphs and a strange stone ball in a cave framed by stucco decorations. The site is believed to date from AD600 to 800. You might make a brief stop in the little Tzeltal village of Ocosingo to take a look at its pretty 18th-century **parish church**.

Comitán, situated some 1,520m (5,000 feet) above sea-level, is an attractive hillside town of white houses and pretty gardens, retaining much of its old Colonial flavor. Once an important center of the Mayan Quiche kingdom, it is now a commercial center for the Tzeltal Indians of the region.

ⅈ Casa de la Cultura

*Continue southeast on **Mex 190** for 16km (10 miles). Turn off at La Trinitaria. Continue east for 37km (23 miles) to Lagunas de Montebello National Park.*

Lagunas de Montebello, Chiapas

4 Shortly before entering Lagunas de Montebello National Park, make a detour to the excavations at Chinkultic, located a short distance off the main road. Once a Mayan ceremonial center, the site lies between two lakes set in lush jungle. From the top of either of the two temples, you can look down into the **Cenote Agua Azul** (Well of Blue Water), a well supposedly used by the Mayas for sacrificial offerings.

Montebello, located on the border with Guatemala, is a region of exceptional beauty. Between 60 and 70 lakes are contained in a national park consisting of wild jungle and hills. The lagoons vary in size and in one group, the **Lagos de Colores** (Colored Lakes), each is a different color, ranging from a delicate pale blue to emerald and shades of violet; the chemical compositions of the crystal-clear waters are responsible for the various hues. There is an atmosphere of quiet isolation here, and if you can stand the cold temperature of the water, going for a swim is an experience. The zone was declared a national park in 1960 to preserve its wild natural beauty.

*Return to La Trinitaria. Take **Mex 190** northwest to San Cristóbal de las Casas.*

San Cristóbal de las Casas, Chiapas

5 San Cristóbal de las Casas, as the oldest Colonial settlement in the state of Chiapas, is Spanish in architecture but strongly Indian in character. The town lies high in pine-forested mountains. Early morning mists, which make it chilly at first, give way to hot, sunny days. San Cristóbal,

Set jewel-like in mountainous jungle scenery, the Lagunas de Montebello are popular for fishing and diving

SCENIC ROUTES

Most of this route through Chiapas offers jungle scenery typical of tropical areas. The stretch between Palenque to San Cristóbal de las Casas is particularly beautiful, over hills and mountains covered by dense green forests. Of particular note, also, is the drive from San Cristóbal to Chiapa de Corzo, which has excellent views.

BACK TO NATURE

The most spectacular resident of the forests of Chiapas is the aptly named resplendent quetzal, a bird which has strong ties with Indian mythology. In spring, the males develop tail plumes several feet long and these were once worn by those of noble birth. Sadly, the quetzals are becoming increasingly rare, partly due to degradation of their forest habitat and partly due to collectors. Visitors will also note the exciting variety of trees, plants and flowers to be seen in the area.

6 The Chamula Indians, noted for their religious ceremonies, hold a number of interesting festivities in San Juan Chamula. Carnival Tuesday (the day before Ash Wednesday) involves a purification rite in which Indians leap dramatically through a sheet of fire in front of the church. This is preceded by days of other colorful ceremonies. To honor the town's patron, St John the Baptist, there are days of pilgrimages and ceremonies leading up to 24 June, with horse races, processions and Indians wearing traditional costumes.

settled in 1528, has been designated a National Monument to preserve its style. Always a bit off the beaten track for the majority of visitors, the place has opened up to tourism only in recent years. A major attraction are the Indians who throng to the main square and marketplace from the surrounding hills to buy and sell their wares. They dress in the colorful costumes of their particular tribe and speak their different languages. Recognizable by their attire, prominent tribes include the Chamulas, the Zinacantáns and the Tzotzil, who all stem originally from the Mayas. A word of advice: many Indians do not like to be photographed, particularly in this region. Make your intentions clear, by sign language if necessary, and respect their wishes if they refuse.

There are a number of notable buildings to visit. The 16th-century **cathedral** on the main square has some fine paintings inside by two prominent Mexican artists, Juan Correa and Miguel Cabrera. The **Templo de Santo Domingo** (Temple of St Dominic) is the most sacred building in San Cristóbal. Dating from the mid-16th century, its façade was built later in typical baroque style and, over the central doorway, has a two-headed eagle, the coat of arms of the Hapsburg Emperor Charles V. The interior is richly decorated with gilded altars and sculptures. Do visit the **Na Bolom Centro de Estudios**, an archaeological and ethnological

museum founded by the late Danish archaeologist Franz Blom. He settled here with his wife Trudy (still living) in the 1920s, and the two of them devoted their lives to studying the Indians. The museum building is in fact the couple's home. For a fine view of the town, drive up to the little church at **Cerro de San Cristóbal**.

Take the road for 12km (8 miles) to Chamula.

Chamula, Chiapas

6 Chamula is the religious center of the Chamula Indians. Although many of them live in the surrounding hills, they come regularly into the village. They are recognizable by their white woolen cloaks, white cotton shirts and trousers, and the flat straw hats with dangling colored ribbons, which they don for special occasions. Large wooden crosses on a hill at the entrance of the town are symbols of the Christian and Mayan cultures. The little white **parish church**, with its painted portal, is very special to the local Indians. Tourists may visit it, but you need a permit and taking photographs is strictly forbidden.

*Return south to San Cristóbal and take **Mex 190** west to Chiapa de Corzo.*

Chamula's parish church: outlying Indian communities all differ in dress, dialect and customs

Chiapa de Corzo, Chiapas

7 The town of Chiapa de Corzo overlooks the Grijalva River (also known as the Río Chiapa). The town was occupied by the Spaniards in 1528, the site of an old Indian settlement formerly used as a trading link between the Mayas to the east and the Zapotecs to the west. Take a look at the Dominican **Convento de Santo Domingo** (Monastery of St Dominic) (1554–1572) and adjoining church, which has since been remodeled. Of special interest is the fountain in the main square, built by the Spaniards in 1562 in the shape of the crown of the Queen of Spain. A specialty of Chiapa de Corzo and other towns in the region is attractive lacquerware, particularly the black gourds painted with bright flowers. It is also known for its interesting masks worn for festivals. The local museum (**Museo de la Laca**) exhibits lacquerware, handicrafts and archaeological pieces found in the area. This is the point of departure for an adventurous boat trip along the river to the Chicoasén Dam. Sheer canyon walls rise up to a great height, and the scenery is very dramatic.

*Take **Mex 190** for 15km (9 miles) to Tuxtla Gutiérrez, then the road north for 22km (14 miles) to Cañón del Sumidero.*

Viewed from the top or from a sightseeing boat below, the Sumidero Gorge is awe-inspiring

Cañón del Sumidero, Chiapas

8 A magnificent rock terrace with several lookout points commands a spectacular view of the Sumidero Gorge. The sight of the churning waters of the Río Grijalva, about a mile below you, is one of those Mexican experiences not to be missed. A small **museum** adds to the interest, and the restaurant may tempt you to linger a while longer and enjoy the breathtaking scenery. Locals believe the area is inhabited by the ghosts of Indians who are said to have flung themselves down into the raging torrents of the canyon rather than surrender to the Spanish conquerors.

*Return to Villahermosa on **Mex 195.***

Villahermosa – Palenque **151 (94)**
Palenque – Agua Azul **82 (51)**
Agua Azul – Comitán **147 (92)**
Comitán – Lagunas de Montebello **53 (33)**
Lagunas de Montebello – San Cristóbal de las Casas **141 (88)**
San Cristóbal – Chamula **12 (8)**
Chamula – Chiapa de Corzo **60 (38)**
Chiapa de Corzo – Cañón del Sumidero **37 (23)**
Cañón del Sumidero – Villahermosa **312 (195)**

FOR CHILDREN

8 About 24km (18 miles) south of El Sumidero, just outside the town of Tuxtla Gutiérrez, is the **Parque Zoológico Miguel Alvárez del Toro** (Municipal Zoo), considered one of the best in Mexico. Several hundred species of animals, birds and fish can be seen here in their natural habitat of woods and rivers. Monkeys, boars, tapirs, ocelots, jaguars, crocodiles, snakes and brilliant tropical birds are among the many creatures to be viewed.

THE YUCATÁN PENINSULA

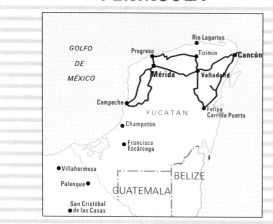

The Yucatán Peninsula includes the states of Yucatán, Campeche and Quintana Roo. This huge land mass rises in a horn shape to the east of the country, bounded on the west and north by the Gulf of Mexico and on the east by the Caribbean. Lagoons and swamps are found in the western and northern regions, while the east coast features white sand beaches and coral reefs.

Much of the region is covered by jungle and scrub forest. The state of Yucatán is a flat limestone plain with henequen plantations, underground wells and charming little villages. To the south, Quintana Roo is a vast wilderness of dense jungle, swamps and lakes, with some beautiful coastlines of fine white sand fringed by palm trees. Campeche, to the west, features gentle hills in the north and tropical rain forests in the south and east. It has rivers, underground lakes and swamp areas, and its abundant wildlife attracts hunters.

Archaeologically, Yucatán is one of the richest areas in Mexico with a heritage of magnificent Mayan ruins set amidst the jungles. The region is believed to be dotted with thousands more unexplored sites. The Mayas built great cities and made important astronomical calculations, devising a calendar claimed to be the most accurate in existence. The peak of their building was in the Early and Late Classic periods (AD300–900). Following a decline towards the end of this period, the arrival of the Toltecs from the central regions brought a revival, when they imposed their influences on the Mayas and built onto existing cities. This post-Classic period lasted from AD900–1450. Human sacrifice was introduced and chac-mool figures used for the rituals. You can see these recumbent stone figures in Chichén Itzá, holding a receptacle to contain the hearts of the unfortunate victims.

From the mid-13th century there was a gradual decline as the inhabitants disappeared mysteriously and the cities crumbled. When the Spaniards arrived in the 16th century, practically all the cities had been abandoned. There was long and bitter fighting during the Caste War (1847–1901), when the Indians tried to regain their lost territories.

The Yucatecans are mainly Mayas and *mestizos* (mixed Spanish and Indian blood). The Mayas are a gentle, courteous people, and many still converse among themselves in the soft Maya tongue. Usually short in stature with broad faces and almond-shaped eyes, the men wear white pin-tucked shirts called *guayaberas*, the women a lovely embroidered garment called a *huipil*, and their children are delightful.

Mérida:

Mérida, although small, is the state capital and the peninsula's major city. Its charm shows a marked European influence. Streets all intersect at right angles and buildings bear numbers rather than names. The main square is very pleasant, with tidily trimmed trees and benches. There are band concerts and lively fiestas on special occasions. Mérida's tempo is decidedly sleepy, with a very friendly and relaxed atmosphere. Horse-drawn carriages called *calesas* wait in a line, ready to take you around town in leisurely fashion. The huge 16th-century **cathedral** overlooks the square. Opposite is the **Palacio Municipal** (Town Hall), a handsome Colonial building with a clock tower. On another side stands the **Palacio de Gobierno** (Governor's Palace), with attractive murals (1971–74) by the famous Yucatecan painter Fernando Castro Pacheco.

Take a look at the **Ermita de Santa Isabel** (Hermitage of St Isabel), set in lovely botanical gardens with a waterfall and a display of Mayan artifacts. Also worth a visit is the **Museo de Arqueología e Historia** (Museum of Archaeology and History) for its fine collection of pre-Columbian art.

The **Mercado Municipal** (local market) is fun for browsing around. You will find hammocks, bags, panama hats made from the local sisal, and the lovely *guayabera* shirts.

Cancún:

Cancún is a new development, dreamed up by computers as an ideal location for a vacation center with its white virgin beaches, palm trees and jungle background. Located on the northeast tip of the peninsula in the state of Quintana Roo, the resort consists of a long, narrow strip of sand wedged between the Caribbean and the Nichupte Lagoon, with a connection to the mainland. Hotels in various modern styles line the strip, overlooking the sparkling emerald seas of the Caribbean on one side and the lagoon on the other. Sunsets can be spectacular. As a change from the hotel pools in their tropical garden settings, the beautiful beaches of powdery white sand and the warm, clear waters offer marvelous swimming – although in certain areas dangerous currents and a strong undertow can be hazardous (a red flag gives the necessary warning). The resort offers excellent scuba diving and snorkeling and every type of aquatic sport. Windsurfing is a favorite sport here, and the colorful sails can be seen all over, together with yachts, parasailers and water skiers. Boat trips are popular, too, especially excursions to the islands of Isla Mujeres and Cozumel and the bird sanctuary on Contoy Island. A glass-bottom boat ride around the Nichupte Lagoon lets you see the exotic marine life in its waters.

Separate from the hotel zone, the downtown area offers many restaurants and shops.

Magnificent even in ruins, the Mayan structures that survive speak of a civilization well advanced in art, architecture and engineering

3/4 days – 442km (275 miles)

WORLD OF THE MAYAS & TOLTECS

Mérida, built over an ancient Mayan site, exudes a certain European air, but the residents still speak Mayan

Mérida • Chichén Itzá • Cuevas de Balankanché
Valladolid • Tizimín • Temax • Dzidzantún
Progreso • Dzibilchaltún • Mérida

This circular tour from Mérida covers the northeastern part of the state of Yucatán, one of the three states that form the Yucatán Peninsula. The long, straight roads that cut through this flat, limestone plain covered by scrub forest make for relaxed driving, but watch out for the odd animal straying across your path. Although the scenery can at times be monotonous, you will be enchanted by the Mayan villages and local people. A major attraction will be your visit to one of Mexico's most impressive Mayan ruins, set in the jungle. Also included are some memorable caves and a quiet little fishing resort on the north coast.

[i] Avenida Itzaes 501, Mérida

From Mérida take **Mex 180** *east (with a brief stop at Izamal) for 120km (75 miles) to the ruins of Chichén Itzá.*

Chichén Itzá, Yucatán

1 On the way to Chichén Itzá you might like to make a brief stop at Izamal, an ancient settlement where Mayan pilgrims came to worship the sky god. Take a brief look at the 16th-century **Church and Monastery of San Antonio de Padua**, which features a huge atrium. It was built with the material used for the old Mayan temples.

The Mayan and Toltec ruins at Chichén Itzá are one of Mexico's splendors. The site extends over a large area and is considered by many to be the most famous and best preserved of the pre-Columbian sites in the country. Its temples, pyramids and columns, spread around a neat clearing in the jungles of Yucatan, form an impressive sight. The name Chichén means 'place of the well' in Mayan, and Itzá refers to a Mayan sect which inhabited the original settlement, believed to have been founded between AD360 and 435. The city went into a gradual decline until the arrival of the Toltecs, around AD980. They built onto many existing structures, and Chichén Itzá developed into a city of great importance, flourishing between the 11th and 12th centuries. Around 1200 the city was abandoned and returned to the jungle; the reasons remain a mystery.

The site is divided into Nuevo Chichén (New Chichén) and Viejo Chichén (Old Chichén). Start your visit in the newer section, which is dominated by the magnificent pyramid known as El Castillo (the Castle). In front is one of the several *Chac-mool* (sacrificial) figures to be seen in Chichén Itzá.

The Castillo (also known as the Pyramid of Kukulkán) has nine terraces and a square temple on top. Four stairways of 91 steps each lead up the four sides of the building. Together with the top step of the summit they total 365, the number of days in the year. It is possible to climb up one set of steps, which has a handrail, but proceed with great care as the steps are steep. Awaiting you at the top is an unparalleled view of the site and the green belt of jungle stretching away into the far distance. A small entrance in one side of the pyramid takes you along a narrow passageway into the interior of the pyramid, leading to a red jaguar sculpture with jade-encrusted eyes.

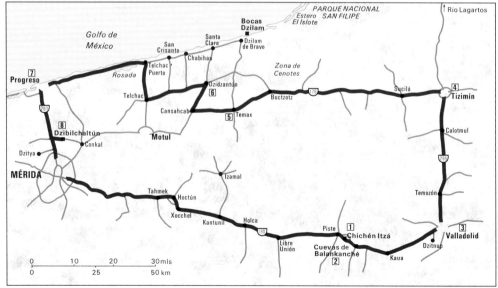

The way is dark and narrow, however, and can be a bit claustrophobic.

The **Templo des los Guerreros** (Temple of the Warriors), behind El Castillo, is another impressive structure of Chac mask carvings and warrior-like columns. Another brooding *Chac-mool* sculpture sits in front. Below is the **Grupo de las Mil Columnas** (Group of a Thousand Columns), with huge feathered serpents and an area called **El Mercado** (the Market). Other buildings include the **Tzompantli** (Wall of Skulls), **Platform of the Eagles and Tigers** and the **Templo de los Jaguares** (Temple of the Jaguars), with jaguar decorations. The **Juego de Pelota** (Great Ball Court) is the largest of its kind found so far in Mexico and has excellent acoustics – clap your hands and you will hear the sound all over the area.

A short walk down a path into the jungle leads to the rather sinister

Chichén Itzá, one of the archaeological wonders of the world: the Group of a Thousand Columns has Toltecan-style square pillars and a Chac-Mool altar

Cenote Sagrado (Sacred Well). The Mayas believed this was the home of the rain god Chac. During times of drought they used the well for sacrificial purposes, throwing young maidens (or so it is believed) into the murky waters as a form of appeasement. Diving operations have revealed human bones, treasures of gold and jade and countless artifacts.

Old Chichén, located on the other side of the road, is a little rougher in appearance but has some buildings of great interest. Of particular note is the Observatory, known as **El Caracól** (the Snail) on account of the spiral staircase inside which leads to the top of the building; it is thought the Mayas studied the solar system there.

SPECIAL TO . . .

1 A fascinating event, noticed some years ago by an archaeologist, occurs in Chichén Itzá twice a year, on the spring and autumn equinoxes. At the exact moment of equal day and night, the sun casts a shadow on the stairway running down the northwest side of **El Castillo**, creating the effect of a huge serpent rising from the carved Quetzalcóatl heads at the base of the pyramid. Great numbers of people come from all over the world to witness this extraordinary phenomenon.

BACK TO NATURE

1 In the vicinity of the famous archaeological site of Chichén Itzá, look for social flycatchers, clay-colored thrushes, black vultures, common ground doves, groove-billed anis and great-tailed grackles. The excellent forest which surrounds the site is home to colorful butterflies as well as mammals such as coatimundis and armadillos, while at the edges, birds including green jays, rufous-browed peppershrikes, plain chachalacas, masked tityras, lineated woodpeckers and, in winter, numerous warblers can be seen.

SCENIC ROUTES

This region is made up of low scrub forest and straight, flat roads. The natural scenery does tend to lack variety, but the little Mayan villages on the route, particularly between Mérida and Chichén Itzá, will more than compensate.

RECOMMENDED WALKS

One of the most agreeable places on this tour in which to enjoy a good walk is the site of Chichén Itzá. Apart from the actual cultural interest, the zone is well laid out, and many paths lead to pleasant shaded areas where you can wander about and explore the fascinating plant life.

They were amazingly advanced in their calculations; before the birth of Christ, they had perfected a calendar more accurate than our present one. The **Edificio de las Monjas** (Nunnery), **Casa Colorada** (the red house) and the **Iglesia** (church) are among other buildings worth looking at.

Chichén Itzá needs a prolonged visit, as the site is extensive and the surroundings pleasant.

Follow **Mex 180** *east for 5km (3 miles) to the Cuevas de Balankanché.*

Cuevas de Balankanché, Yucatán

2 The sacred cave of Balankanché ('throne of the jaguar') was discovered by chance in 1959, after being blocked up for several hundred years. The cave dates back to the time of the Toltecs in the Yucatán (AD900 to 1300). It contains numerous chambers in which artifacts of pottery and ceramics were found. *Metates* (maize-grinding stones) found here are on display. The face of the Toltec rain god, Tlaloc, decorates many of the objects found, suggesting the cave may have been used as a burial ground. In one of the chambers is an altar with an impressive formation of stalactites resembling a ceiba tree, which was sacred to the Mayas. A narrow passage takes you down into the lower chamber with a transparent pool of water and an altar dedicated to the rain god.

Continue east on **Mex 180** *for 37km (23 miles) to Valladolid.*

Valladolid, Yucatán

3 The sleepy little town of Valladolid is a pleasant place in which to browse around and linger awhile. It was founded in 1543 by Francisco de Montejo, one of the members of a prominent Spanish family which more or less ruled over much of the

Valladolid's Church of San Bernardino was built by Franciscans, whom the Indians and landlords fought against continually

Yucatán for a long period. Built on the site of the old Mayan settlement of Zaci, Valladolid is now the second largest town in the state.

An attractive main square has neatly trimmed trees and a scattering of benches for relaxing. All sorts of handicrafts and a variety of goods are to be found in the closed marketplace. The town is known for its *pan dulce*, a sweet-tasting bread almost like cake. Worth a visit is the large **Church of San Bernardino** on the main square. Founded in 1552 by Franciscans, the church is one of the few remaining Colonial buildings from the Civil War, which took place in the second half of the 19th century. On the edge of the town are two *cenotes*, or wells, known as **Sis-ha** and **Zac-hi**, where you can have a swim. Just before entering Valladolid you can make a little detour to the lovely underground well of Dzitnup.

i Palacio Municipal

Take **Mex 295** *north for 52km (32 miles) to Tizimín.*

Tizimín, Yucatán

4 The tiny town of Tizimín is full of tradition and is also known for its production of honey. Its main feature is the 17th-century **Iglesia dedicada a Los Tres Reyes Magos** (Church dedicated to the Three Kings) on the main square. A month of celebrations begins on December 15 in their honor.

Take **Mex 176** *west to Temax for 84km (52 miles).*

Temax, Yucatán

5 Make a brief stop here to have a look at some of the handicrafts it has to offer. Of particular note are the attractive hand-embroidered traditional costumes of the Yucatecan women, called *huipiles*. The **Templo de San Miguel Arcángel** (Temple of St Michael the Arcangel) has some fine *retablos* inside.

Continue on **Mex 176** *west for 17km (10 miles) to Cansahcab. Turn north for 12km (8 miles) to Dzidzantún.*

Dzidzantún, Yucatán

6 The most interesting building in this little town is the **Templo y Ex-Convento de Santa Clara** (temple and former Convent of St Clare). It was built in 1567 under the direction of Friar Francisco Gadéa and proclaimed the finest church of its kind in the region. The building is a splendid example of the Colonial architecture of that time and has an attractively decorated interior. The Festival of Santa Clara is celebrated from August 10 to 13.

A drive north for about 26km (18 miles) will bring you to the little resort of Dzilám de Bravo, noted for its calm waters and beaches of fine white sand. A strange phenomenon of nature produces springs of fresh water from the bottom of the sea. Trips by launch are available to Las Bocas de Dzilám, an area of rich vegetation and canals through mango groves. The place is inhabited by a colony of pink flamingoes, a grand sight when they take flight.

Return to Dzidzantún, then take the road for 23km (15 miles) southwest to Telchac. Turn north to Telchac Puerto, 14km (8 miles). Take the coastal road west to Progreso.

Progreso, Yucatán

7 Progreso is the principal port of the state of Yucatán and the nearest beach resort to Mérida. Its appeal is local rather than international. Many Yucatecans have second homes here, and the place tends to be packed during the summer months and holiday periods. At other times it is quiet and relaxing, offering swimming, sailing and aquatic sports. A pleasant pastime is to stroll along the main pier, or *malecón* as it is called in Spanish, which stretches along the seafront. On either side of the port there are long sandy beaches with houses for rent.

*Take **Mex 262** south for 21km (13 miles). Branch off left to Dzibilchaltún.*

Dzibilchaltún, Yucatán

8 The name of Dzibilchaltún means 'where the flat stones bear writing'. According to experts this was the largest pre-Hispanic town on the

In Mérida's Government Palace on the main square, visitors can see a hall of history and murals by Yucatecan painter Pacheco

Yucatán Peninsula and was occupied for the longest period. Believed to have been settled from about 600BC, the site was still inhabited at the time the Spaniards arrived. Restoration covers only a small part of the archaeological zone, which consists of several different ceremonial centers, formerly connected by *sacbeob* ('white roads' in Mayan). Of particular note is the **Templo de las Siete Muñecas** (Temple of the Seven Dolls), where seven terracotta figures were found. Four stairways lead up a platform to the temple, which has an unusual roof comb in the shape of a truncated pyramid. In the central group of structures is a temple called **Edificio 38** (Building 38) with interesting remains of frescos and carved decorations. There are a few other buildings and a museum containing artifacts from the area. You can have a swim in the **Cenote Xlacah** (Well of Xlacah), where items found here included pottery, jewelry and human bones. The remains of a 16th-century open chapel stand on the main square.

On the way back to Mérida, make a short detour to Dzitya. The **Templo de San Diego** (Temple of St James) here is known for its lovely church bell. Of particular interest is a series of stones on one side of the building. Because these make a special sound when struck, it is thought they could once have been a means of communication between the various villages in the region. The village offers attractive handicrafts, its particular specialty being in woodcarvings.

*Return to Mérida on **Mex 261**, 17km (11 miles) south.*

Mérida – Chichén Itzá	**120 (75)**
Chichén Itzá – Cuevas de Balankanché	**5 (3)**
Cuevas de Balankanché – Valladolid	**37 (23)**
Valladolid – Tizimín	**52 (32)**
Tizimín – Temax	**84 (52)**
Temax – Dzidzantún	**29 (18)**
Dzidzantún – Progreso	**75 (47)**
Progreso – Dzibilchaltún	**23 (14)**
Dzibilchaltún – Mérida	**17 (11)**

FOR HISTORY BUFFS

The Ball Game (*pelota*) was an ancient game played by the Mayas. The object of the game was to propel a small, hard ball through a high ring, using only the elbows, knees and hips. Two teams took part and the game could last for days. Carvings found near the ball courts suggest that the players of one of the teams, presumably the losing team, were sacrificed afterwards.

FOR CHILDREN

Children will probably enjoy stopping off at some of the little Mayan villages, where the local people can often be very friendly. The tour, however, is mainly archaeological and may not appeal to younger children, but they should enjoy one of the nightly *son et lumière* performances in Chichén Itzá (1), where they can learn about the ancient Mayas and Toltecs in the majestic setting of the pyramids and temples. (Performances are cancelled during heavy rain.)

WONDERS OF THE ANCIENT MAYAS

Mérida • Muna • Uxmal • Kabáh • Sayíl • Labná
Hopelchén • Edzna • Campeche • Hecelchakán
Mérida

This tour from Mérida takes you south through the states of Yucatán and Campeche. A highlight of this itinerary is a visit to one of the most famous and splendid of the ancient Mayan centers in this region, with its many relics of the old Mayan cultures. A number of other archaeologiocal sites included in the journey combine with a drive down to the Gulf of Mexico which leads to an attractive old fortified town of historical interest. Here the terrain becomes more tropical and the area rich in flora and fauna. The trip offers a concentration of culture together with the contrasting appeal of nature and wildlife, in regions that, so far, are relatively unpopulated by tourists.

Sayíl's temple: elaborate moldings and grotesque masks of Chac

[i] Avenida Itzaes 501, Mérida

*From Mérida take **Mex 180** southwest for 18km (12 miles) to Umán, where you can stop briefly. Continue south for another 46km (28 miles) on **Mex 261** to Muna.*

Muna, Yucatán

1 Muna is a pleasant little town, typical of so many in the Yucatán. Browse around, and be sure to visit the Iglesia y Convento de la Asunción (Church and Convent of the Assumption), which have some fine chapels. *En route* to Muna you might like to make a stop at Umán to look inside the Iglesia y Convento de San Francisco de Asís (Church and Convent of St Francis of Assisi). Built in the 18th century, it has an interesting wooden pulpit with relief carvings. A road northwest of Muna leads to the village of Calcehtók, with some caves about 3km (2 miles) away. A short distance further on is the small Mayan site of Oxkintoch, believed to be one of the oldest in the Yucatán.

*From Muna continue south on **Mex 261** for 16km (10 miles) to Uxmal.*

Uxmal, Yucatán

2 Uxmal (which means 'thrice built' in Mayan) is one of the most important Mayan cities in the Yucatán.

Uxmal's Pyramid of the Magician, built on an unusual elliptical base

Although much smaller than Chichén Itzá, the other great Mayan center on the peninsula, it is equally significant. Its magnificent pyramids and temples with intricate carvings are elegantly proportioned in the classic Puuc style, and the paleness of its limestone structures gives it a distinctive beauty. Uxmal was once the major city of the Mayan classic period (AD600 to 900) until the gradual development of Chichén Itzá resulted in its decline and eventual obscurity. Some of the buildings are considered to be among the finest examples of pure Mayan architecture.

The **Pirámide del Adivino** (Pyramid of the Magician) rises majestically before you as you enter the site. Some stories say it was built by a magician in one night, while others relate to a dwarf whose mother was a witch. This imposing structure rises to a height of some 38m (125 feet), and you can reach the top by means of a broad stairway adorned with masks of the rain god Chac. The climb up its 118 steps is steep (be careful and use the handrail), but the views of the site and the green jungle below are well worth the effort.

A short walk brings you to an elegant Mayan arch, which leads to the **Cuadrángulo de las Monjas** (Nuns' Quadrangle), a large area surrounded by rectangular buildings decorated with carvings of Chac, double-headed serpents and other symbols and patterns. These build-

ings are renowned for their symmetry and perfect proportions. Another impressive building is the **Palacio del Gobernador** (Governor's Palace). The long rectangular building stands on a series of terraces and has a beautiful façade decorated with thousands of tiny carved stones, giving the effect of fine lacework. Other buildings of interest include the **Casa de las Tortugas** (House of the Turtles), the **Palomar** (Dovecote) and the **Gran Pirámide** (Great Pyramid). The ruins of a ball court can also be seen.

A *son et lumière* (sound and light) show in Spanish and English, on Uxmal's history and structures, is held every evening except Mondays or when it rains during the summer months.

*Continue on **Mex 261** southeast for 20km (12 miles) to Kabáh.*

Kabáh, Yucatán

3 The Mayan site of Kabáh is characterized by the **Codz-Poop** (Palace of the Masks). It stands on a low platform covered with rows of masks with large trunk-like noses, most of which have broken off. Little is known of the site's early history, but it is thought to have been linked to the great city of Uxmal by one of the special limestone ceremonial roads, known as *sacbe*. Other structures are not so well preserved, including the **Palacio** (Palace) and the **Templo de las Columnas** (Temple of the Columns). A striking feature of the site is

BACK TO NATURE

2 The well-known archaeological site of Uxmal is good for birdwatching as well as sightseeing. In the cleared areas look for great kiskadees, great-tailed grackles, turquoise-browed motmots, common ground doves and turkey vultures. Where the vegetation is more luxuriant, Yucatán jays, clay-colored thrushes, plain chachalacas and social flycatchers may be seen. Insect life is abundant and includes butterflies, cicadas and bush crickets.

SCENIC ROUTES

Much of your travels within the state of Yucatán will be through flat, scrub-type forest, but the scenery becomes more interesting when you enter the state of Campeche. Hills appear gradually and the plant life becomes lush and exuberant. There is an attractive stretch of road along the Gulf of Mexico between Campeche and Champotón.

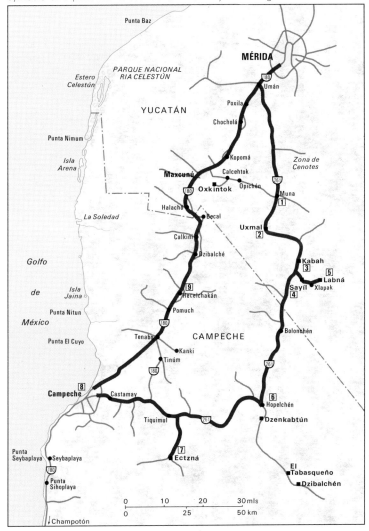

The great, Greek-like palace at Sayíl contains over 50 chambers

SPECIAL TO ...

8 Christmas and New Year are celebrated in Campeche with solemn festivities of music, processions and dancing, which take place in the beautiful 17th-century cathedral. In Champotón, celebrations beginning on November 30 lead up to the **Día de la Immaculada Concepción** (Feast of the Immaculate Conception) on December 8. Each day is marked by a pilgrimage of workers, who attend with their respective guilds.

6 The **Fiesta de la Miel y el Maíz** (Honey and Corn Festival) is held in Hopelchén from April 13 to 17, with bullfights and colorful dances known as *jaranas*.

the **Arco de Kabáh** (Arch of Kabáh) – a fine example of the corbeled arch typical of classic Mayan architecture – formed by a series of overlapping stones and covered by a roof.

Continue south on **Mex 261** *for 5km (3 miles) then branch off southeast to Sayíl.*

Sayíl, Yucatán

4 The Mayan site of Sayíl ('place of ants' in Mayan) is set in dense tropical vegetation. Its early history is obscure. Built in classical Puuc style, it is dominated by a building known as the **Palacio** (Palace), a partly restored structure of three stories with a stairway up one side. Carved masks of Chac decorate the frieze on the western side of the middle structure. A climb to the top gives a good view of the rest of the site, which includes the ruins of a ball court and a temple known as the **Mirador** (Lookout), with a large, decorated roof comb.

Continue east for 9km (5 miles) to Labná.

Labná, Yucatán

5 The main feature of this Mayan site is its magnificent corbeled **Arco de Labná** (Arch of Labná), which forms part of a gate-like structure with ornate mosaic-type decorations on the frieze. Although little is known of its origins, Labná ('broken houses' in Mayan) is thought to have been a city of some importance at one time. Other buildings are a group of structures known as the **Palacio** (Palace) and a group to the south of the area, dominated by a pyramid with a temple on

top called the **Mirador** (Lookout). The architecture shows the fine classic Puuc style.

Return to **Mex 261** *and continue south to Hopelchén.*

Hopelchén, Campeche

6 The little town of Hopelchén, which means 'five fountains' in Mayan, is a good place in which to relax and take a break from archaeology. Worth a visit is the attractive fortified church (el templo), built in the 16th century. But for the really dedicated who don't want to miss a thing, there are many small sites belonging to the Chenes culture, in particular Dzenkabtún, El Tabasqueño and Dzibalchén, located south of Hopelchén.

Continue southwest on **Mex 261**. *After 42km (26 miles) take a left turn and continue for 19km (12 miles) south to Edzna.*

Edzna, Campeche

7 The ruins at Edzna ('house of grimaces' in Mayan) have only been partially excavated. The site lies in scrub forest in a valley surrounded by low hills. Little is known of its early history, but it is attributed to the early classic period. Most notable is the **Edificio de los Cinco Pisos** (Five-Story Building). The pyramid stands on a base with steps leading as far as the fourth story. On top is a temple with a roof comb. Of interest is the **Casa de la Luna** (House of the Moon) and the **Templo del Suroeste** (South-western Temple). Other structures are partly overgrown and in need of restoration.

Return to **Mex 261** *and continue west to Campeche, about 60km (37 miles).*

The palace at Labná, where a well-preserved rainwater cistern on the second story was one of 60 or so in and around the city

RECOMMENDED WALKS

2 You will find there is plenty of walking to be done on this tour as you explore the various archaeological sites. Uxmal is a very pleasant spot in which to take a leisurely stroll in your own good time, as a change of pace from all the scrambling and climbing up the ruins.

8 In the old fortified town of Campeche, you can also enjoy a walk along parts of the massive ramparts, which have been designated a national historic monument.

Campeche, Campeche

8 Campeche, the state capital, lies on the Gulf of Mexico to the west of the Yucatán Peninsula. This fortified town, characterized by its ancient walls and fortress, is an attractive blend of old and new. Hernández de Córdoba landed here in 1517 with his men. The city was formally founded in 1540 by Francisco de Montejo, a member of the prominent Spanish family that settled in Mexico after the Conquest. He named it Campeche, after the old Mayan name *ah-kin-pech*, meaning 'place of the snake and the tick'. The city flourished as a center for exporting hardwood and dyewoods to Europe, becoming the region's major port. In the 16th and 17th centuries Campeche suffered countless raids from pirates, and part of the town was destroyed. In response a wall was built between 1686 and 1704 as a protection against attack. Today the massive walls, with eight fortresses, are Campeche's most attractive feature.

On the main square stands the **Catedral de la Concepción** (Cathedral of the Conception) (1540–1705), noted for its fine baroque façade. Other elegant Colonial houses surround the square. The **Museo de Historia** (History Museum), which has a collection of Mayan artifacts and paintings and relics relating to the history of the town, is located in the Baluarte de la Soledad, one of the old bastions of the town walls. The Baluarte de Santiago houses **botanical gardens**, and the Baluarte de San Carlos, one of the oldest and best preserved of the forts, contains a **Museum of Applied Art**. There is a magnificent view out over the Gulf from the roof of the fort.

The **Iglesia de San Francisco** (Church of St Francis), dating from 1540, is the oldest convent church on the Yucatán Peninsula. Note its five finely carved wooden altars. The convent is built on the spot where the first Mass was celebrated in Mexico in 1517. In total contrast, some very modern buildings are also to be found in Campeche. The **Palacio de Gobierno** (Government Palace) and the **Cámara de los Diputados** (Chamber of Deputies) are such examples, and have been nicknamed 'The Jukebox' and 'The Flying Saucer', respectively, on account of their unusual design.

Do not miss a chance to visit the market, which displays a variety of handicrafts, in particular articles made from alligator skins, seashells and hardwoods. *Jipis* – panama hats – are another local product.

Worth a visit also is the **Fuerte de San Miguel** (Fort of St Michael) located up a hill on the outskirts of the town. Entry is over a drawbridge to a small museum with a good collection of Mayan pieces. Of particular interest are the tiny terracotta figurines from the nearby island of Jaina.

About 66km (40 miles) further south down the coast is the little fishing port of Champotón, with narrow streets and balconied houses. There you can see the remains of an old fort, **El Moro**. It lies on the banks of the Champotón River and offers some good deep-sea fishing.

*From Campeche take **Mex 180** for 28km (18 miles). Turn north onto **Mex 261** for 47km (29 miles) to Hecelchakán.*

FOR HISTORY BUFFS

8 The culture of Jaina is interesting. This little island off the north coast of Campeche was used as a burial place during the time of the Mayas. Many tombs were found here, as well as a number of small, hollow figurines, all finely modeled, with whistles on their backs.

Hecelchakán, Campeche

9 There are two major buildings to visit in the little town of Hecelchakán. The fine 17th-century **Templo Franciscano** (Franciscan church) has imposing twin towers topped by crosses. The **Museo Arqueológico del Camino Real** (Archaeological Museum of the Royal Highway) has a fine collection of artifacts, including more figurines from the island of Jaina, stelae, door lintels and sculpted columns from the region. There are many more Mayan sites in the surrounding area. Among the most interesting are Kocha and Xcalumkin, worth a visit before finishing the tour.

*Return to Mérida on **Mex 180**, a distance of 121km (76 miles).*

Mérida – Muna **64 (40)**
Muna – Uxmal **16 (10)**
Uxmal – Kabáh **20 (12)**
Kabáh – Sayíl **10 (6)**
Sayíl – Labná **9 (5)**
Labná – Hopelchén **75 (47)**
Hopelchén – Edzna **61 (38)**
Edzna – Campeche **60 (37)**
Campeche – Hecelchakán **75 (47)**
Hecelchakán – Mérida **121 (76)**

FOR CHILDREN

Youngsters might find this trip too strong a dose of culture!

62

CARIBBEAN BEACHES & CITIES OF THE PAST

Cancún • Isla Mujeres • Xcaret • Akumal • Xel-Ha
Tulum • Cobá • Felipe Carrillo Puerto • Cancún

This tour from Cancún goes south through the state of Quintana Roo, which borders the Mar Caribe (Caribbean Sea) to the east and Guatemala and Belize to the south. The drive stretches through flatlands among wild tropical vegetation and the scrub-like forests found throughout the region. Many beautiful lakes and large, natural underground wells can be seen along the itinerary. Two impressive Mayan ruins in magnificent settings contrast with a number of delightful little bays and resorts, where you can swim and snorkel in the turquoise waters of the Caribbean or in crystal-clear lagoons abounding with tropical fish. Also included are visits to Mexico's two charming Caribbean islands.

A diver's delight, near Akumal: amazingly patterned tropical fish of every color populate the waters of sea and lagoon

ⅈ Avenida Tulum 81, Edificio Fira, Cancún

*From Cancún take **Mex 307** north for 10km (6 miles) to Puerto Juárez, for the ferry to Isla Mujeres.*

Isla Mujeres, Quintana Roo

1 Puerto Juárez is just a small wharf with some little restaurants and bars, and the point for catching the foot-passenger ferry to the little island of Isla Mujeres, about 10km (6 miles) off the coast (an hour's journey). If you must take your car, continue a bit further up the coast to Punta Sam for the car ferry service. The island is so small, however, that it is preferable to leave your car behind and walk around or rent a bicycle. You can easily spend the whole day there. Isla Mujeres has a rustic charm that has always appealed to young people and escapists. This island of pretty little houses and beaches of fine white sand is surrounded by coral reefs and lagoons, a perfect haven for snorkeling and diving. At the southern end is **El Garrafón**, a beautiful underwater coral reef where you can swim and dive among a stunning variety of brightly colored tropical fish. There are hazardous currents in some areas around the island, so take heed of advice if you plan to swim during your visit. The island has many little open-air restaurants specializing in delicious seafood, and life here is seductively relaxing and informal.

*Return to Cancún and continue south on **Mex 307** to Xcaret, making the side trip to the island of Cozumel if you wish.*

Xcaret, Quintana Roo

2 Before coming to Xcaret, you will see turnings to Puerto Morelos and Playa del Carmen, from which ferries depart to Cozumel, the larger of the two Caribbean islands off this coast. Puerto Morelos has a car and foot-passenger service; Playa del Carmen is for foot passengers only. The crossing takes from about 1½ hours to 2½ hours depending upon the point of crossing. Cozumel, with its palm-fringed beaches of soft white sand, sits in the warm waters of the Caribbean, which offer excellent swimming. One of the best diving areas is the Palancar Reef at the southwestern part of the island, with huge formations of coral. The Chancanab Lagoon in the interior is a small lake of fresh, clear water connected to the sea, with countless tropical fish of every color. The little town of San Miguel de Cozumel has developed in recent years and a lot of activity is centered on the main square. Relax in one of the casual restaurants, or browse in the many shops. Black coral jewelry is available here, as well as many other kinds of attractive handicrafts. Returning to

The beach at Akumal: in summer gigantic turtles come ashore here to lay their eggs

the mainland and continuing south on **Mex 307**, watch out for a sign by a tiny roadside restaurant named Xcaret and turn left. A bumpy track through the jungle takes you past some tiny Mayan shrines to a parking lot by a hut. A short walk from here ends at a small, hidden cove where you can swim in quiet surroundings. Nearby, a concealed path – if you can find it – leads to an enchanting *cenote* or well, typical of hundreds to be found in the region, formed by a crack in the base of protruding limestone rocks. A swim in the cool, dark waters with the jungle around you is an exhilarating experience.

You may like to note that the little restaurant of Xcaret normally serves fresh fish of the day.

*Continue south on **Mex 307** a little further, then turn left to Akumal.*

Akumal, Quintana Roo

3 Akumal is an idyllic spot in which to relax a while over a drink. Its little curved bay, sparkling turquoise sea and silvery beach make it a perfect little Caribbean hideaway. You will no doubt be tempted to take a dip in its warm, clear waters. The hotel houses CEDAM, a Mexican underwater explorers' club, which attracts skin divers from all over the world. Diving and snorkeling lessons are available,

and organized underwater expeditions result in ongoing finds of treasure and artifacts. A small **museum** here displays objects uncovered by divers, including valuable pieces salvaged from local shipwrecks.

*Continue on **Mex 307** for a few miles further, turning left to Xel-Ha.*

Xel-Ha, Quintana Roo

4 A short drive off the main road will suddenly reveal another unexpected delight as you come upon the sight of interlocking lagoons, in varying shades of emerald and turquoise, set like jewels in the jungle. The lagoons' combination of fresh- and salt-water, common to the area, results in a wealth of underwater life. Their warm, transparent waters, rocky inlets and reefs make Xel-Ha a veritable paradise for swimming and snorkeling, and in recent years the place has become popular at weekends. Underwater explorations by members of CEDAM have given rise to the belief that the site was once a Mayan cult center. A strong swimmer with some diving experience can take a look at an underwater cave in the main lagoon, where the remains of an altar can be seen.

*Return to **Mex 307** and continue south for 16km (10 miles) to Tulum.*

BACK TO NATURE

1 From Isla Mujeres special arrangements can be made for a boat trip to the Caves of the Sleeping Sharks. It was here, some years ago, that the famous underwater explorer Jacques Cousteau made the only known discovery of sharks asleep in an underwater cave.

2 Cozumel Island, reached by ferry or plane from the Yucatán mainland, is well worth a visit. Although popular with tourists, a surprisingly large part of the island is unspoilt. Two birds – the Cozumel thrasher and the Cozumel vireo – are unique to the island and visitors may also see bananaquits, black catbirds, rose-throated tanagers and Yucatán vireos.

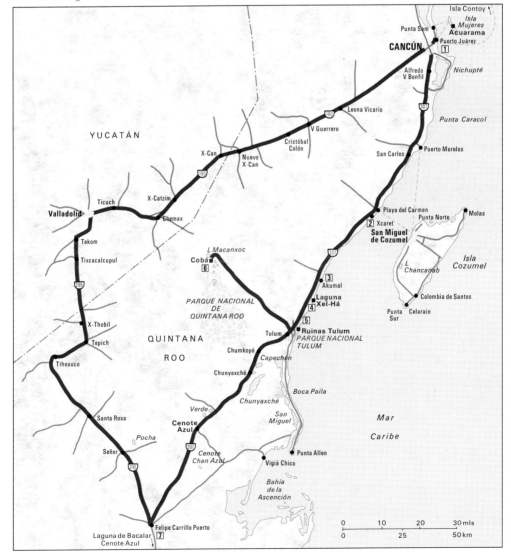

1 When visiting Isla Mujeres, youngsters will enjoy a trip to **Acuarama**, which presents an entertaining show of performing dolphins, seals and elephant seals (now nearly extinct). Programs are normally daily, except on Mondays. On Playa Lancheros, at the southern end of the island, is a turtle farm where visitors can learn how to ride the giant amphibians. Kids and grown-ups alike have fun here, whether taking part or just watching.

Tulum, Quintana Roo

5 The Mayan city of Tulum will surely be a highlight of your trip. The site is small but the setting is magnificent, perched high on a clifftop overlooking the dazzling turquoise seas of the Caribbean far below. Tulum (meaning 'fortress') is the only fortified Mayan town to have been discovered on the coast. Totally different in character from other major Mayan centers, Tulum has a wild, rugged beauty of its own. As with so much of Mayan culture, little is known of Tulum's early history. However, experts believe that it may have belonged to the late post-classic period (700–1500) and that major buildings could have been built as recently as the mid-15th century. The town was first spotted by the Spaniard Juan de Grijalva and his men as they sailed along the coast on an expedition from Cuba in 1518. The Spaniards were astonished at the size and splendor of the city, likening it to Seville in Spain. The place was still occupied when the Spanish Conquistadores arrived in the area.

The most notable building is **El Castillo** (the Castle), also known simply as Building 1, commanding a dominant position on the edge of the cliff. A temple stands on top of other structures linked by a broad stairway. Above the central doorway is a seated figure, known as the Diving

Fortress-like even in ruins, the walled city of Tulum overlooks the Caribbean from its clifftop vantage

God. Another interesting building is the **Templo del Dios Descendente** (Temple of the Descending God), or Building 5. This contains an unusual stucco sculpture of a figure with wings and a bird's tail, also known as the Descending God, which has given rise to strange theories of explanation, including one of visitations in the past by beings from other planets. In the center of the site is the **Templo de los Frescos** (Temple of the Frescos), or Building 16. This also contains a Diving God sculpture and some codice-type paintings with Mayan and Mixtec influences. Other buildings include the **Templo de la Serie Inicial** (Temple of the Initial Series) and others referred to by numbers. There is a sweeping view of the Caribbean from **Building 45**.

If time permits, take a drive down the coast to see beautiful stretches of unspoiled beaches, palm trees and lagoons among green foliage. Boca Paila and Bahía de la Ascensión are two of these beach areas with perfect conditions for swimming and fishing.

Continue south for a short distance, then take the road northwest to Cobá, about 42km (26 miles).

Cobá, Quintana Roo

6 The Mayan site of Cobá ('wind-ruffled waters' in Maya) lies in a region of small lakes set in dense jungle. Although mostly overgrown and with much excavation still to be done, the site is vast and most impressive. It was thought to have been one of the largest settlements in the region at one time, flourishing during the classic period of the Mayan culture (AD600 to 900). The number of sacred white roads found here (called *sacbeob* by the Mayas) indicates the importance of ancient Cobá, as the roads served as a link between major ceremonial centers all over the region. Within the groups of structures known as the Cobá Group, is a building called **La Iglesia** (the Church), with a small temple on top of seven levels. The top of the temple offers a fine view of the site with its surrounding lakes and jungle. An impressive building is the pyramid known as **El Castillo**, which forms part of the Nohoch Mul group. Standing 42m (138 feet) high, it is the tallest accessible structure of its kind on the Yucatán Peninsula, and affords another good view of the surroundings. Two of the recesses in the temple on top contain the figure of a Diving God. A number of stelae were found in this temple, and some of them have been placed in the complex known as **Macanxoc**, between Lakes Macanxoc and Xcantha. Carvings of chieftains and glyphs can be seen on the stones.

*Return to **Mex 307**. Continue south for 95km (59 miles) to Felipe Carrillo Puerto.*

Felipe Carrillo Puerto, Quintana Roo

7 It must be said of Felipe Carrillo Puerto that its historical interest tends to outweigh its attractions as a tourist center. This old Mayan center was the last stronghold of those people during the War of the Castes,

Deep in the jungle, Cobá was never found by the Spaniards: La Iglesia one of its 6,500 structures

which lasted from 1847 to 1901, when the Mayas struggled to maintain their independence. The town became a sanctuary for priests and chiefs and for some 50 years was the center of military operations. Originally called Chan Santa Cruz ('Little Holy Cross'), the town was the center of the so-called Cult of the Speaking Cross. From the large church on the main square came the voice of the Cross, addressing the local Indians and giving them directions. A festival on May 3 marks the Day of the Holy Cross.

There are some other very worthwhile attractions in the vicinity. If you feel adventurous, continue south on **Mex 307** to the beautiful **Laguna de Bacalar** (Bacalar Lagoon), a fresh- and saltwater lagoon with ever changing hues, from turquoise to shades of indigo. Its surrounding white sands and jungle setting make it one of the loveliest in the area, where you can fish and enjoy water sports, and there are some Mayan ruins to be seen. A short distance away is the **Cenote Azul** (Blue Well), named for its deep-blue translucent waters. The plunging roots of neighboring trees have formed an exotic underwater forest, making it a great place for divers to explore.

*Take **Mex 295** north to Valladolid. Continue on **Mex 180** northeast and return to Cancún.*

Cancún – Isla Mujeres	**10 (6)**
Isla Mujeres – Xcaret	**81 (50)**
Xcaret – Akumal	**34 (21)**
Akumal – Xel-Ha	**7 (4)**
Xel-Ha – Tulum	**16 (10)**
Tulum – Cobá	**45 (28)**
Cobá – Felipe Carrillo Puerto	**137 (85)**
Felipe Carrillo Puerto – Cancún	**301 (188)**

FOR HISTORY BUFFS

2 Cozumel appears to have had some importance in the period between AD1000 and 1200 and is thought to have served as a sanctuary dedicated to the rising sun. The island was discovered in 1518 by the Spanish explorer Juan de Grijalva, and was later used as a base by Francisco de Montejo in his efforts to conquer the Yucatán. The Montejos became virtual rulers of the Yucatán for a long period after that.

RECOMMENDED WALKS

6 The vast archaeological zone of Cobá is a good place for walking. You could spend hours here wandering among the Mayan ruins in a wonderful setting of lakes and jungle.

SPECIAL TO...

Carnival takes place all over Mexico in an atmosphere of fun and jollity. Lively pre-Lenten celebrations in Isla Mujeres (1) and Cozumel (2) start a week before Ash Wednesday, with festive parades, floats, music, fireworks and dancing everywhere, and all and sundry taking part.

SCENIC ROUTES

Most of this journey is through flat, sparsely populated scrub forest and jungle terrain without much scenic variety. There is a pretty stretch of road, however, along **Mex 307** between Felipe Carrillo Puerto and Laguna de Bacalar to the south, where you will pass , through some attractive little Mayan villages.

THE WEST

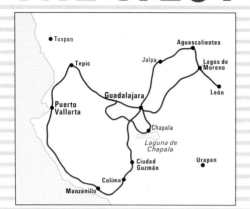

Jalisco, Colima and Nayarit are the states that feature mainly in this section, with the inclusion of parts of Aguascalientes, Guanajuato and Zacatecas. The region is mostly hot and tropical. Spectacular landscapes are created by the mighty mountains of the Sierra Madre Occidental, which sweep down western Mexico covered by dense tropical vegetation. The state of Jalisco is characterized by rugged mountain peaks and deep gorges, combined with open plains and cactus plantations. Further south, Colima is dominated by the two majestic volcanoes of Nevado de Colima and the Volcán de Fuego. Nayarit features mountainous terrain, jungles and valleys, with coastal swamps and lagoons. A major attraction of the region is its magnificent coastline of beaches, bays and rocky inlets set against luxuriant jungle foliage; among the delightful beach resorts and hotel complexes is the popular Puerto Vallarta.

Little is known of the region's early civilizations, which are simply referred to as the cultures of the west. They are thought to have reached their peak in the Classic period (AD200–850) but were never as advanced as some other cultures, as demonstrated by their fairly crude terracotta figurines, vessels and strange, fattened dogs.

Manzanillo was already an important seaport before the arrival of the Spaniards. After the Conquest of 1521, the Spanish Conquistadores built galleons here and set off on expeditions, resulting in the conquest of the Philippines. Trading links were established with the Orient and the area prospered. But resistance from the Indians was relentless, and the area took long to settle. The discovery of precious minerals led to further development of the area, which became known as Nueva Galicia. In 1889 it was divided into the states of Jalisco and Nayarit.

Jalisco is rich in folklore. Its music, traditional dances and costumes are among the most colorful and lively in the country. This is the home of the famed *mariachis*, renowned for their magnificent costumes and vibrant music, and also of Mexico's famous national drink, tequila, produced from the blue agave cactus plants that grow in the region. Its capital, Guadalajara, is the second city of Mexico, and Lake Chapala is the largest in the country. The population is made up of whites, *mestizos* and a large proportion of Indians, including the Nahuas, Huicholes and Tarascans. The state of Colima has a large population of Huichol Indians, who live mainly in the hinterland, and Cora Indians, who dwell in the coastal regions.

Guadalajara:

Guadalajara is the state capital of Jalisco and Mexico's second city, with a population over two million. Graced with elegant buildings, lovely churches, flower-filled squares, fountains and parks, Guadalajara is a modern, thriving town that retains its Colonial character. In the center of town four grand plazas form the shape of a cross. Overlooking this area is the **cathedral**, an impressive building with magnificent Byzantine towers. Fine murals by Orozco, one of Mexico's major painters, can be seen in the splendid **Palacio de Gobierno** (Government Palace), in the former orphanage Hospicio Cabañas and at the State University. Also worth a visit is the **Museo Regional de Guadalajara** (State Museum), with archaeological artifacts and paintings. Guadalajara has an excellent cultural life. Plays,

Best explored on foot, Guanajuato still mines the silver that once made it famous

concerts and operas are held in the elegant neoclassical **Teatro Degollado**, built in the late 1850s, along with performances of the colorful Folkloric Ballet of the University of Guadalajara.

A pleasurable pastime is to relax in one of the cafés on the Plazuela de los Mariachis and let the strolling musicians entertain you. You can also view the town by horse-drawn *calendrías*. The local market is good fun, while fashionable shops and boutiques are to be found in the **Zona Rosa** (Pink Zone). A big occasion in Guadalajara is the October Festival, with countless events and displays of the beautiful traditional dances of the region.

Puerto Vallarta:

Not so long ago Puerto Vallarta was a sleepy little fishing village, practically unknown. It was the filming of *The Night of the Iguana* here that attracted publicity and put it on the map. Today it is one of Mexico's major resorts. The old village is still a pretty cluster of white houses, red roofs and tiny cobblestoned streets wending their way up the hillside, where donkeys amble along carrying their loads. From here there are fine views of its picturesque surroundings. Set on the beautiful **Bahía de Banderas** (Bay of Flags) and ringed by mountains, it boasts miles of lovely beaches shaded by palms. The lush tropical vegetation and casual atmosphere are part of Puerto Vallarta's allure. Hotels of all categories have sprung up along the coast, and open-air bars and beach-front restaurants add to the ambience of fun. The shoreline is the scene of constant activity, with swimming, water skiing, parasailing, boating and other water sports. Donkey polo is also a favorite beach game. An enjoyable boat trip can be made across the bay to the beach of Yelapa, in a dramatic mountain setting. Apart from good swimming, excursions can be made into the interior of the jungle. Evenings in Puerto Vallarta are lively, with plenty of cafés, restaurants and discos to choose from.

4 days – 315km (193 miles)

LAKE CHAPALA & SURROUNDINGS

Guadalajara • San Pedro Tlaquepaque • Tonalá
Laguna de Chapala • Ajijic • Jocotepec • Ahualulco
Etzatlán • Magdalena • Tequila • Guadalajara

This tour from Guadalajara introduces you to some delightful little towns within the state of Jalisco, a number of which are dotted about the shores of Laguna de Chapala, Mexico's biggest lake. The scenery is interesting and varied, combining mountains, wide open plains and vast regions of the agave cacti, so characteristic of the region. The area is famed for its attractive arts and crafts, which you can see in some of the picturesque villages that produce them. Beautiful Colonial churches complete the trip, which is rounded off by a visit to the town that produces Mexico's fiery national drink.

[i] Lázaro Cárdenas 3289, 1st Floor, Col Chapalita, Guadalajara

From Guadalajara take the road southeast for 6km (4 miles) to San Pedro Tlaquepaque.

San Pedro Tlaquepaque, Jalisco

1 This small picturesque suburb of Guadalajara is renowned throughout Mexico as an arts and crafts

Handweaving near Chapala, one of several handicraft centers on Lake Chapala's north shore

center. Among the wide variety of attractive products it is particularly noted for its ceramics and pottery, blown glass, papier-mâché and tinware. The place is crammed with shops and boutiques offering all sorts of beautiful native crafts. There are still potters plying their trade in tiny workshops, but much is now produced in factories. You can watch some of the remaining skilled craftsmen at work, and a visit to the glassblowers will prove a fascinating experience. The marvelous selection of colorful goods is very tempting. Tlaquepaque is a pretty place with cobbled streets, attractive Colonial houses and abundant flowers. You can pass the time very pleasantly by installing yourself around **El Parián**, the main square, edged by little restaurants, arcades and a splendidly ornate bandstand. 'Mariachis' are likely to come along and play their lively tunes under the portals.

*Take **Mex 110** or **Mex 3**, southeast for 10km (6 miles) to Tonalá.*

Tonalá, Jalisco

2 Tonalá is renowned for its distinctive style of pottery, with its painted and polished ceramics instantly recognizable. The town has a long tradition of pottery, dating back to pre-Hispanic times. When the Spaniards arrived in the area, they noticed that the finished pottery gave off a faint odor, hence it was known as *loza de olor* or aromatic pottery. Here you can also enjoy watching skilled craftsmen creating beautiful original objects. Many work in their own homes, which have been converted into workshops, and many are family-run. Worth a visit is the **Museo Nacional de la Cerámica** (National Ceramic Museum), which has a whole range of exhibits, from pre-Columbian times through the Colonial period and contemporary

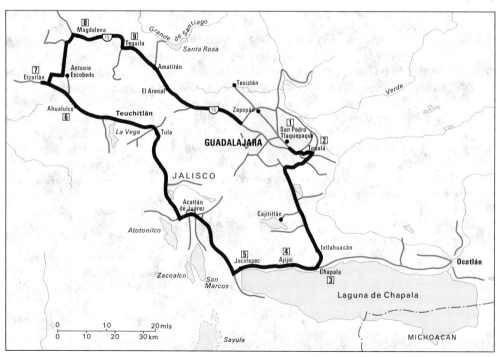

The gates to the market at Tlaquepaque, renowned for its distinctive painted pottery

products. The museum is in the home of artist Jorge Wilmont, who succeeded in combining the talents of other local artists with modern technology. The result has been fine and original pottery of a distinctive style, some inspired by Oriental designs. At **El Santuario** (the Sanctuary) on the outskirts of town is a huge monument to Pope Pius IX, erected in the 18th century. A lookout point from the Cerro de la Reina (Hill of the Queen) offers an impressive view of the city of Guadalajara.

Take the road southwest. Join the road going southwest to Laguna de Chapala (Lake Chapala), about 46km (28 miles) away (making a short stop at Cajititlán en route if you wish).

Laguna de Chapala, Jalisco

3 On the way to Chapala a turnoff to the right takes you to Cajititlán, a pretty little village with two churches of note, both built in the 17th century. Take a look at the **Santuario de los Reyes** (Sanctuary of Guadalupe), in popular baroque style, and the **Parroquía de los Reyes** (Parish Church of the Three Kings), which has some fine gilded *retablos*.

Continue on to Laguna de Chapala, Mexico's largest natural lake, measuring 82km (51 miles) long by 28km (17 miles) across. Set in a range of hills, it is beautiful at all times, but is renowned for its lovely sunrises and spectacular sunsets, when the whole lake can become a huge reflection of crimson and orange. The tranquillity of the surroundings, coupled with its

ideal climate, has attracted many foreigners who have settled in the region, particularly Americans, Canadians and some Europeans. The lake is also a very popular weekend resort for the residents of Guadalajara.

Chapala (which means 'splashing waves' in Náhuatl) is the biggest town. The main square is very charming, with a bandstand for concerts, and the local market merits a visit. An open mall runs from the center of town down to the pier on the lake, attractively laid out with pink tiles and adorned with colorful flowers and plants. A walk along the waterfront is very enjoyable – shops, bars and restaurants line the front, and mariachi musicians stroll along in their striking outfits, playing their lovely tunes and adding to the atmosphere.

Facilities are readily available for water sports. Swimming is possible, but check on the condition of the water, which is variable. Chapala is also an active boating center. You may wish to rent a launch and explore the lake, perhaps visiting some of the picturesque villages around its shores. Of the three largest islands in the lake, the most interesting is Mezcala. The ruins of a fort there mark the spot where Indian rebels held a siege against the Spaniards between 1812 and 1816.

Chapala holds colorful pre-Lenten festivities for Carnival Week.

Back on the mainland, you can drive east along the lakeshore towards Ocotlán and make a stop by the **Barranca del Toro** (Gorge of the Bull), where there are pre-Hispanic cave paintings.

Take the road west along the lakeshore for a few miles to Ajijic.

BACK TO NATURE

3 From the marshy shores of Laguna de Chapala, especially near Chapala and Jocotepec, the birdwatcher can scan the open water for black-necked (eared) grebes, western grebes, pied-billed grebes and American coots. Marshy areas attract white-faced ibises, American bitterns, tricolored herons, little blue herons and great egrets and, in winter, a variety of ducks is also present.

FOR CHILDREN

About 6km (4 miles) north of Guadalajara are **jardines zoológicos** (zoological gardens) covering a large area overlooking the Rio Santiago Canyon. Children will enjoy the wide variety of animals, birds and reptiles to be seen here. There is a children's zoo and an auditorium offering special presentations.

RECOMMENDED WALKS

3 The little lakeside towns on the shores of Laguna de Chapala offer pleasant walking areas. The waterfront of Chapala itself is a delightful place for a stroll. The hustle and bustle of the street vendors and musicians contrasts with the peaceful view of the boats on the lake, set against a background of distant hills.

Ajijic, Jalisco

4 The little town of Ajijic lies on the northern shore of the lake. Its waterfront, cobblestoned streets and lovely mansions make it an attractive place in which to linger a while. It is a great favorite with many North Americans, who have made their home in this haven for artists and writers.

Many shops and boutiques here offer a variety of attractive handicrafts, and the town is especially noted for its weaving and embroidery. The small **Museo de Artesanías** (Museum of Arts and Crafts) has a good selection of ceramics, jewelry and embroidered garments on display. Have a look, too, at the little **Iglesia de San Andrés** (Church of St Andrew), which was built in the 1500s in typical neoclassical style.

Continue on the same road west for about 28km (17 miles) to Jocotepec.

Jocotepec, Jalisco

5 Lying on the western shore of the lake is the little fishing town of Jocotepec, another longtime favorite of artists, who appreciate its tranquillity and rustic charm. Originally a settlement of the Náhua people, it was taken over by the Spaniards and founded officially in 1529. Have a look around the little **Iglesia de San Pedro Tesitán** (Church of St Peter). Some attractive handicrafts are produced locally and Jocotepec is noted for its finely woven white *serapes* (shawls). Market day is on a Thursday.

Take the road northwest to Acatlán de Juárez. Continue north, then at Tala take the road northwest to Ahualulco.

Ahualulco, Jalisco

6 Just before reaching Ahualulco, you can make a stop at Teuchitlán, where there are ruins consisting

A taste of Old Mexico awaits you at the western end of Lake Chapala in Jocotepec. One of the lesser-known pueblos on the lake, it has kept its character intact as a retreat for artists and writers

mainly of a group of platforms and terraces overgrown by vegetation. An altar found in the rocks is thought to be somehow related to the sacrifices of the Ball Game.

A little further on, among plantations of maguey cactus so common in the state of Jalisco, lies the picturesque village of Ahualulco. Founded in 1542, it was once an active mining center. An interesting feature of the village is the huge stone standing in front of the **church**; in the region is an area where these huge, round stones – a natural phenomenon – can be seen.

Continue on the same road for 13km (8 miles) to Etzatlán.

Etzatlán, Jalisco

7 Etzatlán, a pleasant little mining center, has a number of buildings worth visiting. Of special note is the **Monasterio Franciscano** (Franciscan monastery) dating from the 16th century, built with thick walls as a protection against the local Indians. The fountain in the atrium is adorned with cherubs. In front of the main square is another attractive 17th-century **church**. A festival on 3 May honors the town's patron saint, while the Festival of Our Lady of Guadalupe is held on 12 December.

Take the road north to Magdalena.

Magdalena, Jalisco

8 Magdalena lies in the valley of the Santiago River. The village is renowned for its semiprecious stones, including opals, turquoise and agate, and you can visit the mines that produce them. Numerous shops offer

The Degollado Theater, in Guadalajara, presents plays, concerts and operas year round

a wide selection of jewelry. A couple of buildings worth a visit are the 16th-century **Templo del Señor de los Milagros** (Temple of the Man of Miracles) and the 17th-century **Templo de la Purísima** (Temple of the Purest One) with an attractively tiled cupola. Many of the more remote villages, inhabited by the Huichol Indians, are barely accessible by road, but it is sometimes possible by special arrangement to visit some of them by means of small aircraft.

Take **Mex 15** *southeast for 19km (11 miles) to Tequila.*

Tequila, Jalisco

9 The name of this town is literally on almost everyone's lips, for it is a center for the production of the famous fiery drink tequila. A visit to one of the town's distilleries is an interesting experience. Supplies of cactus – the basis of the drink – are obtained from the agave plantations in the region.

The **Templo de la Purísima** (Temple of the Purest One), built in the 18th century in the neoclassical style, is worth a visit. So, too, are the thermal springs known as **La Toma de Tequila** and **Las Termas de Tequila**, surrounded by orchards of fruit trees. Festivals here focus on the local firewater: 13 May is the Tequila Fiesta, while the Annual Tequila Fair is held from 30 November to 12 December.

On your return journey, about 7km (4 miles) before Guadalajara, make a stop at Zapopán. The **Basílica de la Virgen de Zapopan** was built in the 17th century and is dedicated to the Virgin of Zapopan, who is believed to have performed miracles here. The tiny statue of the Virgin is displayed in various churches in Guadalajara for periods of time and returned to Zapopán on 12 October amid great festivities of dancing and music. Handicrafts of the Huichol and Cora Indians from the surrounding region are displayed in a small museum.

Return to Guadalajara on **Mex 15**.

Guadalajara – San Pedro Tlaquepaque	**6 (4)**
San Pedro Tlaquepaque – Tonalá	**10 (6)**
Tonalá – Laguna de Chapala	**46 (28)**
Laguna de Chapala – Ajijic	**8 (5)**
Ajijic – Jocotepec	**28 (17)**
Jocotepec – Ahualulco	**103 (64)**
Ahualulco – Etzatlán	**13 (8)**
Etzatlán – Magdalena	**22 (13)**
Magdalena – Tequila	**19 (11)**
Tequila – Guadalajara	**60 (37)**

SCENIC ROUTES

There is some very attractive scenery along this route. Of particular note are the stretches from Tonalá to Laguna de Chapala, especially the last part of the journey as the road makes its descent and a lovely view of the lake unfolds; the drive along the lakeshore from Chapala to Ajijic and on to Jocotopec; the road from Magdalena to Tequila, which is very mountainous, with hairpin curves in and out of vast plantations of blue agave cactus.

FOR HISTORY BUFFS

7 Some 7km (4 miles) west of Etzatlán in the grounds of the former hacienda of San Sebastian is an archaeological site known as **El Arenal**. This was explored in the mid-50s and includes underground chambers resembling tombs, similar to those found in the states of Nayarit and Colima. Ceramics found here are now exhibited in the Museum of Guadalajara.

4 days – 630km (391 miles)

CHURCHES, COLONIAL TOWNS & RANCHLANDS

Guadalajara • Jalpa • Aguascalientes
Lagos de Moreno • León
San Juan de los Lagos • Guadalajara

This second tour from Guadalajara sets out to the north and northeast of the city in a circular route, passing through the states of Zacatecas, Aguascalientes, Guanajuato and Jalisco. You will be driving through some very varied scenery, which includes dramatic mountain passes with deep gorges and valleys, as well as many rivers and waterfalls. You will also have the opportunity to explore several of Mexico's attractive towns, with their elegant Colonial-style buildings. This is an area of large ranches, where the fighting bulls are bred. Some fine churches are included and one of Mexico's important pilgrimage centers.

FOR CHILDREN

4 The **Parque Zoológico** is a good zoological garden located near León, which has a special appeal to children with its variety of animals, including lions and pigmy hippos. Equestrian events are held here every week in a fortlike building that looks like something out of the Wild West.

SCENIC ROUTES

Much of the scenery along this route is impressive. There is a magnificent stretch between Guadalajara and Jalpa, as the road passes through the Barranca (gorge) of the Río Grande de Santiago. The route continues through superb landscapes of mountain ranges and deep valleys. Also notable is the stretch from San Juan de los Lagos back to Guadalajara.

ⓘ Lázaro Cárdenas 3289, 1st Floor, Col Chapalita, Guadalajara

*Take **Mex 54** north toward Jalpa, making a short detour to the Barranca de los Oblatos. Then continue to Jalpa, for a total of about 161km (100 miles).*

Jalpa, Zacatecas

1 On the way to Jalpa make a detour to the **Barranca de los Oblatos**, a spectacular gorge, where you can stop and look down into the ravine or descend by cable car to its depths, some 660m (2,170 feet) down.

The little town of Jalpa is a pleasant place in which to make your first major stop and admire a few of its attractions. Buildings of note are the 18th-century **Church of the Señor de Jalpa**, which boasts a fine façade in the baroque style, and the **Presidencia Municipal** (Town Hall), from the Colonial era. A fine-looking bandstand sits in the middle of the main garden square.

*Take **Mex 70** northeast for 96km (60 miles) to Aguascalientes.*

Aguascalientes, Aguascalientes

2 Aguascalientes is the state capital and a handsome town of lovely parks, fine buildings and churches. Known for its thermal springs (its name means 'hot waters' in Spanish), the town plays host to many visitors who come to take a cure. Lying among vineyards and orchards, Aguascalientes is right in the middle

Ranch country, where the proud tradition of horsemanship and roping is shown off in charreadas, the Mexican forerunner of the rodeo. The charro (cowboy) is expected to display dexterity and elegance

of ranchlands where bulls are bred for bullfights. One of Mexico's best-known bull-breeding ranches is **Peñuelas**, where it may be possible to arrange a visit. Other ranches in the vicinity are also often ready to welcome a visitor.

Aguascalientes is one of Mexico's prominent wine-producing areas, and you may like to have a look around one of the local wineries; it is best to make inquiries on arrival. The town is also noted for its pottery, hand embroidery and textiles, and its famous annual fair, the **Feria de San Marcos**, held from 25 April to 5 May. Another annual festival celebrates the Assumption of the Blessed Virgin Mary on 15 August.

The main square is surrounded by some beautiful buildings. Of special note are the 17th-century **Palacio Municipal** (Town Hall) and the 18th-century **Palacio de Gobernación** (Government Palace), which has some fine murals by Osvaldo Barra, a pupil of Mexico's famous painter Diego Rivera, in the courtyard. Other buildings worth a visit are the **cathedral** (1730) with some interesting paintings; the **Iglesia de San Antonio** (Church of St Anthony) with its unusual towers; and the 18th-century **Temple of Guadalupe**, a fine example of the Churrigueresque style. The **Casa de las Artesanías** (Arts and Crafts Center) offers a display of arts and crafts. In the **Museo J Guadalupe Posada** (J Guadalupe Posada Museum) you can see some fine engravings and paintings, and the **Museo de Aguascalientes** (City Museum) has a good collection of artifacts and relics. A lovely old former convent is now the **Casa de Cultura** (House of Culture), where various evening events are staged.

In the vicinity are a number of old mining towns, long fallen into decline. Worth a visit are the little mining centers of Tepezalá and Asientos, which have been restored since they were deserted some 200 years ago.

ⓘ Avenida de las Americas 502

*Take **Mex 45** southeast to Lagos de Moreno.*

Lagos de Moreno, Jalisco

3 Once an important stagecoach stop, Lagos de Moreno is now a sleepy little town surrounded by orchards. A number of its churches and buildings merit a visit. The **Iglesia Parroquial** (parish church) is impressive: inside are 18 cupolas where you can see the changes of style from Churrigueresque to neoclassical. The **Iglesia del Calvario** (the Church of Cavalry) features 12 huge statues representing the Apostles. The **Teatro Rosas Moreno** is a center for education with a fine reputation, earning it the nickname of the Athens of the Bajio (the local region). Take a look too, at the 18th-century bridge spanning the Lagos River. If you are in the vicinity of the town around 28

The Government Palace in Aguascalientes, formerly a feudal castle, boasts this historical mural

July to 6 August, you can see how the people celebrate their annual fiesta. The spa of La Laguna is nearby.

*Continue on **Mex 45** southeast to León.*

León, Guanajuato

4 León de los Aldamas (to give it its full name) is the largest town in the state of Guanajuato. Situated on the banks of the Turbio River in a wheat-growing area, it is an important commercial center known mainly for its shoe-manufacturing industry. Saddles and other leather goods are also produced here. The town is

SPECIAL TO . . .

2 The **Feria de San Marcos** takes place in Aguascalientes from 25 April to 5 May each year, in honor of the town's patron saint. It is one of the oldest fairs in Mexico and also one of the most famous. People dress in colorful costumes and the whole town is taken over by a variety of entertainments, which include music and dancing, fireworks, bullfights and cockfights, **charreadas** (Mexican-style rodeos) and parades. The event attracts visitors from many parts.

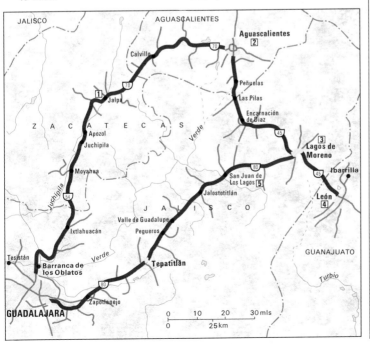

FOR HISTORY BUFFS

2 The town of Pabellón de Hidalgo 40km (25 miles) north of Aguascalientes, features a fine **church** with an impressive altar built in the baroque style. Of historical interest is the **Hacienda San Blas** which now houses the **Museo de la Insurgencia** (Museum of the Insurgency). It was here that Father Miguel Hidalgo, hero of the Independence War against the Spaniards, lost his command after suffering defeat in two important battles and was replaced by another prominent figure, Ignacio Allende. The hacienda is known for its woven goods produced on hand looms.

mainly made up of attractive Colonial buildings, although a large part of it has been rebuilt – several floods, the worst in 1888, have caused severe damage in the past. Old buildings blend happily with modern boulevards to create a harmonious combination. The main square, with trees and flowers, is surrounded by the portals typical of the Colonial era. This is overlooked by the 18th-century **Catedral de Nuestra Señora de la Luz** (Cathedral of Our Lady of the Light) and has some artistic treasures inside, including a fine painting of the Virgin. The **Palacio Municipal** (Town Hall), also facing the square, has a richly decorated exterior and presents a fine example of Colonial architecture. Also of note is the **Templo Expiatorio**, built in neo-Gothic style, with a great number of altars and chapels. Other buildings of interest are the **Casa de Los Monos** (House of the Monkeys), with columns representing indigenous figures, the **Panteón Taurino** and the **Teatro Doblado**. There is a good **Museo de Antropología** (Museum of Anthropology), housed in the Presidencia Municipal, and a lively market that offers a variety of goods.

Near León is the archaeological site of **Ibarrilla**. The ruins consist mainly of some pyramids and structures of Tarascan origin, very overgrown by dense vegetation. A number of artifacts found here are now on display in the Museum of Guadalajara. Also of interest in the vicinity is the ancient Otomí settlement now called **Silao**. The 18th-century **parish church** has some fine *bas-reliefs*. Near here is the pleasant spa resort of Comanjilla. Further away, about 42km (26 miles), is a spot known as the **Vergel de la Sierra** (Flower Garden of the Sierra), an area of several small lakes with facilities for fishing, golf and tennis in a pleasant setting and with a lovely old hacienda converted into a hotel.

Return northwest on **Mex 45** *to Lagos de Moreno. Then take* **Mex 80** *southwest to San Juan de los Lagos.*

Built in 1665 as the mansion of the feudal baron the Marqués de Guadalupe, the Government Palace, with its stunning courtyard, is the most outstanding example of Colonial architecture in Aguascalientes

RECOMMENDED WALK

4 The **Vergel de la Sierra** (Flower Garden of the Sierra) is 38km (24 miles) north of León, just off **Mex 37**. There are several small lakes and an oak forest which provide a pleasant area for a quiet walk.

In San Juan de los Lagos, the parish church contains a miraculous statue of the Virgin. The flocks of pilgrims who arrive here for religious festivals outnumber even Acapulco's Holy Week crowd

San Juan de los Lagos, Jalisco

5 The small town of San Juan de los Lagos (St John of the Lakes) is famed throughout Mexico as a pilgrimage center and renowned for its religious festivals. Multitudes of pilgrims come from all over the country to pay homage to the Virgen de la Candelaria, whose statue is in the parish church and to whom miracles are attributed. The town was founded in the early 17th century by the missionary Antonio de Segovia, who brought the image of the Virgin to the town. There are many fine churches and Colonial buildings worth visiting. The **Basílica de San Juan de los Lagos** is an impressive church built in the 18th century, with twin towers in the neoclassical style. Inside are some fine works of art. The **Palacio Municipal** (Town Hall), the old **Palacio del Colegio** (Palace of the College) and the **Parián** are among the lovely Colonial buildings in the town. The annual pilgrimages begin on 20 January and continue until 5 February accompanied by lively celebrations with music, dancing, bullfights and cockfights.

On the way back to Guadalajara on Mex 80, you might like to stop at one or two interesting places. After Pegueros turn left and continue through San Ignacio to Arandas, a little town that boasts the biggest church bell in Mexico. It was discovered in the Sanctuary of San José but had to be taken down, as the towers could not bear the weight. The bell now stands before the imposing Gothic-style church of Arandas.

Soon after returning to Mex 80 you will come to Tepatitlán. This small town is characterized by its attractive Colonial-style main square surrounded by arcades. The **Temple of San Antonio** has lovely gilded *retablos* and an impressive wooden carving of the patron of the city, the Señor de la Misericordia (Lord of Mercy). A lively fiesta takes place here in the last week of April, with mariachi music, bullfights, horse racing, rodeos, regional dancing and a car race dedicated to the Lord of Mercy.

*Return to Guadalajara on **Mex 80**, about 156km (97 miles) from San Juan de los Lagos.*

Guadalajara – Jalpa **161 (100)**
Jalpa – Aguascalientes **96 (60)**
Aguascalientes – Lagos de Moreno **84 (52)**
Lagos de Moreno – León **44 (27)**
León – San Juan de los Lagos **89 (55)**
San Juan de los Lagos – Guadalajara **156 (97)**

BACK TO NATURE

Away from the city center, residential gardens and parks attract a surprising array of birds. Diminutive Inca doves feed on the ground alongside house sparrows and brown towhees, while the trees should be searched for vermilion flycatchers and house finches. Further away from built-up areas, visitors should find rough-winged swallows, Bewick's wrens, loggerhead shrikes and eastern meadowlarks.

5/6 days – 1,019km (634 miles)

GOLDEN PACIFIC TROPICS OF THE WEST

Puerto Vallarta ● Bahía Chamela ● Melaque
Barra de Navidad ● Manzanillo ● Colima
Parque Nacional Volcán de Fuego
Ciudad Guzmán ● Tepic ● Puerto Vallarta

This itinerary, starting from Puerto Vallarta, passes through the states of Jalisco, Colima and Nayarit. The tour commences with a drive down this beautiful Pacific coastline of sandy beaches, rocky coves, banana and coconut plantations and lush, tropical vegetation, with stops at various resorts and attractive areas along the way. The route then continues into the dense jungles of the interior, where some spectacular scenery awaits you as you cross the mighty mountain ranges of the Sierra Madre Occidental. Included in the itinerary are major towns of interest, as well as little villages inhabited by some fascinating Indian groups.

FOR HISTORY BUFFS

4 It is believed that junks from the Orient called at Manzanillo before the Spanish came. When Hernán Cortés visited the port for the first time in 1526, he named it after the lovely manzanilla trees he found here, and chose it for his place of retirement. Cortés founded the first Latin American shipyard in Manzanillo, and vessels were fitted out here for expeditions across the Pacific. Today the town continues as Mexico's most important West Coast port.

Mismaloya Beach, Puerto Vallarta: palm-frond huts sell lobster meals

[i] Presidencia Municipal P B, Puerto Vallarta

*From Puerto Vallarta take the coastal **Mex 200** southeast to Bahía Chamela.*

Bahía Chamela, Jalisco

1 This beautiful bay extends for several miles. Stop at this point to admire the view of silvery beaches and clear blue waters which teem with exotic marine life. A number of small islands are sprinkled about the bay, which is set against luxuriant green terrain. Chamela is known for its excellent beaches, lovely seashells and turtles, and has a reputation for good oysters. In February and March the area is invaded by vast flocks of migrating seabirds. There are a few hotels, bars and restaurants and camping facilities. The tranquillity and beauty of the place could easily tempt you to linger awhile.

*Continue along coastal **Mex 200** to Melaque.*

Melaque, Jalisco

2 On your way to Melaque you might like to make a stop or two to admire the view along the route. The **Costa de Careyes** (Turtle Coast) has miles of beautiful coastline, with bays edged in pure white sand and palm trees, and lagoons set in lush tropical foliage. Tenacatita is another fine bay with ideal conditions for swimming, fishing and snorkeling. Not so long ago the area was mostly virgin land. In recent years, however, new hotels have been springing up along the

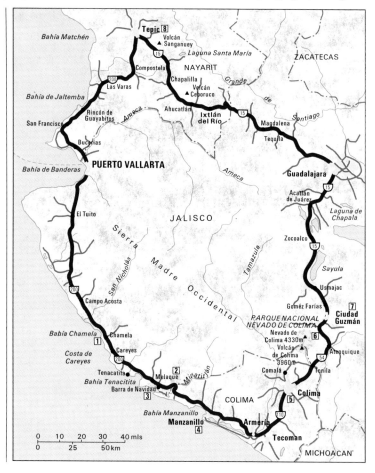

The beach at Barra de Navidad is perfect for watery pursuits, especially with youngsters. Boogie boards and windsurfing boards can be rented at a nearby hotel

coast, which offers swimming and fishing in tropical surroundings. Many quiet coves and bays offer good swimming, but there are also expanses of open beach, where the big rollers are suited to surfers. Watch out for strong currents.

The picturesque little town of Melaque has long been a popular resort for Mexicans and North Americans. Situated on the Bahía Navidad, the resort consists of a collection of small sandy beaches, with a few hotels, bars and restaurants. Its charms lie chiefly in its unsophisticated simplicity and informal way of life. Facilities for water sports on the bay are readily available.

Continue east on the coastal Mex 200 for 5km (3 miles) to Barra de Navidad.

Barra de Navidad, Jalisco

3 This tiny fishing village lies on a sandbar and is another favorite resort for Mexican families, who arrive mostly at weekends and during holiday periods. With its sandy beaches and large lagoon, the village offers boat trips and fishing. The old port played an important role in the history of the Philippines, as expeditions set out from here in the 16th century to find a route to the Spice Islands, leading to the discovery and conquest of the Philippines. The area was very remote until roads were built linking Guadalajara to Tepic and Puerto Vallarta, and then the coastal roads.

Continue on Mex 200 southeast for 67km (42 miles) to Manzanillo.

Manzanillo, Colima

4 The port of Manzanillo is situated on a narrow isthmus at the southern end of the Bays of Santiago and Manzanillo. Known as the sailfish capital of Mexico, Manzanillo is a good base for fishing expeditions in the vicinity. One of its main attractions lies in its setting among lush plantations, with a backdrop of beautiful mountains sweeping down to the coast. The town has plenty of bars, restaurants and shops, and a cheerful zócalo (main square), where the evenings are lively. Fishing boats can be rented for fishing excursions to catch sea bass, snapper and catfish, and for deep-sea fishing for sailfish, bonito, devil ray and shark. Sailing across the Bay of Manzanillo on a warm tropical night is an unforgettable experience, with the bay shimmering under a starlit sky. Try asking one of the local fishermen.

i Juárez 244, 4th floor.

Continue on Mex 200. Take Mex 110 inland for 98km (62 miles) to Colima.

RECOMMENDED WALK

6 Fire Volcano Park is a beautiful area for walking among the scented pine forests. Serious climbers who wish to ascend the Nevado de Colima must start from El Fresnito. There is a mountain hut at La Joya and the climb could take two days. From the summit, which is normally covered by snow, the view is spectacular. The climb up the Volcán de Fuego is via Atenquique and El Playon. The Volcán's crater is still active. The climb up here is also rewarded with fine panoramic views.

Popular (Museum of Masks, Dance and Popular Arts of the West).

Other notable buildings in the town are the **Palacio de Gobierno** (Government Palace), the **cathedral** and several other churches, including those of **El Sagrado Corazón**, **San José** and **Fátima**.

While in the vicinity you may like to visit the little health resort of Agua Caliente, a few miles southeast, and Comalá, a pretty little village of white houses and red roofs, set among small lagoons. Comalá is noted for its wrought-iron work, painted furniture and other fine crafts.

Near Los Ortices is a resort called **Las Cascadas de Tampumacchay** (Tampumacchay waterfalls) in a beautiful setting overlooking a deep gorge and some waterfalls. There is an archaeological zone, a cactus garden and an open-air museum with a collection of pre-Hispanic artifacts from the area.

*Take **Mex 54** in the direction of Guadalajara. About 30km (19 miles) before Atenquique, branch off on a minor road for 27km (17 miles) to Parque Nacional Volcán de Fuego (Fire Volcano National Park).*

Parque Nacional Volcán de Fuego, Jalisco

6 This park, also known as Fire Volcano National Park or Nevado de Colima, covers an extensive area of beautiful pine forests, which grow in profusion on the lower slopes and gradually disappear as the higher ground becomes covered with snow. There are magnificent views of the two volcanoes. The **Nevado de Colima**, also known as Zapotépetl (which means 'mountain of the sapodilla trees') reaches a height of 4,380m (14,371 feet) and is the sixth highest mountain in Mexico. The **Volcán de Fuego** (Fire Volcano), also known as the Volcán de Colima, is 3,960m (12,989 feet) high with an awesome crater some 1,800m (5,908 feet) across and 250m (820 feet) deep. Its last eruption in 1941 caused considerable damage. To this day it shows signs of activity, emitting smoke and sulphur vapors, and the occasional rumble can be heard.

At the foot of the mountains, the lovely Lake Carrizalillo nestles in beautiful coniferous woods. Boat trips and horseback riding are available here.

*Return to **Mex 54**. Continue northwest for 20km (12 miles) to Ciudad Guzmán.*

Ciudad Guzmán, Jalisco

7 Ciudad Guzmán is an agricultural center and an important town in the region. One of Mexico's most prominent painters of the 20th century, José Clemento Orozco, was born here, and the local museum (**Museo Regional de las Culturas**) contains some of his paintings, as well as archaeological exhibits. The town has several fine churches to visit. These include the **cathedral**, which was built in 1866 and has four notable paintings inside; the **Iglesia del Sagrado Corazón** (Church of the Sacred Heart), from the 17th century and the first to be built in the town; and the

BACK TO NATURE

5 The whole area surrounding Colima is a deer sanctuary. A relaxed drive around here should afford plenty of opportunities to see these beautiful creatures. Many of the trees are colonized by epiphytes – plants which grow on other plants – and are covered in creepers. In clearings look for owl butterflies and birds such as motmots, trogons, hummingbirds and woodpeckers.

SCENIC ROUTES

The coastal drive from Puerto Vallarta down to Manzanillo is very beautiful, with miles of silvery beaches and tropical vegetation against a background of hills and mountains covered by dense forests. There are some very scenic stretches of road between Colima and Ciudad Guzmán, passing through ravines and deep valleys as you approach the area of the Nevado de Colima and Volcán de Fuego. Most of the drive from Guadalajara to Tepic is spectacular as you pass over the Sierra Madre del Sur mountain range. The steeply rising mountains are slashed by deep gorges and valleys thickly covered by jungle vegetation.

Not everyone is on vacation in Puerto Vallarta: local women wash clothes in the time-honored way

Colima, Colima

5 Colima, the state capital, lies in a fertile valley at an altitude of 458m (1,502 feet), within sight of two magnificent volcanoes, the **Nevado de Colima** and the **Volcán de Fuego** – the latter caused much devastation in 1941, when it last erupted. Two rivers run through the slopes that surround the valley. The town is pleasant and tranquil, featuring Colonial buildings and tropical gardens. Of special interest to the visitor is the **Museo de las Culturas del Occidente** (Museum of the Western Cultures), part of the House of Culture complex. Among the fine displays of pre-Columbian artifacts is a notable collection of the curious 'Colima dogs' (strangely shaped models of fattened dogs made by potters in pre-Hispanic times). Some may be interested in seeing the collection of old cars, dating from the early 1900s to the 50s, in the **Museo de Automóviles Antiguos** (Museum of Old Cars). Other centers worth a visit include the **Casa de Artesanías** (House of Crafts) and the **Artesanías Cooperatíva Comalá** (Comalá Crafts Cooperative), where you can see handicrafts, Colonial furniture and paintings. The **House of Culture** has theaters and an art school and stages concerts, plays and art exhibitions. Take a look at the interesting collection of masks in the **Museo Nacional de la Máscara, la Danza y el Arte**

A tropical paradise that has yet to be overwhelmed by tourism, Puerto Vallarta caters for every budget – here, pleasant condominiums

19th-century neo-Gothic **Templo de San Antonio**, decorated in part with Italian mosaics. Several days of celebration honor St Joseph, from 22 to 25 October (Dia de San José).

Take **Mex 54** *northwest for 144km (90 miles) to Guadalajara. An overnight stay here is recommended before continuing your journey on* **Mex 15** *west to Tepic, 227km (141 miles), stopping at the suggested detours as desired.*

Tepic, Nayarit

8 Before reaching Tepic, there are a few places that merit a detour. The ruins at Ixtlán de Río are only partly excavated, but considered the most important in northwest Mexico. This ancient ceremonial center is believed to have been inhabited from about the 6th century AD. Dwellings, platforms and various buildings can be seen, including a temple thought to be dedicated to the god Quetzalcóatl. Markets in the town sell a variety of leather items, including sandals and furniture.

Continuing towards Tepic, a turning to the right leads up through volcanic terrain to the **Ceboruco Volcano**, which erupted in 1885. From the top you can take in the superb view of the strange landscapes around you.

Branch off to the right a little further on to **Laguna Santa María**, an attractive crater set in wooded hills. You can swim in its lovely clear waters, fish or rent a launch.

Tepic, capital of the state of Nayarit, is a combination of old and new. It lies in the valley of Matatipac, overlooked by the Sanganguey Volcano and surrounded by forest-clad hills and plantations of tobacco and sugarcane. It was formerly an old Indian site and was occupied by the Spaniards in 1542, but owing to its isolation, development was slow until the arrival of the railroad at the beginning of the century.

Buildings of note include the 18th-century **cathedral**, with its fine Gothic towers, and the **Iglesia de la Cruz de Zacate** (Church of the Cross of Zacategras), which has a cross much venerated by the local Indians. The **Museo Regional de Antropología** (Regional Anthropology Museum) contains archaeological items from the area and material relating to the Colonial period and to the Cora and Huichol Indians from the surrounding country. Shops stock colorful items made by these Indians. Tepic is a good base for excursions into the hinterland to visit little villages inhabited by the Huichol and Cora Indians. The area is barely accessible by road, but at certain times of the year special arrangements can be made to visit some of these Indian communities by small charter plane. Check locally for details.

[i] Avenida Mexico Sur 253A, 1st floor

Take the road south and southwest to join **Mex 200***. Return to Puerto Vallarta.*

Puerto Vallarta – Bahía Chamela	**149 (92)**
Bahía Chamela – Melaque	**62 (38)**
Melaque – Barra de Navidad	**5 (3)**
Barra de Navidad – Manzanillo	**67 (42)**
Manzanillo – Colima	**98 (62)**
Colima – Parque Nacional Volcán de Fuego	**57 (36)**
Parque Nacional Volcán de Fuego – Ciudad Guzmán	**47 (29)**
Ciudad Guzmán – Tepic	**371 (231)**
Tepic – Puerto Vallarta	**163 (101)**

SPECIAL TO...

5 Colima celebrates several festivals over the year. One of the most enjoyable is **Día de la Virgen de la Salud** (the Festival of Our Lady of Health). There are nine days of celebrations, with music and dancing, religious events, bullfights and fireworks, culminating with the feast day itself on 2 February.

FOR THE CHILDREN

8 There is a **zoo** at Las Piedras, near Las Varas, 67km (42 miles) southwest of Tepic (**Mex 200**) on the return to Puerto Vallarta. It has a magnificent collection of fauna from the region. Among exhibits are large alligators, racoons and coral snakes. The setting is attractive and is a great place for children.

THE NORTH & NORTHWEST

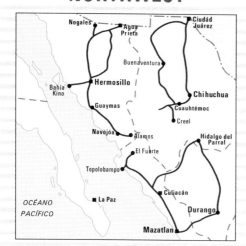

Chihuahua:

Chihuahua, the capital of the largest state in Mexico, lies on a high plateau set against the impressive backdrop of the Sierra Madre Occidental. The city is a prosperous industrial center for silver mining, cattle raising and timber. It has wide avenues and elegant squares, and some of the buildings are worth visiting, primarily for their historical significance. The **catedral** (cathedral) (1724–1825) on the main square is a fine example of baroque architecture; the **Palacio Federal** (Federal Building), preserves the tower where a hero of the Independence War, Father Hidalgo, was kept prisoner in 1811; and the **Palacio de Gobierno** (Government Palace) was the scene of his execution. The **Museo de la Revolución** (Museum of the Revolution) was formerly the home of the revolutionary outlaw Pancho Villa, and it displays items related to that period. In an elegantly restored mansion the **Museo Regional de Chihuahua** (Regional Museum) has material on the history of the religious communities of the Mormons and Mennonites who settled in the region.

This region includes the northern border states of Chihuahua and Sonora, with Durango and Sinaloa to their south. Together they make up an area of vast deserts, mighty mountain ranges and a long coastline. The Río Bravo, or Río Grande, forms a natural frontier between much of Chihuahua and Texas. The Sierra Madre Occidental range dominates the southern part of this region, with some of the most spectacular scenery in Mexico. The Barranca del Cobre (Copper Canyon) is an area of soaring mountains, deep gorges and dense vegetation. Sonora combines deserts and plains with mountains, forested areas and a sandy coastline. Durango's wild scenery is highlighted by arid plateaus of lava rock divided by deep gorges. Sinaloa, bordering the Mar de Cortés in the west, has mountain slopes rising in the east.

Various tribes, mostly nomadic, inhabited Mexico's northern regions in pre-Hispanic times. Present-day Indian tribes include the Tarahumaras, who live in the Copper Canyon region, and the Guarijo and Tepehuano peoples. The Yaquis, Mayos and Seris are among the other tribes in Sonora and Sinaloa.

The north was historically subject to frequent raids from the Apache and Comanche Indians, and these continued long after the Conquest. During the 17th century a number of missions were established here by the Jesuits, who succeeded in pacifying the area for a period of time. Chihuahua was finally founded in the early 1700s, and the area began to prosper when mineral deposits were found. Over the years Chihuahua has seen some significant events. Father Hidalgo and other leaders of the Independence War were courtmartialed and shot here in 1811. The town was temporarily occupied by US troops during the Mexican-American War (1846–48). The Revolutionary, Pancho Villa, made the town his headquarters in the early part of the 1910–20 Revolution; he was ambushed and shot in Hidalgo del Parral, in the southern part of the state, in 1923. In the north, evidence of an early civilization dating back 700 years can be seen at Casas Grandes.

Mazatlán is an important port and tourist destination in Sinaloa. Together with Bahía Kino, in Sonora, it attracts visitors with an interest in fishing. Good hunting is found in the hinterland. It can be extremely hot in the summer. In winter the climate normally remains sunny and pleasant, reaching cold temperatures in the high sierras. Rainfall is minimal year round.

Hermosillo:

Hermosillo is the capital of the large and prosperous state of Sonora. It lies on the shores of a lake at the confluence of the San Miguel and Sonora Rivers, with a background of bare mountains. The town has developed into a modern commercial center with wide boulevards and a good selection of shops. The main square has a beautiful white bandstand for concerts. This is overlooked by the 19th-century **Catedral de la Ascensión** (cathedral), built of white stone in the neoclassical style. Of the few Colonial buildings left in Hermosillo, the **Palacio de Gobierno** (Government Palace), with its colorful courtyard murals, is worth a visit, as well as the **Museo Regional de Historia de Sonora** (Regional Museum) on the University campus. One item of particular note is a mummy believed to date back some 12,000 years, found near the village of Yécora.

There is a sweeping view of the city and its surroundings from a hilltop lookout post in Madero Park, located on the Cerro de la Campana just outside town.

Mazatlán:

Mazatlán is an important deep-sea fishing center. It lies on a small peninsula in a lovely setting of hills and mountains, with a string of beaches and coves that offer excellent swimming, surfing, scuba diving, water skiing and sailing. Deep-sea fishing is a long-established attraction.

Mazatlán is also a major port, and there is constant activity around the docks. Young boys dive into the sea from a tall rock called El Mirador. Curious little three-wheel taxis called *pulmonias* can take you around town. The *malecón*, a long seafront promenade, offers lovely walks along the shores of the Pacific, spectacular at sunset and also beautiful by night.

The resort has a lively atmosphere with its many cafés and restaurants, known for their fresh seafood. The Mazatlán Carnival, just before Lent, rates as one of the liveliest fiestas in Mexico.

Aglow from the setting sun, the year-round resort of Mazatlán was where Spanish galleons took on great shipments of gold

7/8 days – 1,529km (946 miles)

COPPER CANYON COUNTRY

Chihuahua • Cuauhtémoc • Creel
Cascada de Basaseachic • Buenaventura
Nuevo Casas Grandes • Casas Grandes
Ciudad Juárez • Parque Nacional Cumbres de Majalca
Chihuahua

This tour starts from Chihuahua and takes you through some formidable cactus-studded desert terrain characteristic of northern Mexico. It can be extremely hot here, so be prepared. The itinerary leads you to the brink of Copper Canyon, which has some of the most spectacular scenery imaginable, with the option of taking the famous Chihuahua Pacífico railroad trip through the dramatic landscapes of the canyons. You will see magnificent waterfalls and one of the few archaeological sites in the area, as well as visit a completely contrasting border town.

FOR HISTORY BUFFS

7 Ciudad Juárez has played an important role during certain periods of Mexico's turbulent history. Founded in 1659 by the Spanish and called Paso de Norte, it was renamed Ciudad Juárez in 1888 in honor of Benito Juárez, considered one of Mexico's greatest Presidents. Juárez used the town as his headquarters during the War of Intervention from foreign powers (1865–66). During the troubled times of the Revolution of 1910–20, Ciudad Juárez was also used as a base by the revolutionary figure Pancho Villa. You can visit the **Cuartel del Quince** (Headquarters of the Fifteenth) which was taken by fire and much blood-spilling when the town fell to the revolutionaries in 1911.

ⓘ Calle Cuauhtémoc 18000, 3rd Floor, Chihuahua

*Take **Mex 16** southwest to Cuauhtémoc.*

Cuauhtémoc, Chihuahua

1 Cuauhtémoc is an agricultural center — with a difference. Here you will come across something quite unexpected in Mexico: a town founded by Mennonites, who established a community here back in 1921. This religious sect, dating back to the mid-1500s, seeks the freedom to hold certain beliefs and live as their religion dictates. A number of Mennonites, mainly German, found their way to Mexico in the early 1920s and were granted the right to live according to their religious principles. They have their own schools and are exempt from military service. They keep within their own community, do not intermarry, and do not speak Spanish. The Mennonites are excellent farmers known for their cheese and sausages. With their blond hair and blue eyes they are distinctive, the men with wide-brimmed hats and the women in long skirts.

About 24km (15 miles) away is Cusihuiriáchic, where you can take a quick look at the little 18th-century **Temple of Santa Rosa de Lima**, with a modest but well-proportioned vestibule and a fine *retablo* inside. The nearby **Laguna de los Mexicanos** (Lagoon of the Mexicans) has water sports facilities.

Detail of Chihuahua's cathedral: although begun in 1724, it was not completed until 1826 because of continual Indian wars

*Take **Mex 16** west to La Junta, then travel southwest for 138km (86 miles) to Creel.*

Creel, Chihuahua

2 The small logging village of Creel is an excellent base for excursions into the interior of one of the most fascinating regions of Mexico. You are on the edge of the famous **Barranca del Cobre** (Copper Canyon), a vast region of huge canyons and deep gorges, created by ancient erosions and eruptions of nature. This impressive canyon is actually larger than Arizona's Grand Canyon. It is also the home of the Tarahumara Indians.

From Creel you can explore this beautiful canyon country and visit some of the Tarahumara villages, little missions and lovely waterfalls in the vicinity. Excursions on horseback are also organized. Another option is the Chihuahua Pacífico railroad trip from Creel, often called the world's most scenic railroad. The journey starts at Chihuahua, but you can board the train at Creel; it takes a day to reach Los Mochis, down on the Pacific coast. The stretch from Creel to Los Mochis is the most scenic of the whole journey, as the train winds its way over miles of rugged terrain with deep canyons and gorges. The line covers 653km (406 miles) and is a remarkable feat of engineering, with 39 bridges and 86 tunnels. Various stops *en route* allow access to views of the area. At Divisadero, with an altitude of 2,300m (7,546 feet), a stop of about 20 minutes offers a magnificent panorama of Copper Canyon. You can also stop off for a night or two at various points, where accommodation is available and organized excursions visit places inhabited by the Tarahumaras, an area also known as the Sierra Tarahumara.

Return north then southwest to Cascada de Basaseachic.

Cascada de Basaseachic, Chihuahua

3 These falls are situated in the Parque Nacional Cascada de Basaseachic (Basaseachic Falls National Park), in a beautiful setting of wooded mountains, gorges and streams. The waterfalls are among the most magnificent in Mexico, with an impressive sheet of cascading water that drops some 310m (1,020 feet) into a gorge far below on the Basaseachic River.

*Return east on **Mex 16** to Cuauhtémoc. Take the road north to Alvaro Obregón, then continue northwest via Gómez Farías and Zaragoza to Buenaventura, 80km (50 miles) from Gómez Farías to Buenaventura.*

Buenaventura, Chihuahua

4 Buenaventura is a small agricultural town known for its excellent dairy products. Although the town has little to offer in the way of obvious tourist attractions, it is a convenient place to stop before continuing with your journey northwards.

*Take **Mex 23** northwest for 85km (52 miles) to Nuevo Casas Grandes.*

Nuevo Casas Grandes, Chihuahua

5 Nuevo Casas Grandes is a modern farming settlement and commercial center for the surrounding valley. Worth a visit is the small **Museum of Ancient Indians**, with a collection of items and maps relating to the history of the Indians who inhabit the region. Some of the artificial lakes nearby offer fishing and have facilities for water sports. In addition to Casas Grandes (the next stop on your itinerary), other pre-Columbian sites can be visited in the area, either by jeep or on horseback. The going can be tough and some of the places difficult to find, so a guide is recommended. Some suggestions are Huaynopa, Vallecito and Cuarenta Casas (around Ciudad Madero) and El Willy and Cueva de Olla (near Pacheco). Cueva de Olla is a bizarre-shaped cave dwelling.

Take the road southwest for 5km (3 miles) to Casas Grandes.

Basaseachic Falls plunges through a natural bridge into an open cylinder of gigantic rock columns

RECOMMENDED WALKS

3 The **Parque Nacional de Basaseachic** (Basaseachic National Park) provides a wonderful setting in which to spend some time. There are lovely walks in this area of woods, rocks and boulders. One path leads down to a point known as **La Ventana** (The Window), where there is a good view of the magnificent waterfall, which is the highest in Mexico. Two streams from the mountains join together before tumbling down the sheer rock cliff to the gorge below.

8 The **Parque Nacional Cumbres de Majalca** (Majalca National Park) is also a fine place for the car-numbed traveler to have some exercise. The scenery is very impressive, with its pine forest set among the great dramatic peaks and strange rock formations that characterize the area.

7 From Ciudad Juárez make a side trip along **Mex 2** southeast towards Zaragoza. This leads to the **Bosque Petrificado** (Petrified Forest), an extraordinary natural phenomenon where, millions of years ago, a whole forest of trees was covered by sand and turned into stone through the action of salt.

SPECIAL TO . . .

2 The area around Copper Canyon is inhabited by the Tarahumaras. Related to the Apache family, they call themselves the Raramury (running people) on account of their practice of long-distance running. Sometimes they challenge each other to races, which can last for days, through the tough terrain of mountains, canyons and rivers. They generally run barefoot, kicking a small ball in front of them as they go. The Tarahumaras are seminomadic and live in caves in the highlands during the summer, moving to the lower ground among the canyons in the winter. They maintain their independence and each village is governed by three elected chiefs. They are a shy, proud race, to be treated with courtesy and respect.

SCENIC ROUTES

2 There is some very spectacular scenery in parts of Chihuahua. The Copper Canyon region (also known as the Sierra Tarahumara) is incomparable, with its wild, rugged mountains, canyons and gorges covered by cacti, forests and lush vegetation. The most scenic journey of all is the railroad trip from Creel to Los Mochis – you can let someone else do all the driving as you travel in relative comfort through the fantastic landscapes of Copper Canyon.

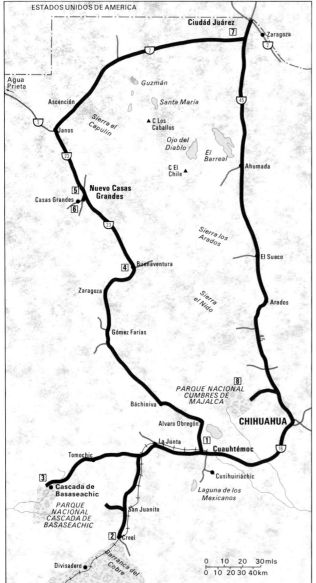

Chihuahua is the center of a rich cattle-raising, silver-mining and lumbering district

Casas Grandes, Chihuahua

6 The Casas Grandes ruins, also known as the **Paquimé ruins**, were explored at the end of the 19th century. The last known inhabitants were the Paquimé Indians. It is thought to have been established in the 7th or 8th century AD and reached its peak between 1000 and 1200. Experts have found evidence of different cultures here, including traces of the Pueblo culture of the Rio Grande Valley and the Mesoamerican cultures of the Central Plateau. The reasons for its collapse around the 15th century are not known, but there may have been some connection with the Apaches.

The complex is made up of a lot of low adobe walls, giving it a curious, sun-baked appearance. Only part of the site has been excavated. A large **ball court** has been uncovered and traces of an irrigation system and a partially restored market place can be seen. Many artifacts were also found here during explorations.

*Return to Nuevo Casas Grandes. Take **Mex 23** north, then at Janos take **Mex 2** northeast to Ciudad Juárez 273km (169 miles).*

Ciudad Juárez, Chihuahua

7 Ciudad Juárez is one of Mexico's largest and most important border towns, and there is quite a lot to do here. Shopping is a great lure to visitors; several markets offer a wide variety of goods, ranging from native handicrafts to modern necessities. At the other end of the spectrum, attractions include bullfights, horse and dog races, and lively night life. *Charreadas* are also held regularly from spring through fall. These colorful events are the equivalent of

The sun-baked walls of the Casas Grandes ruins: the wise visitor wears a sombrero and brings water

American rodeos, but have a very definite Mexican flavor and include intervals of music and dancing. The costumes of the riders – both male and female – are very colorful and attractive. Horsemen compete with each other in tests of skill.

Rounding off the town's attractions are some places of interest to visit. Take a look at the **Museo de Arte e Historia** (Museum of Art and History), which houses archaeological exhibits and Mexican handicrafts; films and lectures are also presented in Spanish and English. The **Centro Nacional Artesanía** (National Arts and Crafts Center) displays and sells a variety of handicrafts from all over the country, including ceramics, textiles, glassware, jewelry and leather goods. The new **Centro Cultural** (Cultural Center) houses an archaeological and historical museum with a display of folk art, pottery from Casas Grandes and relics of the Revolutionary Wars. Take note of the grand old **Aduana Fronteriza** (Customs Building), built in French style around 1800. The **Monumento a la Revolución** (Monument to the Revolution) is an impressive bronze sculpture by the

artist Ignacio Asunsolo.

*Take **Mex 45** south toward Chihuahua. Turn right on a minor road to Parque Nacional Cumbres de Majalca (Majalca National Park), 30km (18 miles) away.*

Parque Nacional Cumbres de Majalca, Chihuahua

8 Rising dramatically from the plains, Majalca National Park presents a magnificent sight of high peaks, boulders and strange rock formations among forests of fir and oak. There are facilities for eating and camping, and horseback riding is also available.

*Return to **Mex 45** and continue south for 30km (18 miles) to Chihuahua.*

Chihuahua – Cuauhtémoc	**100 (62)**
Cuauhtémoc – Creel	**138 (86)**
Creel – Cascada de Basaseachic	**141 (87)**
Cascada de Basaseachic – Buenaventura	**378 (234)**
Buenaventura – Nuevo Casas Grandes	**85 (52)**
Nuevo Casas Grandes – Casas Grandes	**5 (3)**
Casas Grandes – Ciudad Juárez	**273 (169)**
Ciudad Juárez – Parque Nacional Cumbres de Majalca	**379 (235)**
Parque Nacional Cumbres de Majalca – Chihuahua	**30 (18)**

FOR CHILDREN

2 No doubt the biggest attraction for children on this journey would be the railroad trip on the **Chihuahua Pacifico** through the Copper Canyon. Boarding at Creel, it takes you through some of the most dramatic scenery in the country.

BACK TO NATURE

Lying in the northern highlands of Mexico at an altitude of nearly 1,525m (5,000 feet), Chihuahua is surrounded by arid semi-desert. Around city gardens and parks, look for birds such as Inca doves, canyon wrens, boat-tailed grackles and cliff swallows. Further away from habitation, cactus scrub predominates comprising species such as chollas, prickly pears and candelabra cacti. Lizards, scorpions and kangaroo rats are largely nocturnal but during the daytime look for birds such as ladder-backed woodpeckers, cactus wrens, curve-billed thrashers, turkey vultures and black-throated sparrows.

4/5 days – 973km (603 miles)

DESERT LANDS & CACTI

Hermosillo ● Bahía Kino ● Guaymas
Ciudad Obregón ● Navojóa ● Alamos ● Hermosillo

This tour sets off from Hermosillo and takes you southwest, south, southeast and east of this wealthy, modern city, where you can explore part of the large state of Sonora. This is a region of desert, semidesert and mountains of the Sierra Madre Occidental, with vast forested areas, irrigated valleys and rocky bays with sandy beaches. Cacti, in all their fascinating variety of shape and size, are a common feature of the scrub-covered landscape. Included in the itinerary are major coastal resorts and fishing ports, areas with Indian interest and a pretty little Colonial town, one of the few to be found in this part of Mexico. Be prepared for intense heat during much of the year and take suitable precautions.

Guaymas is probably best known as a beach resort and a deep-sea fishing port, famous for its marlin, red snapper, sailtail, yellowtail and sea bass

ⁱ Blvd Eusebio Kino/Pitic – 6, Hermosillo

From Hermosillo take the road southwest for 102km (63 miles) to Bahía Kino.

Bahía Kino, Sonora

1 Bahía Kino is one of the finest bays on the **Mar de Cortés** (Gulf of California), with long stretches of sandy beaches. The town is divided into Viejo (Old) Kino and Nuevo (New) Kino. It is named for a famous Jesuit missionary, Eusebio Francísco Kino, who was responsible for establishing a number of missions around the turn of the 18th century. About 25 missions were founded all over the state of Sonora during this period, and the area gradually began to open up.

The place was relatively undeveloped until recent years, but things are now changing. Although Viejo Kino remains a dusty little fishing village, Nuevo Kino is more geared up for the tourist, with condominiums and many other facilities. It is an excellent center for camping, swimming, fishing and water sports.

The region is inhabited by the Seri Indians, known for the little wooden animals and figures they carve. You are likely to find them around town trying to tempt you with their wares.

Return to Hermosillo and take **Mex 15** *south to Guaymas, a distance of 141km (88 miles).*

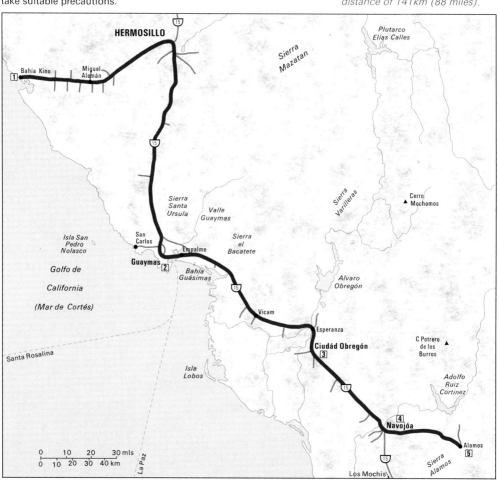

Guaymas, Sonora

2 The busy port of Guaymas lies in a bay on the Mar de Cortés, backed by a ring of bare mountains that descend sharply to the water. Set against the deep blue skies of this northern part of Mexico, the place has a rare beauty of its own. A mountainous ridge divides the port area from the popular beaches of Bacochibámpo and San Carlos, among other excellent spots. Guaymas is well known to fishermen as a deep-sea fishing center; catch includes sea bass, sailfish and swordfish. Facilities are available for fishing expeditions, as well as for all kinds of aquatic sports. In the town a couple of buildings that merit a look are the **Iglesia de San Fernando** (Church of St Ferdinand) and the **Palacio Municipal** (Town Hall). The Yaqui Indians produce and sell their wood carvings in the town. Boat trips can be taken to the small islands of San Nicolás, Santa Catalina and San Pedro, where there is excellent diving and nature lovers can observe the birds and sea lions.

Guaymas holds a number of sailing regattas and fishing competitions, as well as religious events. Carnival (the week before Ash Wednesday) is a

Bahía Kino, a desert community on the Gulf of California, is becoming more popular for sportfishing and camping. Local Seri Indians sell hardwood carvings

lively affair, while festivals on 18 May and 24 June honor, respectively, St Joseph and St John the Baptist.

[i] Avenida Serdan, between streets 13 and 14

*Take **Mex 15** southeast for 124km (77 miles) to Ciudad Obregón.*

Ciudad Obregón, Sonora

3 Ciudad Obregón is an agricultural town lying in the heart of the Yaqui Valley. Formerly called Villa Cajeme, after a prominent Yaqui chieftain of the 19th century, it received its present name in 1924. Noted for its ultramodern agricultural equipment, it is now an important center for processing the region's produce. The city is spacious, modern and neatly laid out. The Alvaro Obregón Dam, northeast of the city, irrigates the valley and has made possible the cultivation of wheat, cotton, corn, rice and many other crops. You can rent a boat or go fishing on the reservoir.

*Continue southeast on **Mex 15** for 65km (40 miles) to Navojóa.*

Navojóa, Sonora

4 In recent years Navojóa has developed into an important agricultural center, with cotton being the principal crop, but the town was formerly a settlement of the Mayo Indians, related to the Yaqui tribe. The

BACK TO NATURE

1 Off the coast of Bahía Kino is Isla Tiburón (Shark Island), which lies in the Mar de Cortés. Once inhabited by Seri Indians, it is now one of Mexico's finest nature reserves, and an exciting variety of wildlife, game and plant life can be seen here. Although a special permit must be obtained to visit the island, this does not normally present any problems. Birds to be expected include magnificent frigatebirds, brown pelicans, Heermann's gulls and great blue herons.

SPECIAL TO . . .

2 The region southeast of Guaymas is inhabited by the Yaqui Indians. Little is known of their origins, but they are thought to be related to one branch of the Aztec tribe. Dancing plays an important role in their ceremonies, and the dramatic **Danza del Venado** (Stag Dance) is considered one of the highest forms of art in Mexico. The movements of the dancer, who wears a deer's head with antlers, relate to the creature's life and finally its death. The stag is sacred to them as the incarnation of good.

FOR HISTORY BUFFS

2 Guaymas was first settled by the Spanish in 1535 and named Guaima, which related to a tribe of Seri Indians. Around 1700 Father Eusebio Francísco Kino established a mission nearby. The town of Guaymas was officially founded in 1769. For a long period after that it was subject to frequent raids from pirates who sought the precious metals shipped here. The town was occupied for a time by US troops during the Mexican American War in the mid-19th century. A few years later history took a curious twist when a Frenchman by the name of Count Gaston Raousset de Boulbon, together with a band of followers, tried to take over Guaymas and set up an independent colony in Sonora. The attempt failed and the Count lost his life as a result. In 1865, during the War of Intervention, French troops occupied the town.

RECOMMENDED WALKS

2 Some 80km (50 miles) north of Guaymas on **Mex 15**, a right turn onto a minor road leads to **La Pintada** (the Painted One) a few miles further on. You must leave your car and proceed on foot. It is recommended you ask at one of the local ranches to enlist the services of a guide to accompany you. A climb of about 20 minutes or so, along the side of a gorge, leads to some varicolored rock paintings showing scenes of daily activities, animals and some interesting heraldic symbols. The paintings are believed to be the work of Seri Indians.

SCENIC ROUTES

In this region you will be driving through a combination of arid desert, wide open plains and mountainous terrain, with the familiar sight of cacti growing all over. There are also pleasant areas of forest and irrigated valleys. There are attractive stretches of road around Guaymas, where the silhouette of the stark mountains against the deep blue of the sea and sky creates some beautiful landscapes.

FOR CHILDREN

1 This is one tour which is not particularly suitable for children as there is a considerable amount of traveling, though the coastal areas are a welcome break. In particular, the beach at Nuevo Kino has good facilities for swimming, fishing and boating.

Seen from a bridge, the Rio Fuerte as it snakes beside the foothills of the Sierra Madre Occidental

Indians fiercely resisted the Spaniards after the Conquest, and the area was settled only at the turn of the 18th century, when Father Kino came to the area and established a Jesuit mission. In 1923 Navojóa received the status of a city. On the outskirts of town is the **Hacienda Siquisiva**, birthplace of General Alvaro Obregón, who was President of Mexico after the Revolution, from 1920 to 1928.

Navojóa is still a center for the Mayo Indians, and there are some interesting festivals in which they participate. These include Holy Week as well as other religious festivals: 24 June, marking the Día de San Juan Bautista (St John the Baptist); 2 November, honoring the dead (Día de los Muertos); and 12 December, Our Lady of Guadalupe.

Take the road southeast for 54km (33 miles) to Alamos.

Alamos, Sonora

5 Alamos is a little Colonial gem, considered the prettiest town in Sonora and protected as a national monument. It began to flourish after the Spaniards found gold and silver deposits here and became a prosperous mining center. But a combination of repeated attacks by local Indians, the fall in silver prices, and the turmoil of the 1910–20 Revolution led to the gradual decline and eventual closure of the mine. Residents moved away and the town became a relic of the past. After World War II there was a revival of sorts. Artists from the United States began to settle here, and many of the old run-down Colonial buildings have been restored to their former glory. Some have been converted into attractive hotels. One building of note is the parish **Church de Nuestra Señora de la Purísima Concepción**; begun in 1763 and completed in the early part of the 19th century, it was built in a moderate baroque style. The **Palacio Municipal** (Town Hall) is another interesting building, with a red brick façade and a somewhat modern look. The **Casa de Artesanía Mexicana** (House of Mexican Folk Art) and the pottery center of **La Uvulama** are also worth a visit.

A famous export of Alamos are Mexican jumping beans — seeds gathered locally from wild shrubs of the spurge family — whose curious tumbling movement is caused by the hyperactive larva of a small moth.

$\boxed{i}$ Palacio Municipal

*Return to Navojóa. Join **Mex 15** and return to Hermosillo.*

Hermosillo – Bahía Kino **102 (63)**
Bahía Kino – Guaymas **243 (151)**
Guaymas – Ciudad Obregón **124 (77)**
Ciudad Obregón – Navojóa **65 (40)**
Navojóa – Alamos **54 (33)**
Alamos – Hermosillo **385 (239)**

Agua Prieta has some historic interest as well as the usual border town offerings

ℹ Blvd Eusebio Kino/Pitic – 6, Hermosillo

*Take **Mex 15** north for 172km (107 miles) to Santa Ana.*

Santa Ana, Sonora

1 The small town of Santa Ana dates back to 1688 with the founding of **Mission Santa Ana el Viejo** a short distance away. Yaqui Indians are seen here frequently as they sell the little carved wooden figures and animals for which they are known. The Indians feature prominently in the local festivals, taking part in colorful regional dances. The major festival takes place from 16 to 25 July and is dedicated to the patron saint of the town. Celebrations include music, dancing, and horse racing.

*Continue on **Mex 15** north for 81km (50 miles) to Nogales.*

Nogales, Sonora

2 Nogales is Sonora's principal border town with the US and a continuously busy transit point. Just across the border, the neighboring town of the same name is also a busy commercial center. Both towns were named after the walnut trees (*nogales* in Spanish) that grow in

In Magdalena de Kino, the tomb of Jesuit Father Eusaebio Kino, who founded many missions in the region

BORDER TOWNS & MISSIONS

Hermosillo ● Santa Ana ● Nogales ● Cananea
Agua Prieta ● Arizpe ● Huépac ● Aconchi ● Ures
Hermosillo

This second tour from Hermosillo takes you to the northern areas of the large state of Sonora. You will travel through another region of hot, dry desert lands, always accompanied by the sight of the many varieties of cacti that characterize much of northern Mexico. You will get to see a number of the small missions founded by the Jesuits in the 17th century, which played such an important role in the development of the region. As well as some old towns of historic interest, there is a look at two of Mexico's frontier towns with the US, which have a different sort of appeal to the traveler.

RECOMMENDED WALKS

8 On the way to Hermosillo from Ures, make a stop at the **Parque Nacional de Topahue**, a lovely wooded area with a man-made waterfall. The park is a little oasis in the Sonoran desert, where you can stretch your legs in lovely surroundings.

FOR HISTORY BUFFS

2 On the way to Nogales, you may wish to stop at Magdalena de Kino, a town rich in the tradition of Sonora. The **Misión Santa María Magdalena de Baquivaba**, along with the town, was founded here in the 17th century by the Jesuit Father Kino. His remains were discovered here in 1966, and a mausoleum and replica of the old **Palacio Municipal** (Town Hall) were built and dedicated to him.

FOR CHILDREN

1 This tour has limited appeal to youngsters. But you can stop at Benjamin Hill, between Hermosillo and Santa Ana, to give them a treat. The **Parque Infantil** has a large man-made lake, zoological gardens, a miniature railway and mechanical toys.

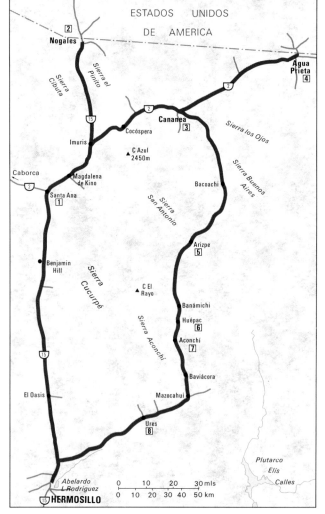

A university town and state capital, Hermosillo, with its grand cathedral, has many cultural and social amenities

profusion in the area. The town is crammed with shops and markets offering pottery, leather goods, glassware and a wide variety of other goods. These, combined with the multitude of bars and restaurants, ensure there is plenty to do at all times. Once, the big attraction of Nogales was its cheap liquor, but this all changed when customs restrictions were imposed. Sonora seemed to lose some of its personality for a while, but today, the scene is again lively.

*Return along **Mex 15** south to Imuris, then take **Mex 2** northeast to Cananea 133km (82 miles).*

Cananea, Sonora

3 If you want to break the journey to Cananea, you can make a brief stop at Imuris. The **Mission of San José de los Himeros** was established here in the 17th century and was important in its time. Further along the route, on the winding **Mex 2**, you will come across Cocóspera, with the ruins of another old mission, **Nuestra Señora del Pilar y Santiago de Cocóspera**, which dates back to 1691.

Cananea, an old Indian settlement taken over by the Spanish in the mid-17th century, is today a major mining center. Back in 1760 Jesuit missionaries discovered rich deposits of copper in the region and began exploration for the mineral. Cananea received the status of a city in 1901. A few years later, in 1906, an unusual

Coming or going, this sign for used car parts makes its point above the streets of Agua Prieta

event took place here when American miners went on strike, complaining of low salaries and bad working conditions. It was a surprise to many when their cause was recognized and their demands for equal rights for Mexican workers was met by the Government.

You can visit the spot where the Spanish missionaries first initiated work on the mine, which is known as the **Cobre Grande** (Big Copper). The local museum, the **Museo de Antiguedades**, has a display of items relating to Cananea's past. The **Feria del Cobre** (Copper Fair) is held from 25 to 27 June.

*Continue on **Mex 2** for 89km (55 miles) to Agua Prieta.*

Agua Prieta, Sonora

4 Agua Prieta, named after the nearby river, is another typical frontier town, just across the border from the town of Douglas, Arizona. It has some pleasant parks and offers plenty of entertainment with its shops, bars, restaurants and nightclubs. The town has some historic interest as well: 1920 saw the signing here of the Plan of Agua Prieta, an agreement of non-recognition of the newly formed government of Venustiano Carranza at the end of the Revolution of 1910–20. The **Aduana Fronteriza de Agua Prieta** (Customs Office) is a very handsome red-brick building topped by a large square tower.

Return to Cananea, then take the road southeast to Arizpe, a total of 188km (117 miles).

Arizpe, Sonora

5 The town of Arizpe was founded in 1646 by the Jesuits and became the capital of the independent state of Sonora-Sinaloa in 1776. The town's most notable building is the **Iglesia de la Asunción** (Church of the Assumption), built in the 17th century, where lie the mortal remains of Juan Nautista de Auza (1735–88), founder of the city of San Francisco, California. The church has an adobe exterior and good *retablos* inside.

Continue south for 51km (32 miles) to Huépac.

Huépac, Sonora

6 The main features of Huépac are the **Misión de San Lorenzo** (Mission of St Lawrence), established in the 17th century and now the parish church, and the **Palacio Municipal** (Town Hall), where you can see some old paintings relating to the War of Independence against the Spanish.

Continue southeast for 10km (6 miles) to Aconchi.

Aconchi, Sonora

7 The **Misión de San Pedro Aconchi** (Mission of St Peter Aconchi) dates from the 17th century. On each side of the central part of the building are two towers forming a pyramid shape. Of special interest is the statue of the **Cristo Negro** (Black Christ) in the interior of the church, whose origins and significance remain a mystery.

Continue southwest for 71km (44 miles) to Ures.

Ures, Sonora

8 This picturesque little village is also known as La Olvidada Atenas ('Athens forgotten') for having been the birthplace of a number of intellectuals and illustrious people. It is one of the oldest towns in the state and was its capital from 1838 to 1842.

There are some fine Colonial buildings in the villages. One of the most notable is the **Misión de San Miguel Arcángel** (St Michael the Archangel) dating from the 17th century. In the main square, the **Plaza de las Armas**, there are four imposing bronze statues depicting figures from Greek mythology. Ures has a big festival in honor of St John the Baptist, 20 to 29 June.

Return to Hermosillo, a distance of 70km (43 miles).

Hermosillo – Santa Ana 172 (107)
Santa Ana – Nogales 81 (50)
Nogales – Cananea 133 (82)
Cananea – Agua Prieta 89 (55)
Agua Prieta – Arizpe 188 (117)
Arizpe – Huépac 51 (32)
Huépac – Aconchi 10 (6)
Aconchi – Ures 71 (44)
Ures – Hermosillo 70 (43)

SCENIC ROUTES

8 Sonora is a combination of arid deserts, mountains and forests characterized by cacti in all shapes and forms. The ubiquitous cacti lend drama to the landscape, and between Ures and Hermosillo you will pass an area of interesting cactus shapes.

BACK TO NATURE

8 Between Hermosillo and Ures is a region strewn with magnificent cacti. The most dramatic is the soaring saguaro cactus, a common feature of the northwestern landscapes of Mexico and the peninsula of Baja California. The cactus, which bears white flowers and edible fruit, takes about 20 years to reach its full height, which can reach 18m (60 feet). Its simple columnar or sparsely branched trunks dominate the landscape and are a most dramatic sight. Other specimens growing in abundance include the palo verde and the ocotillo, which produce brightly colored flowers at certain times of the year. There is a surprising amount of vegetation and flower life in these desert areas, if you have the time and energy to look for it.

SPECIAL TO ...

2 A very special festival takes place in Magdalena de Kino. The **Día de San Francisco Xavier** (Festival of St Francis) starts on 22 September and finishes on 4 October. San Francisco Xavier is a much revered saint among many local Indian tribes from both sides of the border, and the fair is attended by groups of Yaquis, Seris, Papagos, Pimas and Sioux, who make a pilgrimage here each year in large numbers. The **Venado** (Deer Dance) features among the exciting dances performed.

8/9 days – 1,734km (1,074 miles)

THE WILDS OF THE NORTHWEST

Mazatlán • Concordia • Copalá • La Ciudad
El Salto • Durango • Hidalgo del Parral
Topolobampo • El Fuerte • Culiacán • Cosalá
Mazatlán

This tour takes you from the Pacific resort of Mazatlán on a circular route to the northeast and north, passing through the states of Sinaloa, Durango and Chihuahua. While parts of the journey will be through bare and sparsely populated areas, other sections will offer outstanding scenery as you traverse the wild, rugged mountain ranges of the Sierra Madre Occidental, with deep canyons and gorges, valleys and forests. On the way there is the opportunity of visiting some charming little rural towns and a region of striking landscapes that have provided the setting for many a well-known Western, with the options of visiting some of the sets.

FOR HISTORY BUFFS

6 On 20 July 1923 the flamboyant revolutionary Pancho Villa was ambushed and killed by a group of men who opened fire with a burst of rifles and pistols. Villa and four of his bodyguards were killed, although Villa, riddled with bullets, managed to shoot one of his killers before dying. A small plaque placed on the outside of the **Museo del General Francisco Villa**, in Hidalgo del Parral, marks the spot where he died. In the museum there is a library and good photographic archives relating to the leader.

ℹ️ Avenida del Mar 1000, Mazatlán

*From Mazatlán take **Mex 15** east, then at Villa Unión take **Mex 40** northeast to Concordia, 42km (26 miles).*

Concordia, Sinaloa

1 In the picturesque town of Concordia, set in lush tropical

With practised hand and careful eye, women work their colorful stitches

vegetation, little white houses are grouped around a tiny main square overlooked by the **Iglesia de San Sebastián** (Church of St Sebastian). Built in the 18th century in baroque style, it features an attractive pink portal and richly decorated columns. The town is noted for its finely crafted pottery and Colonial-style wooden furniture. In the vicinity are a number of thermal springs, among them Zarate, Sante Fe and Arrona.

*Take **Mex 40** northeast for 18km (11 miles) to Copalá.*

Copalá, Sinaloa

2 The charming little town of Copalá is surrounded by the gently rolling slopes that form the foothills of the Sierra Madre Occidental. Low-lying houses with wrought-iron balconies line the narrow cobblestoned streets. The main square features a marvelously ornate bandstand, and the 16th-century **church** is noted for its beamed portico and atrium, as well as some fine *retablos* inside.

About 20km (12 miles) away is the delightful little Colonial town of Panuco. Nearby is the **Presa de los Herreros** (Blacksmith's Dam), built at the turn of the 19th century in a natural crater amidst lovely forest surroundings.

*Continue northeast for 40km (25 miles) on **Mex 40** to La Ciudad.*

La Ciudad, Durango

3 The tiny hamlet of La Ciudád is a base from which to visit the **Parque Nacional Puerto de los Angeles** (National Park of Mexiquillo). This is an extensive area of beautiful forest-land of firs and many other varieties of trees, curious rock formations and lovely waterfalls. El Mirador Buenos Aires is a lookout point which offers a matchless view of the surrounding mountains and **El Espinazo del Diablo** (Devil's Spine) gorge.

*Continue on **Mex 40** east for 62km (38 miles) to El Salto.*

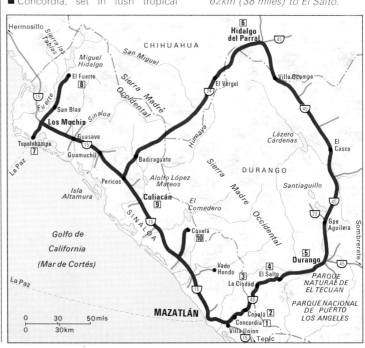

El Salto, Durango

4 The small village of El Salto nestles among the folds of the Sierra Madre Occidental mountains at an altitude of over 2,000m (6,562 feet) above sea level. With its beautiful setting it serves as a good base for excursions into the forests. The waterfall and huge canyon have made it an ideal place to film Westerns. In the hills nearby there are some recreation centers with various types of accommodation and tourist attractions. The region has plenty of streams, which offer good fishing.

*Continue on **Mex 40** northeast for 84km (52 miles) to Durango.*

Durango, Durango

5 The city of Durango lies in a rich mining area in the valley of Guadiana 1,880m (6,166 feet) above sea level. Capital of the state of Durango, this is basically a provincial town with Colonial architecture. The pleasant main square has attractive gardens and a pretty circular bandstand where concerts are held on Sundays. A few buildings are of interest to the visitor. The **cathedral**, begun in 1695 and completed in 1750, dominates the principal square with its massive structure and two square towers. Its richly decorated interior is in the baroque style. Take a look at the 18th-century Jesuit **Templo del Sagrario** (Church of the Sanctuary) and the **Instituto Juárez** (Juárez Institute) housed in the adjacent convent, with its elegant cloisters. The **Palacio del Gobierno** (Government Palace) is a handsome Colonial building of the 17th century, and the **Casa del Conde Suchil** (House of the Count of Xuchíl) is a fine example of 17th-century Colonial architecture.

Innumerable Westerns have been filmed in and around Durango, as the area's wild and rugged landscapes provide the perfect setting for this type of movie. For people interested in visiting some of the film sets, two major permanent sets are located on Mex 45 about 14km (8 miles) away; one includes part of the village of Chupaderos. Tours are often organized at weekends; check with the local tourist office. The **Iglesia de los Remedios** (Church of Los Remedios), built by the Franciscans in 1640, is to be found up the hill called **Cerro de los Remedios**. From here you have a sweeping view of the town, deserts and mountain ranges. The **Cerro del Mercado** (Mercado Hill) dominates the city. The hill is of high-content iron ore and is said to be one of the largest single iron deposits in the world, rising some 213m (699 feet) above the plains around it. There are a number of man-made lakes in the vicinity, most of which offer fishing.

i Bruno Martínez 403 Sur 305

*Take **Mex 45** northwest for 395km (245 miles) to Hidalgo del Parral.*

The jagged contours of the Sierra Madre Occidental repeat into the distance along the climb from the coastal lowlands of Mazatlán to Durango, where the air is thin

BACK TO NATURE

7 Nature lovers will enjoy a visit to **El Farallón**, a rocky island about 27km (18 miles) off the coast of Topolobampo that is a natural refuge for seals and sea lions. A number of other islands are conservation areas for various species of water birds.

Around the coast are lagoons and mangroves where ospreys plunge-dive in search of fish while white ibises and little blue herons wade in the shallows.

RECOMMENDED WALKS

3 There are a number of areas on the tour where you can go for a walk in magnificent surroundings. The Parque Nacional Mexiquillo is a beautiful place with lovely wooded areas, rocks and waterfalls.

4 More enjoyable walks can be taken in the vicinity of El Salto.

SCENIC ROUTES

Impressive scenery is not in short supply on this tour. The drive between Mazatlán and Durango is one of the most scenic in Mexico, with some striking landscapes around **El Espinazo del Diablo**.

Hidalgo del Parral, Chihuahua

6 The old mining center of Hidalgo del Parral lies some 1,676m (5,500 feet) above sea-level. The town began to flourish in the mid-1500s when rich deposits of silver, lead, copper and iron ore were found in the area. In the 1860s it was occupied briefly by troops of Napoleon III during the French occupation of Mexico. The town gained notoriety as the place where Pancho Villa, flamboyant figure of the 1910–20 Revolution, was killed in 1923.

*Take **Mex 24** southwest toward the coast. At Pericos take **Mex 15** northwest to Topolobampo.*

Topolobampo, Sinaloa

7 The little fishing village of Topolobampo lies on the beautiful Bay of Ohuira. Waterfront restaurants specialize in seafood. Across the bay is Punta de Copas, a long sandbar with excellent beaches. The shore along this stretch invites a leisurely search for seashells, and just general beachcombing. Some areas also offer water skiing. Ferries leave here for trips across the Mar de Cortés to La Paz in Baja California.

*Continue on **Mex 15** west to Los Mochis, where you can stop if you wish. Then take the road northeast to El Fuerte, some 90km (55 miles) further on.*

With its rugged terrain and formidable cacti, Durango has been the scene of many Western movies

El Fuerte, Sinaloa

8 On the way to El Fuerte you pass through the bustling, modern town of Los Mochis. This is the starting point (or terminus, as the case may be) for the spectacular Chihuahua Pacífico train ride, which journeys through the breathtaking mountains and gorges of the **Barranca del Cobre** (Copper Canyon) northeast to Chihuahua.

The quaint town of El Fuerte lies on the banks of the El Fuerte River in a rich agricultural valley. It was founded by the Spaniards in 1564 and called San Juan Bautista de Carapoa. Some time after this the town was attacked and destroyed by the Indians. In 1610 a fort was built as a means of protection, and the town has been known as El Fuerte (the Fortress) ever since.

There is a strong Colonial feel to the town. An elaborate wrought-iron bandstand adorns the main square, the Plaza de las Armas. Take a look at the 18th-century **Templo de Sagrado Corazón de Jesús** (Temple of the Sacred Heart of Jesus) and the **Palacio Municipal** (Town Hall) from the 19th century. Take a pleasant stroll along the river bank, sampling, if you can, some of the tasty seafood in the local restaurants.

Nearby are some good fishing centers, in particular, Miguel Hidalgo and Josefa de Ortíz de Domínguez, which are noted for black bass.

*Return to Los Mochis and take **Mex 15** southeast to Culiacán, 293km (182 miles).*

Culiacán, Sinaloa

9 Culiacán, capital of the state of Sinaloa, lies in a fertile valley. Founded in 1531, Culiacán was once a mining town but has since developed into an important agricultural center. Among its leading attractions are the 18th-century **cathedral**, the modern **Centro Cívico Constitución** (Civic Center) – which houses a theater, hospital, swimming pool and administrative offices – and the **Museo Arqueológico** (museum), with a collection of archaeological artifacts discovered in the region. Culiacán is known for its particular brand of music, a very pleasing combination of Dixieland jazz and lively Cuban rhythms.

For relaxing, there are a number of spas in the immediate surroundings and some good hunting and fishing in the region.

*Take **Mex 15** southeast, branching off north to Cosalá, 156km (97 miles).*

Cosalá, Sinaloa

10 Cosalá is a small Colonial town of whitewashed houses, red-tiled roofs and cobblestoned streets. Founded in 1550 as the 'Royal and Ancient Site of the Immaculate Conception of the 11,000 Virgins of Cosala', it became the state capital

Projecting stone formations on the Mazatlan-Durango route pierce the landscape with a gap-toothed bite

shortly after Mexico gained independence from the Spanish. Its main church, the 18th-century **Templo de Santa Ursula** (Temple of St Ursula), is dedicated to the town's patron saint. In an old mansion is the **Museo de Minería e Historia** (Museum of Mining and History), with a collection of documents and material relating to the old mining days.

Among the most enjoyable places to visit in the vicinity are the resort of Vado Hondo, the Caudal del Arroyo del Sabinál, with a large natural pool and waterfalls, and the Gruta México, a large cave with beautiful stalactites and stalagmites.

*Return south to **Mex 15** and head southeast to return to Mazatlán.*

Mazatlán – Concordia	42 (26)
Concordia – Copalá	18 (11)
Copalá – La Ciudad	40 (25)
La Ciudad – El Salto	62 (38)
El Salto – Durango	84 (52)
Durango – Hidalgo del Parral	395 (245)
Hidalgo del Parral – Topolobampo	362 (224)
Topolobampo – El Fuerte	124 (76)
El Fuerte – Culiacán	293 (182)
Culiacán – Cosalá	156 (97)
Cosalá – Mazatlán	158 (98)

SPECIAL TO...

9 Carnival is a very colorful time in Culiacán. The whole town becomes alive with parades and gay floats, bands, traditional music and dances, fireworks, masked balls, a battle of flowers, masquerades and numerous amusements. Carnival, or Mardi Gras, starts a week before Ash Wednesday and celebrations last for about a week.

FOR CHILDREN

5 A highlight for youngsters on this tour would be a visit to one or two of the film sets around Durango. One of the most important sets is located in Villa del Oeste, approximately 10km (6 miles) north of Durango on **Mex 45**. The area has become an amusement center and is an attraction for locals and tourists. About 2km (1½ miles) further north on **Mex 45** is Chupaderos, where most of the Westerns were filmed.

THE NORTHEAST & THE GULF REGION

This area centers on the states of Nuevo León, Tamaulipas, San Luis Potosí and Veracruz and includes parts of Puebla and Zacatecas. The scenery here matches the climate in its diversity: arid deserts and irrigated farmlands in the north, humid subtropical areas and tropical jungle in the Gulf regions. The Sierra Madre Oriental, standing to the east, forms beautiful landscapes of mountains, forests and valleys, while the central and western area is a bare plateau. The ranch country around San Luis Potosí is where the fighting bulls are bred. The eastern coastline on the Gulf of Mexico has long stretches of sandy beaches punctuated by lagoons. The states of Veracruz and Puebla are characterized by exuberant vegetation and a profusion of brilliantly colored flowers. Coffee and tobacco plantations are to be found in Veracruz, and magnificent snow-covered volcanoes are a feature of Puebla.

The population varies according to region. The north consists mainly of whites and *mestizos*. In San Luis Potosí there is a proportion of Creoles (descendents of Spaniards born in Mexico), *mestizos* and Indian tribes including Otomí, Nahua, Huastec and Pame Indians. Huastec Indians inhabit the states of Tamaulipas and Veracruz, as do descendants of Totonac and Nahua Indians. The Negroid characteristics to be seen in Veracruz are evidence of the slaves who were brought over in the past to provide labor. Culturally, there is a great archaeological heritage in the Gulf regions, with important Olmec sites in the vicinity of Lake Catemaco. The influence of the Olmec civilizations, which existed from about 1200 to 400BC, extended over a vast area of Mexico and affected subsequent cultures. The Olmecs were followed by the Huastecs and Totonacs, who left the important remains of El Tajín.

In 1519, Cortés and his soldiers landed at Veracruz. The northern areas of Mexico, formerly inhabited by nomadic tribes, were settled by the Spaniards at the end of the 16th century. A vast province known as Reino de Nuevo León included Nuevo León, Tamaulipas, Coahuila, Zacatecas, Durango, part of San Luis Potosí, Texas and New Mexico. Independent states were formed at the conclusion of the Independence War in 1820. In more recent times, major oil and gas industries in the Gulf region have inevitably brought about great changes. The city of Veracruz is renowned for its folklore. The typical music and traditional dances of the region are among the liveliest in Mexico.

Monterrey:

Monterrey, with a population of 830,000, is the third largest city in Mexico and an important industrial center of the north. Lying in a valley beneath the dramatic peaks of the Cerro de la Silla (Saddle Mountain), its modern buildings blend with lovely Colonial mansions and churches and squares adorned with flowers. The Gran Plaza is a vast area of lawns, fountains and sculptures together with government buildings and theaters. The **Fuente de la Vida** (Fountain of Life) is an outstanding sculpture in bronze. An unusual landmark in Monterrey is the tall monument built to commemorate 100 years of successful industry; a laser beam on top puts on a show in the evening. Facing this is the 19th-century **cathedral** (begun in 1603), which features an impressive tower and a richly decorated façade. There is a fine view of the city from **El Obispado** (the Bishop's Palace), which perches on top of a nearby hill. Other places of interest include the **Monterrey Planetarium**, the **House of Crafts** and the **Crafts Market**, which have a variety of items for sale. The **Zona Rosa** (Pink Zone) is an open pedestrian mall with boutiques, restaurants and nightclubs.

Above: The city museum of Veracruz concentrates on pre-Hispanic history and the Revolution

Right: Jalapa's Anthropological Museum has artifacts from Olmec and Totonac civilizations

Below: Textiles are a primary product of Saltillo, capital of Coahuila. It is possible to see serapes and small rugs being woven

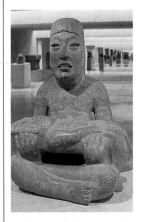

Veracruz:

The old port of Veracruz has played a significant role in Mexico's history, beginning with the landing of the Spanish Conquistadores in 1519. It was important as a trading link with Europe during the 16th and 17th centuries, and in the 1800s it was occupied at various stages by US and French troops. The importation of African slaves in the Colonial era has left its mark and given the town a distinctive Afro-Caribbean flavor. The main square is surrounded by attractive arcades and sidewalks, with many cafés and restaurants that specialize in fresh seafood. The scene is a very lively one, with street vendors, musical groups and constant activity. The exuberant *jarocho* music of the Veracruzanos competes with the soft strains of the marimbas and numerous other groups.

Among the few Colonial buildings worth visiting are the **Catedral de Nuestra Señora de la Asunción** (Cathedral of Our Lady of the Assumption) on the main square, and the 17th-century **Palacio Municipal** (Town Hall), which has a fine façade and attractive patio. The **Museo Regional** (Regional Museum) has an interesting collection of pre-Hispanic artifacts. Take a look at the former fort and prison of San Juan Ulua, located on an island in the port.

Veracruz is Mexico's busiest port. A stroll along the *malecón*, or waterfront boulevard, lets you see all the colorful activities of a major harbor town. Shops and restaurants line the way, and you may like to sample the local shrimp dishes served in a spicy sauce. *Huachinango a la Veracruzana* is a well-known Mexican dish of red snapper served Veracruz-style.

Veracruz's festivities before Lent (Carnival) are reputed to be the most exciting in Mexico, when the vibrant strains of the town's traditional music fill the air and there's dancing everywhere. The whole town explodes with pageants, floats, fireworks and numerous events.

6 days – 1,196km (740 miles)

MEXICO'S OLD MINING HERITAGE

Monterrey • Cañon Huasteca
Grutas de García • Saltillo • Zacatecas
San Luis Potosí • Santa María del Río • Linares
Cola de Caballo • Monterrey

This tour sets out from Monterrey and takes you to the south and southeast. The journey is through the states of Nuevo León, Coahuila, San Luís Potosí and Zacatecas. The tour combines attractive Colonial towns in the heart of ranching country, old mining towns and little villages renowned for their handicrafts. Some of nature's marvels include a spectacular canyon, beautiful waterfalls and fascinating caves full of stalactites and other formations. In this region of subtropical areas and forest-clad mountains, the scenery is magnificent.

> [i] Marco Plaza, Monterrey
>
> *Take **Mex 40** west in the direction of Saltillo. After 18km (11 miles) turn south to Cañon Huasteca.*

Saltillo's cathedral, in super-baroque style, has an elaborately worked façade and doors

Cañon Huasteca, Nuevo León

1 The magnificent Cañon Huasteca is a rock gorge with sheer walls rising up to a great height. All around are dramatic rock formations created by erosion. The canyon is located in the **Parque Nacional Cumbres de Monterrey** (Monterrey National Park), a beautiful setting of coniferous trees and small streams at the bottom of the gorge.

> *Return to **Mex 40**. Continue towards Saltillo for 7km (4 miles), then turn off right to Villa de García. Take the road north to the Grutas de García (García Caves).*

Grutas de García, Nuevo León

2 These caves are among the most impressive sights in the region. A cable car takes you from the parking lot to the entrance to the caves, which go deep into the mountain. A tour of the caves includes a subterranean lake and forests of stalactites and stalagmites. The caves are dramatically lit.

Continuing along the itinerary, make a stop *en route* at Villa de García and take a look at the 19th-century **Temples of San Juan Bautista** and **Cristo Rey.**

> *Return to **Mex 40** and continue southwest to Saltillo.*

Saltillo, Coahuila

3 Saltillo, capital of the state of Coahuila, lies in a large valley surrounded by mountains. This Colonial town is renowned for its colorful *serapes,* or woolen shawls. The market has a variety of attractive handicrafts, which include *serapes,* pottery and silverware. Dominating the main square, the Plaza de las Armas, is the **Catedral de Santiago** (Cathedral of St James). Built between 1746 and 1801, it represents a fine example of the Churrigueresque style of architecture. It features a richly decorated exterior and a huge tower, from which there is a good view of the town. The **Palacio de Gobierno** (Government Palace) houses an interesting museum. On the Coahuila University campus is the **Ateneo Fuente** (Fuente Atheneum), whose art gallery features paintings by prominent artists from both Mexico and Europe.

An unusual but fun side trip is a ride on the Zacatecas and Coahuila Railroad to the old mining town of Concepción del Oro. The excursion, in railcars built at the end of the last century, passes along a scenic route of narrow mountain ridges.

> *Take **Mex 54** south for 364km (226 miles) to Zacatecas.*

Zacatecas, Zacatecas

4 Zacatecas, the state capital, lies in a narrow gorge on the slopes of the Cerro de la Bufa, a hill that rises to

The García Caves, discovered by a parish priest in 1843, have a 2½ km (1½-mile) route through 16 lighted chambers

some 2,667m (8,750 feet). Zacatecas is an attractive Colonial town of churches and monasteries. Its huddled houses, steep streets and stone steps lend it a medieval air. Formerly an Indian mining center, Zacatecas was taken over by the Spaniards in 1548, when they transported huge quantities of silver to Spain. The 200-year-old **El Bote** mine is still in operation, and Zacatecas remains an important mining center.

A number of fine buildings can be seen in the town. The **cathedral** on Plaza Hidalgo was built between 1612 and 1760 and is a good example of the Churrigueresque style, with a richly ornamented façade.

The 18th-century **Palacio de Gobierno** (Government Palace) has pretty wrought-iron balconies. A mural up the staircase inside depicts the history of Zacatecas.

The **Museo Pedro Coronel** (Pedro Coronel Museum) houses archaeological artifacts and a fine art collection, and the **Museo Francisco Goitia** (Francisco Goitia Museum) displays work by this Mexican painter, who studied in Europe. An old aqueduct from the Colonial era passes nearby.

A short trip up the Cerro de la Bufa takes you to the 18th-century Patrocinio Chapel, where there is a rewarding view of the town and its surroundings. The **Museo de la Toma de Zacatecas** (Museum) at the top of the hill gives an account of Pancho Villa's capture here in 1914.

There are some interesting ruins at La Quemada (The Burnt One), about 53km (33 miles) southwest. The pre-Columbian site, also known as Chicomoztóc ('seven caves' in Náhuatl), stands on a bare mountain overlooking a plain. The ruins may date back to around AD700. The center flourished between the 10th and 11th centuries and was destroyed in the early 13th century, possibly by fire. The site consists of several groups of buildings, mainly of adobe brick and flat stone. Major structures include the **Palacio del Rey** (King's Palace), which leads to the **Salón de las Columnas** (Great Pillared Hall), the **Pirámide del Sol** (Sun Pyramid) and the **Templo de los Sacrificios** (Temple of Sacrifices), which stands atop the Citadel and offers a panoramic view of the area.

ⓘ Viajes Mazzoco, Enlace 113

*Take **Mex 45**, then **49** east for 205km (127 miles) to San Luis Potosí.*

SCENIC ROUTES

Dramatic mountainous scenery is to be found in Monterrey, Zacatecas and San Luis Potosí. Between Zacatecas and San Luís Potosí you will drive through moonscapes of wild, rugged mountains and bare terrain, which have a strange and compelling beauty.

FOR HISTORY BUFFS

3 You may be interested in taking a short drive of about 30 minutes on **Mex 54** south of Saltillo to La Angostura. A fierce two-day battle took place here, **La Batalla de Angostura** (the Battle of Angostura) in February 1847, between the Mexicans and Americans during the Mexican-American War. A monument to the east of the highway marks the battleground.

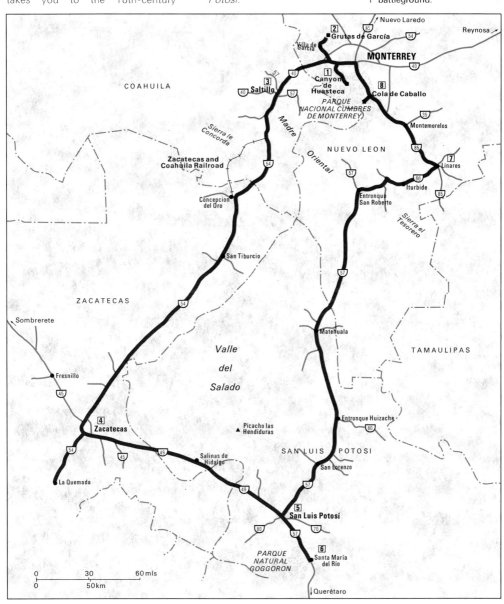

SPECIAL TO...

4 In Zacatecas the Festival of the Moors (**Día de la Morisma**) on 17 August is held in a large meadow called El Bracho, where the battle between the Moors and the Christians is re-enacted. Charlemagne, Mohammed and St John the Baptist feature in the events, and the battle ends with the defeat of the Moors and the beheading of Mohammed amidst great jubilation.

For the Festival of Our Lady of the Protection (**Día de Nuestra Señora del Patrocinio**) there are 10 days of pilgrimages, when members of the various guilds climb up the Cerro de la Bufa to the sanctuary, culminating on 14 September. The Matachine dancers perform every day in the atrium of this old church. The worshippers bring offerings, and hundreds of candles add to the spectacle. This coincides with the town's annual fair, so September is a good time to visit.

FOR CHILDREN

8 Children can enjoy some time in the lovely **Parque Nacional Cumbres de Monterrey**, which offers camping, horseback riding, and a swimming pool in a beautiful setting of woods and gardens, centered around the magnificent Cola de Caballo waterfall.

RECOMMENDED WALKS

6 In Santa María del Río there is a very pleasant walk past the old aqueduct by the river. A road also leads to the **Sanctuary of the Señor del Amparo** and on to a waterfall, which cascades down into a pool where you can have a swim. You can also climb up the hill to the **Cerro El Original**, where there is a good view of the surrounding countryside.

BACK TO NATURE

1 There are plenty of opportunities for birdwatching *en route* to Cañon Huasteca and García Caves. Thickets of live oak and riverine woodland can be seen along the way. In more disturbed areas, look for great kiskadees, boat-tailed grackles, Inca doves and groove-billed anis. Turkey vultures and black vultures are common, while beside the rivers look for green kingfishers, brown jays, social flycatchers, cardinals and pyrrhuloxias.

San Luis Potosí, San Luis Potosí

5 Although it has developed into a busy commercial town, the state capital has retained much of its Colonial charm. It became established as a mining town in the 15th century and is still a center for the production of gold, silver and copper.

The old sector has lovely parks and elegant Colonial buildings. The main **cathedral** (1670–1740), standing on the main square, has an interesting façade depicting the Apostles, richly carved wooden altars and some fine paintings inside. The **Iglesia de la Virgen del Carmen** (Church of Our Lady of Mt Carmel) is a real gem of baroque architecture, with a beautiful dome of different-colored tiles. Take a look also at the **Palacio de Gobierno** (Government Palace), a handsome neoclassical building dating from the mid-18th century. Other places of interest are the **Museo Regional de Artes Populares** (Regional Museum), the **Casa de la Cultura** (House of Culture) and the **Museo de la Mascaras** (National Museum of Regional Masks). Near the main square is the colorful local market, the **Mercado Hidalgo**.

San Luis Potosí, right in the middle of ranching country where the fighting bulls are bred, has an important bullring. Some visitors might be interested in the **Museo del Centro Taurino Potosino** (Bullfighting Center Museum), where the history of the bullfight is presented. The town is known for its finely woven *rebozos* (long scarves worn chiefly by women).

ⓘ Jardín Guerrero No 14

*Take **Mex 57** southeast for 49km (30 miles) to Santa María del Río.*

Santa María del Río, San Luis Potosí

6 The little town of Santa María del Río is famous for its high-quality *rebozos* and other fine handicrafts. Take a look at the weavers at work in

The sheer walls of Huasteca Canyon reach up to 305m (1,000 feet)

their workshops. The main square is pleasant, surrounded by Colonial buildings and a Franciscan church with a large atrium.

*Return to San Luis Potosí, then continue on **Mex 57** heading north. At Entronque San Roberto branch off northeast for 98km (61 miles) to Linares on **Mex 60**.*

Linares, Nuevo León

7 The farming center of Linares lies in the fertile valley of the Pablillos River. Buildings of interest include the 18th-century **Catedral de San Felipe** (Cathedral of St Phillip), the **Templo del Señor de la Misericordia** (Church of Our Lord of Compassion) with its finely decorated façade, the **Palacio Municipal** (Town Hall), and the French-style **Casino**. A small **museum** contains ancient rock paintings. The **Parque Nacional Ojos de Vista Hermosa** is a lovely place with luxuriant vegetation.

*Continue northwest on **Mex 85**, then turn off west to Cola de Caballo.*

Cola de Caballo, Nuevo León

8 Situated in the **Parque Nacional Cumbres de Monterrey** are the magnificent waterfalls called Cola de Caballo (Horsetail Falls). Cascades of water tumble down more than 25m (80 feet) over rocks and boulders. A road leads up the mountain to a parking lot and from there you can proceed on foot – or on horseback – down a path that leads to the base of the falls.

Return to Monterrey, 44km (27 miles) north.

*A sign of Monterrey's prosperity –
shoemaking – paired with the
mystique of the bullfight*

ℹ️ Marco Plaza, Monterrey

*Take **Mex 85** north for 94km
(58 miles) to Sabinas Hidalgo.*

Sabinas Hidalgo, Nuevo León

1 The little town of Sabinas Hidalgo is
situated on the banks of the
Sabinas River. Founded in 1693, it
developed into an important mining
center, and silver, lead and zinc are
still mined in the area. The town is also
an important farming and textile
center, and has some thermal springs
known as Playa Azul. Its most interesting building is the distinctively
styled 18th-century **Templo de San
José** (Church of St Joseph), which
contains the only *retablo* in the state.

Among other pleasant places in the
vicinity are the **Ojo de Agua** spa,
about 10km (6 miles) east, and **La
Cascada Park**, with an artificial waterfall. Located 36km (22 miles) west are
the **Bustamante Caves**, where you
can visit the few chambers that have
been explored. The beautiful stalactites and stalagmites have formed
fascinating shapes. Nearby, the
Cañon de Bustamante offers some
impressive landscapes.

*Continue northeast on **Mex 85**
for 130km (81 miles) to Nuevo
Laredo.*

*The city of Monterrey, founded three
times before it succeeded as a
settlement, has a fine cathedral with
a tiered bell tower*

A TRIP THROUGH HUASTECA COUNTRY

Monterrey • Sabinas Hidalgo • Nuevo Laredo
Matamoros • Tampico • Tamuín • Ciudad Valles
Ciudad Victoria • Monterrey

This second tour from Monterrey includes the states of Nuevo León,
Tamaulipas and San Luis Potosí. On the first part of the trip there is
the opportunity of visiting two of Mexico's most important border
towns with the United States. Combined with this is a visit to an
archaeological area relating to the Huastec Indians, early inhabitants
of the region. Included in the itinerary is a major port and fishing
center, together with charming regional towns where you will get the
flavor of northeastern Mexico. In a more restful vein, there are
beautiful gardens to visit, with woods and waterfalls and a number of
thermal springs.

BACK TO NATURE

4 Wetlands in the Tampico
area hold a good range of
bird species. Waders such as
lesser yellowlegs, least
sandpipers, western sandpipers,
long-billed dowitchers and
American avocets are
particularly numerous in
spring and autumn around the
water margins. Depending on
the size of the water body,
also look for belted
kingfishers, great blue herons,
little blue herons, egrets and a
variety of ducks.

FOR HISTORY BUFFS

4 Tampico was thought to
have been an early
settlement of the Huastec
Indians, as indicated by
pottery found here. Before the
arrival of the Spaniards,
Tampico had fallen under the
domination of the Aztecs.
After the Conquest, a convent
was built by the Franciscans
on the site of the old Aztec
settlement, and in 1560 it was
given the status of a town. Oil
was discovered here at the
beginning of this century,
bringing growth and
prosperity to Tampico and the
surrounding area. Today it is
one of Mexico's leading ports
and large oil tanks and
refineries stretch along the
southern banks of the Río
Pánuco.

FOR CHILDREN

7 Southwest of Ciudad
Victoria is the **Parque
Tamatán**. Children will enjoy
a visit to these zoological
gardens, which contain a
great variety of animals from
both the region and all over
the world. There is also a
pleasant section of lawns,
with games for younger
children, and a lake with boat
trips. The **Parque Infantil
Estefanía Castañeda** in
Ciudad Victoria is said to be
the best amusement park for
young children in Mexico.

Nuevo Laredo, Tamaulipas

2 Nuevo Laredo is the major point of
entry between the US and Mexico
and is linked to Laredo in Texas, by
two international bridges across the
famous Río Grande, known as the Río
Bravo in Mexico. Nuevo Laredo offers
the sort of entertainment and activity
typical of a busy frontier town.
Mexican and US immigration and
customs offices are open 24 hours a
day and life goes on around the clock.
The town bursts with shops and markets, which stock an enormous variety
of goods, from typical Mexican handicrafts – ceramics, wrought iron and
glassware – to saddles and any
number of tourist-oriented goods.

Entertainment includes bullfights
and horse and greyhound racing. The
town is also an important center for
cattle and agricultural trading and
border industries.

*Take **Mex 2** southeast for 326km
(202 miles) through Reynosa to
Matamoros.*

Matamoros, Tamaulipas

3 This is Mexico's easternmost
border town. It lies on a coastal
plain on the **Golfo de México** (Gulf of
Mexico), with the Río Grande separ-

ating it from Brownsville, Texas. The
town is pleasant and has a few cultural attractions that are worth a visit.
The **Museo Casa Mata** (Casa Mata
Museum) is housed in an old fort
which saw some fierce fighting
during the Mexican-American War.
Here you can take a look at some relics
of the Mexican Revolution and some
Indian artifacts. The state-run **Centro
de Artesanías** has attractive displays
of regional handicrafts. Of interest
also is the **Museo del Maíz** (Museum
of Maize), also known as the **Casa de
Cultura**, which focuses on the importance of this cereal crop in the history
and development of Mexico. Shopping is one of the tourist's major
pleasures, and you will enjoy the
attractive shopping mall. The huge,
enclosed marketplace called **Mercado
Juárez** offers a wide variety of indigenous handicrafts and is also a good
place for browsing. Matamoros's best
swimming beach is located some
miles away, east of the town, and has
a few restaurants that offer good
seafood.

*Take **Mex 180** south to
Tampico, a total of 488km
(303 miles).*

Tampico, Tamaulipas

4 The port of Tampico lies on the
north bank of the Panuco River.
Second largest seaport after Veracruz
on the Gulf of Mexico, it is also an
important petroleum center. Tampico
has that indefinable air of a grand old
tropical port that's seen better days.
The discovery of oil in the region
affected the character of old Tampico,
but it still has its attractions. Fishing is
a major one, and it draws many
visitors. There is usually plenty of
activity and atmosphere along the
waterfront around the Plaza de la
Liberación. The main square, the
Plaza de las Armas, is quite grand,
adorned with tall palm trees and with
a handsome **Palacio Municipal**
(Town Hall) on one side. Popular
beaches are Playa Miramar and
Altamira, located north of the town
amidst wild, tropical vegetation. To
the south is the **Laguna de Tamiahúa**
(Tamiahúa Lagoon), good for fishing
and shrimping. Boat trips visit the
mangrove swamps and little islands.

It is worth the short side trip to
the **Museo de la Cultura Huasteca**
(Huastec Museum) housed in the
Instituto Tecnológico in neighboring
Ciudad Madero, about 7km (4 miles)
north of the main square. It has a very
interesting collection of pottery, terracotta sculptures, jewelry, semiprecious stones, weapons and costumes from the Huastec culture.

ℹ️ Carranza and Olmos Altos

*Take **Mex 70** southwest to the
banks of the Tamuín River.*

Tamuín, San Luis Potosí

5 Along the banks of the Río Tamuín
is an archaeological zone, extend-
ing for 17 hectares (42 acres). Tamuín
was once a ceremonial center of the
Huastec people and is believed to
date back to between AD900–1500.
Only part of this zone has been
explored, and it consists mainly of
a series of platforms, altars and
courtyards. Major finds so far have

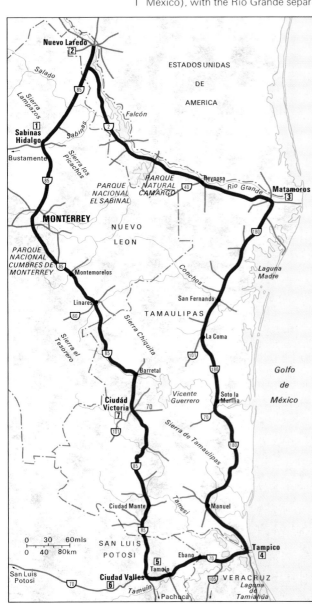

Though apparently docile, such bulls as these can kill in the ring

included a platform with a large stairway, some conical-shaped altars and traces of frescos. A notable piece of sculpture found here, now in the Museum of Anthropology in Mexico City, is a fine statue of a young man, with symbols of the wind god Ehécatl.

*Take **Mex 70** for 27km (17 miles) to Ciudad Valles.*

Ciudad Valles, San Luis Potosí

6 Ciudad Valles is a little agricultural town located in the center of a citrus- and sugarcane-growing region. Worth a visit is the local museum, the **Museo Regional Huasteco de Antropología**, which has interesting displays relating to the culture of the Huasteca people. Nearby is the spa resort of **El Bañito** with thermal springs.

*Take **Mex 85** northwest to Ciudad Victoria.*

Ciudad Victoria, Tamaulipas

7 Ciudad Victoria, the capital of the state of Tamaulipas, is named after General Guadalupe Victoria, who

Ringed by mountains, Monterrey is a fascinating and unique example of modern urban Mexico

became the first President of the Republic of Mexico in 1824, following independence from the Spanish. Principally an agricultural center, the town is modern and clean, with tree-lined boulevards and colorful markets offering a multitude of local handicrafts. The main square is flanked by the **cathedral** and the modern **Palacio de Gobierno** (Government Palace). The Alameda Central is a pleasant little square that invites a leisurely stroll. Take a look at the **Palacio Municipal** (Town Hall), built in 1898 and one of the city's most elegant buildings. And pay a visit to the **Museo de Antropología e Historia** (Museum of Anthropology and History) housed in the University of Tamaulipas. It has a very good collection of Huastecan art and sections dedicated to the Colonial era, Independence Wars and the Revolution.

*Return on **Mex 85** northwest to Monterrey, 287km (178 miles).*

Monterrey – Sabinas Hidalgo **94 (58)**
Sabinas Hidalgo – Nuevo Laredo **130 (81)**
Nuevo Laredo – Matamoros **326 (202)**
Matamoros – Tampico **488 (303)**
Tampico – Tamuín **107 (66)**
Tamuín – Ciudad Valles **27 (17)**
Ciudad Valles – Ciudad Victoria **246 (153)**
Ciudad Victoria – Monterrey **287 (178)**

SPECIAL TO ...

4 Tampico is known for its very lively **Carnival Week**. The celebrations leading up to Ash Wednesday feature parades, floats, music, competitions, masquerades and dancing in the streets.
There is also a fiesta on 12 April, when civic ceremonies are held to commemorate the re-establishment of the city in 1823. There is a big parade through the streets and an equestrian troupe from Altamira, and people wear elegant costumes of the 19th century.
On 3 November the **Festival of St Martin of Porres** is celebrated with music and dancing in the atrium of the church.

RECOMMENDED WALKS

5 You will have the opportunity to stretch your legs and have a good stroll as you take a look at the archaeological zone along the shores of the Tamuín River.

6 There are also fine walks round the lovely waterfall **La Cascada Micos**, 18km (12 miles) northeast of Ciudad Valles. Here the falls drop 80m (260 feet) in a tumbling series of cascades.

SCENIC ROUTES

Much of the northern section of this route is through rather bare, arid terrain, but there are pleasant drives south from Tampico, along the Tamuín River to Ciudad Valles and returning through Ciudad Victoria, where the surroundings become lush and tropical.

5 days – 839km (521 miles)

THE TROPICAL LANDS OF THE GULF

Veracruz ● Santiago Tuxtla ● San Andrés Tuxtla
Laguna de Catemaco ● Córdoba
Fortín de las Flores ● Orizaba ● Tehuacán ● Jalapa
Zempoala ● Veracruz

This tour from Veracruz travels through the states of Veracruz and Puebla. There you will see areas of lush tropical vegetation, with an abundance of flowers everywhere, exciting jungle terrain, and lovely lakes and mangrove swamps, combined with pretty little mountain towns set amidst plantations of coffee beans, fruit and such like. As with much of Mexico, there will also be some archaeological interest. Mingled with all this are the lively rhythms of the typical music from Veracruz which add to the enjoyment. Much of the area will be hot and tropical, but temperatures are cooler at higher altitudes.

🛈 City Hall, Zaragoza 20, Veracruz

*Take **Mex 180** southeast to Santiago Tuxtla, 122km (76 miles).*

Santiago Tuxtla, Veracruz

1 The ancient pre-Hispanic town of Santiago Tuxtla is thought to be the oldest in the region. Lying at the foot of the **Volcán San Martín** (St Martin Volcano) it is surrounded by green mountains in an area of abundant

On Mandinga Lagoon, near the city of Veracruz, a local fisherman works from his traditional craft. There are good seafood restaurants in Mandinga, and boats can be rented to explore the area

tropical flowers and birds. An intriguing feature of the town is the large Olmec head that stands in a corner of the main square. The small regional museum, **Museo Tuxteco**, has a good display of artifacts from the Olmec culture, including an interesting collection of stone pieces found at the archaeological site of Tres Zapotes, located some 24km (15 miles) southwest of the town. At this site two huge heads and a stela – bearing the earliest date so far known in the history of the Olmec culture, 31 BC – were found. A small museum (**Museo Arqueológico**) here has an impressive Olmec head, stone figures and stelae.

*Take **Mex 180** east for 8km (5 miles) to San Andrés Tuxtla.*

San Andrés Tuxtla, Veracruz

2 San Andrés Tuxtla ('enclosed place' in Náhuatl) is an old Colonial town set in the mountains of the Volcán San Martín. Its central square, shaded by a variety of trees, has a splendid bandstand. Take a look at the **Catedral de San José y San Andrés** (Cathedral of St Joseph and St Andrew), built in a pale-colored stone, and the elegant **Palacio Municipal** (Town Hall) which face the square. This is the tobacco-growing region of Mexico, and the local cigar factories can be visited. The countryside here is very green and lush. A short distance away is the **Laguna Encantada** (Enchanted Lagoon) in the crater of an extinct volcano. Along the coast to the north there are some pretty, unspoiled beaches where the mountains sweep down to the water. Nearby, too, is the waterfall known as Salto de Eyipantla, whose cascading waters have a drop of over 40m (130 feet).

🛈 Hotel del Parque, Zócalo

*Continue on **Mex 180** southeast for 14km (9 miles) to Laguna de Catemaco.*

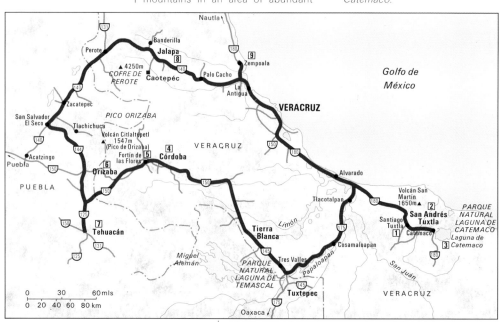

Laguna de Catemaco, Veracruz

3 Laguna de Catemaco (Lake Catemaco) is one of Mexico's most beautiful lakes, set in the cone-shaped peaks of the Tuxtla Volcano with two small islands breaking its surface. The area of the lake was formed long ago by the eruption of several volcanoes, and it covers some 130sq km (78 square miles). The well-known explorer Alexander von Humboldt, who came here at the beginning of the 1800s, was very taken by this area, with its pleasant climate and European-looking land-scapes, calling it the 'Switzerland of Veracruz'. The old town of Catemaco, on the lake shore, lives principally by fishing. Catemaco has a reputation for good seafood, and fish from the lake is among its specialties.

Among the buildings of note is the **Basílica de Nuestra Señora del Carmen** (Basilica of Our Lady of Mt Carmel), patron saint of the town. It has a lovely white stone façade and a much venerated image of the Virgin, made of gold and stone, placed over the altar. Paradoxically, Catemaco is renowned for its witchcraft. Here you can have a curse removed or purchase a love potion.

Some 18km (10 miles) away is the delightful village of Sontecomapán, right in the heart of the jungle by a small, isolated lagoon.

Return west on **Mex 180** *via San Andrés Tuxtla. Branch off south on* **Mex 175** *towards Tuxtepec. Take* **Mex 145** *northwest. Join* **Mex 150** *and turn left to Córdoba.*

Córdoba, Veracruz

4 The pretty little town of Córdoba lies in a fertile agricultural region, surrounded by lush natural vegetation and an abundance of flowers. Tropical fruits, coffee and tobacco are the main products here. The houses, with their strong wooden doors, window grilles and wooden balco-nies, are reminiscent of the style of architecture in Spain's Andalucía region. The main square is sur-rounded by arcades and shops, cafés and restaurants. The 17th-century iglesia parroquial (parish church), standing on one side of the square, features an enormous bell known as Santa María. Also on the square is the **Palacio Municipal** (Town Hall), built in the impressive neoclassical style. Take a look at the local museum, the **Museo de la Ciudad de Córdoba**, whose interesting material includes a collection of artifacts from the Totonac culture. The local market, the **Mercado Juárez**, is lively and colorful, especially at weekends.

Continue west on **Mex 150** *for 6km (4 miles) to Fortín de las Flores.*

Fortín de las Flores, Veracruz

5 The delightful town of Fortín de las Flores deserves its name, which in Spanish means 'little fortress of flowers'. Famous for its gorgeous flowers, vast plantations of coffee and tropical fruit, it has a pleasant climate. Gardenias, camellias, azaleas and orchids grow in profusion and adorn all the houses, squares and gardens, sweetly scenting the evenings. Tropical and semitropical flowers are cultivated in the surrounding area. It may be possible to arrange a visit to one of the fruit or coffee plantations. Look out for the curious plant that closes up when touched. The attract-ive main square is divided into two areas and overlooked by the **Palacio Municipal** (Town Hall) and the **Biblioteca Pública** (Public Library). On a clear day there is a superb view of the snow-capped volcano Pico de Orizaba, rising in all its might to a height of 5,700m (18,700 feet).

In the vicinity is the **Puente de Metlác** (Metlác Bridge). Over 100m (330 feet) in length, it spans a huge canyon and is an impressive piece of engineering.

Continue on **Mex 150** *southwest to Orizaba.*

The Palacio Municipal in Veracruz, which houses the tourist office on the ground floor. The city is famed for cigars, gourmet cuisine, coffee, embroidered capes, and the popular song 'La Bamba'

BACK TO NATURE

3 On the Laguna de Catemaco, boat trips are available to the Isla de los Monos (Island of Monkeys). A colony of monkeys lives here and their habits are being studied. Spider monkeys and various other species are imported from Thailand and they have learned to fish and swim. On boat trips, visitors should also look for ringed, belted, green, Amazon and pygmy kingfishers as well as American coots and several species of wildfowl.

RECOMMENDED WALKS

6 Experienced climbers who wish to ascend Pico de Orizaba should take the route running southeast from San Salvador El Seco on **Mex 140** or alternatively the route via Tlachichuca, from where you can drive to a mountain hut and stay overnight. The ascent of Mexico's highest mountain can be done in a day, but expert guidance is usually necessary. Pico de Orizaba, also known as Volcán Citlaltépetl ('Mountain of the Star') is 5,700m (18,700 feet) high.

SCENIC ROUTES

The scenery on this tour ranges from green tropical regions to beautiful landscapes offering views of Mexico's great mountains, some snow-covered. The whole drive from Fortín de las Flores to Orizaba and up to Jalapa affords excellent views of Pico de Orizaba and the square-topped Cofre de Perote, assuming you have good, clear weather. There can be a lot of heavy cloud around Jalapa in particular, but this can come and go. The scenery is also lovely around Laguna de Catemaco.

FOR HISTORY BUFFS

9 Between Zempoala and Veracruz is La Antigua, the old Veracruz, founded by the Spaniards in 1524. A small chapel, built in the 16th century and dedicated to **Santo Cristo del Buen Viaje**, stands on the shores. In the **parish church** on the main square can be seen a little wooden statue of Santo Cristo, brought to the New World by Cortés.

Orizaba, Veracruz

6 Orizaba is one of the most important towns in the state of Veracruz. It lies in a valley surrounded by mountains, at an altitude of 1,285m (4,215 feet) above sea level. Although now a busy agricultural and commercial center, it has retained some of its old Colonial flavor. The **Parroquia** (parish church) **San Miguel** is a vast fortress-like structure (1620–1729) with a bell tower which is used as a weather station. The **Palacio Municipal** (Town Hall) is a unique green and yellow building made of steel. Constructed in Belgium and used as the Belgian pavilion for the International Fair of 1889 in Paris, it was bought by Orizaba and reassembled. Other buildings of note include the churches of **El Calvario**, a neoclassical building, **El Carmen** and **San José de Gracia**, formerly part of a Franciscan monastery.

About 6km (4 miles) east is the reservoir of **Presa de Tuxpango** on the Blanco River. A cable car descends to the village of Tuxpango, about 1km (½ mile) below.

*Take **Mex 150** then **125** southwest for 60km (37 miles) to Tehuacán.*

Jalapa's Anthropology Museum is among the best in Mexico, its spacious layout sympathetic to the large pre-Hispanic collection

Tehuacán, Puebla

7 Tehuacán is one of Mexico's best-known spa resorts and a great favorite with Mexicans, who take advantage of its mineral water cures. Most of the famous brands of purified water consumed in the country come from here. Visits to the bottling plants can be arranged.

Buildings of note are the monastery church, **Iglesia de la Concepción** (Church of the Conception), with an attractive tiled dome, and the **Iglesia del Carmen** (Carmelite Convent). The Saturday market specializes in sombreros, baskets, leather goods and onyx.

*Take **Mex 125** north, then continue on **Mex 144**. Join **Mex 140**, turning northeast at El Seco to Jalapa.*

Jalapa, Veracruz

8 Its name is derived from the old name of Xall-apan, which means 'river in the sand' in Náhuatl. Jalapa is the capital of the state of Veracruz and is situated in a series of hills surrounded by lofty mountains. The Cofre de Perote dominates the landscape, while the Pico de Orizaba can be seen to the south. In this area, subject to heavy cloud and mist, Jalapa is known for its light drizzle, called the *chipichipi*. These weather conditions create a kind of greenhouse atmosphere and promote the

In the mangroves of Mandinga Lagoon, the brackish waters can be navigated in a rented boat

lush vegetation and tropical flowers of the region. Jalapa is often referred to as 'The Flower Garden of Mexico'. The town combines old narrow streets, gaily painted houses and tropical gardens with wide, modern boulevards and new buildings. Among the buildings of interest are the late 18th-century **Catedral Metropolitana de Jalapa** (cathedral) near **Parque Juárez** (Juárez Park) and the **Palacio de Gobierno** (Governor's Palace), an attractive structure of pale-colored stone with some interesting frescos inside. The **Museo de Antropología de Jalapa** (Museum of Anthropology) has a fine collection including Monolithic Olmec heads and other pieces of sculpture from various cultures are displayed in its landscaped park.

For a side trip, go along to Perote, situated at the foot of the square-topped Cofre de Perote volcano, the centerpiece of a national park.

*Continue on **Mex 140** southeast. Turn north along **Mex 180** to Zempoala.*

Zempoala, Veracruz

9 On the outskirts of the village of Zempoala (also known as Cempoala) are the ruins of an old Totonac ceremonial center. Cortés and his men gained support from the Indians here in the first stages of his conquest of Mexico.

There are six remaining structures. The main buildings are the **Gran Pirámide** (Great Pyramid), which stands on 13 platforms and is partially covered by palm trees. The **Templo de las Chimeneas** (Temple of Chimneys) was named for its series of semicircular pillars. The **Templo Mayor** (Principal Temple) is also known as the Temple of 13 Steps. On top stand the remains of a rect-angular temple. The **Templo de las Caritas** (Temple of the Little Heads) is an interesting structure, with wall niches that were once filled with small terracotta heads. A small museum displays a few exhibits.

*Return to **Mex 180** and continue sou:heast back to Veracruz.*

Veracruz – Santiago Tuxtla **122 (76)**
Santiago Tuxtla – San Andrés Tuxtla **8 (5)**
San Andrés Tuxtla – Laguna de Catemaco **14 (9)**
Laguna de Catemaco – Córdoba **275 (171)**
Córdoba – Fortín de las Flores **6 (4)**
Fortín de las Flores – Orizaba **17 (11)**
Orizaba – Tehuacán **60 (37)**
Tehuacán – Jalapa **218 (135)**
Jalapa – Zempoala **76 (47)**
Zempoala – Veracruz **54 (33)**

SPECIAL TO ...

3 On 15 July the **Día de la Virgen del Carmen** (Festival of Our Lady of Mt Carmel) is celebrated in Catemaco, and pilgrims come from all over, even as far away as Oaxaca, to pay her homage. Festivities last for two days and traditional costumes are worn by the Indians. Celebrations include music and regional dancing.

FOR CHILDREN

3 While at Laguna de Catemaco, children would probably very much enjoy a boat trip to the **Isla de los Monos** (Island of Monkeys). Among the many breeds to be found here are spider monkeys and macaques. The colony was imported from the jungles of Thailand.

BAJA CALIFORNIA

La Paz:

La Paz is the capital of Baja California Sur. From a quiet little fishing port it has gradually grown into a sizeable town. It was once renowned for its black and pink pearls, but the industry declined and the town now relies mainly on fishing, processing and tourism. In pre-Hispanic times the area was inhabited by various Indian tribes, who fought bitterly against the Spaniards when they attempted to settle the area (it was not finally settled until 1800). La Paz became the capital in 1830.

The present-day town is very relaxed, with handsome Colonial buildings and pleasant squares with trim laurel trees. The palm-shaded waterfront boulevard (*malecón*) is perfect for strolling, and on Sunday evenings concerts are held on the esplanade. There are fine, sandy beaches for swimming, and scuba diving and water skiing are also popular. Deep-sea fishing is another big attraction (catch includes yellowtail, rooster fish and bonito), and a

Baja California – a rugged finger of land that points southward for 1,216km (760 miles) – is washed by the Pacific Ocean to the west and the Mar de Cortés (Gulf of California) to the east. The narrow Sea of Cortés, distinctive for its shades of emerald and deep blue, is considerably warmer than the Pacific.

With California abutting its northern border, the peninsula is divided along the 28th parallel into Baja California Norte and Baja California Sur. Dominating the north are the jagged peaks of the Sierra San Pedro Martir, while the Sierra de la Giganta runs south. Baja, as it is often called, has a coastline of long, sandy beaches, rocks and coves, and an interior typified by barren, lunar-like deserts bristling with towering cacti. But there is a more hospitable side to Baja: agricultural regions in the north, and the brilliant flowers and lush vegetation of the tropical south. The climate of the peninsula also varies regionally, from the dry heat of the interior deserts to the more humid coastal areas in the south. Baja's climate is perhaps at its best in the winter months, with warm, sunny days and cool nights.

Little trace remains of Baja's earliest inhabitants, and no important cultures were established here. Hernán Cortés first set foot in Baja in 1535, at the spot that was to become La Paz. Subsequent visits by the Spaniards met with fierce resistance by the Indians. At the end of the 17th century Jesuit missionaries came to the peninsula, and one of their number – Father Francisco Eusebio Kino – played a leading role in establishing missions all over Baja California, as well as mainland Mexico. The Jesuits, expelled by order of Carlos III of Spain in 1767, were followed by Franciscans and, later, by Dominicans. The remains of many of these missions can be seen dotted about the countryside.

Baja California was separated from California in 1804, but was occupied by American troops during the 1846–8 War of Intervention between Mexico and the US. In 1931 the peninsula was divided into two territories, and they later became independent states.

Until recent years virtually all visitors to the area came only for the excellent fishing and hunting. The development of new resorts in the south, however, has done much to attract more tourism. The winter months see many visitors come to the breeding grounds of the gray whale on the west coast. This area is a haven for fishermen, hunters, birdwatchers and those who appreciate remote landscapes of unusual beauty.

number of restaurants offer fresh sea-food. Shopping in La Paz has benefits, too, as it is a duty-free port.

Places of interest include the 19th-century **parish church** on the main square and the 20th-century **Palacio Gobierno** (Government Palace), the **Museo de Antropología** (Museum of Anthropology) and the **House of Folk Art**.

Tijuana:

Mexico's most famous border town, Tijuana, is a busy port of entry to Baja California and the rest of Mexico. The town has always had a reputation for being brash and seedy and, although neatened up by new industry and booming tourism, its somewhat tarnished image lives on. Perhaps that is part of its attraction, for visitors continue to come in droves. Of the millions Tijuana receives each year, a large number come for the day to stock up on shopping or merely to enjoy the atmosphere. For Tijuana is great fun. The city has broad avenues, huge department stores and high-rises, yet retains the hustle and bustle of its streets, the noise and color of its heritage. There are numerous bars, restaurants and nightclubs, and the place teems with activity in the evenings. Performances of the colorful Ballet Folklorico, mariachi bands and plays are given in the **Centro Cultural Tijuana** (Tijuana Cultural Center) where there is also a museum of archaeological and historical interest, with a display of handicrafts.

Other entertainments include bull-fights and *charreadas* (Mexican-style rodeos) during the summer months, jai alai, golf, and horse and dog racing. There are facilities for golf and tennis and good swimming at the beaches a few miles away. The **Feria de las Californias**, featuring many sports events and exhibitions, is a colorful festival from August to September.

Stunning shades of azure delight the eye at this bay in Baja. The warm, narrow gulf between the peninsula and the mainland attracts migratory gray whales

7 days – 1,880km (1,168 miles)

LUNAR LANDSCAPES OF BAJA CALIFORNIA

La Paz • San José del Cabo • Cabo San Lucas
Loreto • Bahía Concepción • Mulegé
Santa Rosalía • San Ignacio
Laguna Ojo de Liebre • La Paz

Commencing in La Paz, this itinerary takes you on an exploratory trip around the southern part of the peninsula, Baja California Sur. The area, sparsely populated, is one of lunar-type landscapes, with arid desert and rugged outlines of distant mountains. The intense blue of the sky and the surreal silhouettes of the desert cacti add to the drama of the scenery. As a welcome change, you can visit the main resorts on the southern shores of this magnificent coastline of wild, sandy beaches, sheer cliffs and emerald waters. Deep-sea fishing and wildlife are major attractions of this trip, together with the quaint towns and old missions you will encounter on your journey.

At home in the heat near La Paz, cacti happily populate the land

ℹ️ Paseo Alvaro Obregon 2130, La Paz

> *From La Paz take **Mex 1** southeast to San José del Cabo, about 164km (102 miles).*

San José del Cabo, Baja California Sur

1 The old mission station of San José del Cabo is still a rather sleepy little fishing village, which has not changed much in spite of the development of the area. In recent years the Mexican government has launched an ambitious development program to attract tourists to this somewhat isolated part of Mexico, and a number of hotels have sprung up around the area. The majority of visitors come for deep-sea fishing: all facilities for fishing expeditions are available. The area is characterized by long, sandy beaches and wild, jagged rocks and boulders. Most beaches are exposed to the huge waves of the open sea. Many parts have heavy surf and a dangerous undertow, making them unsuitable for swimming. Excellent surfing locations do exist, though; a particularly good spot south of here is Mirador Point.

The little town of San José has gaily painted houses and a pleasant beachfront. Take a look at the 18th-century Jesuit **Misión Vieja** (Old Mission) and the attractive **Palacio Municipal** (Town Hall). The shopping center

At Cabo San Lucas, jagged rocks and a natural arch mark the place where ocean and gulf converge

sells a good variety of handicrafts and nice clothes. The **Casa de la Cultura** (House of Culture) contains a small museum and library.

> Continue on **Mex 1** southwest for 30km (19 miles) to Cabo San Lucas.

Cabo San Lucas, Baja California Sur

2 This bay is located at the southernmost tip of the 1,222km (760-mile) long peninsula of Baja California. In the 16th and 17th centuries it was a hideout for pirates. The area has been developing over recent years with the building of a number of attractive hotels. Its long beaches and magnificent rock formations are a big attraction. Deep-sea fishing is the big lure, however. Catches include marlin and sailfish, among many other species. All facilities are offered for deep-sea fishing, as well as for diving and snorkeling. Beaches on either side of the resort fulfil different needs. The Costa Azul and Acapulquite are surfing beaches. Punta Palmilla offers good diving and snorkeling, and the secluded beach of Santa María is perfect for a picnic. The color of the sea is beautiful here, in varying shades of emerald and blue, but the temperature of the water can be cold.

A feature of Cabo San Lucas is **El Arco**, a famous natural arch of white stone carved out of steep rocks that rise dramatically from the sea, marking the point where the Mar de Cortés (Gulf of California) meets the Pacific Ocean. Organized boat trips tour the bay, where you can have a closer look at the impressive arch and observe the colonies of sea lions lazing about on the rocks. There are also plenty of pelicans and other birds around.

Cabo San Lucas is a point of departure for ferries to the mainland, and cruise ships also stop here. When they dock, temporary markets are set up on the beach and there is a burst of lively activity. There is good shopping in the resort, with a choice of handicrafts and other goods available, including black coral jewelry.

The sparkling stretch of gently shelving beach at San José del Cabo complements the quaint town with its Spanish-style buildings

For something different, you can make an excursion by jeep or horseback to the **Faro de Cabo Falso**, a lighthouse built on sand dunes at the very tip of the peninsula. Experienced divers may want to see the interesting 'sand falls', underwater cascades of sand emerging from the ocean floor.

> Take **Mex 9** north to La Paz. Continue on **Mex 1** northwest, then northeast to Loreto.

Loreto, Baja California Sur

3 Loreto is a quaint little town with pleasant, shaded plazas. It lies on the Sea of Cortés among palm groves, against a backdrop of the rugged peaks of the Sierra de la Giganta to the west. The town relies on farming and fishing, and is also a good center for scuba diving and deep-sea fishing, attracting a great number of fishermen who come for the sailfish, marlin, rooster fish and other species.

A few miles south of Loreto is the new tourist development of Nopolo. Further along is Puerto Escondido, a port that offers good fishing and diving and is also being developed for tourism. It has a small marina for boats and camping facilities.

> Continue on **Mex 1** northwest to Bahía Concepción.

Bahía Concepción, Baja California Sur

4 This is a truly exceptional spot and well worth a stop to admire the breathtaking view of the bay. Small islands are dotted about in the distance, and there are a number of beautiful beaches. Those of El Coyote, El Resquesón, Santispác and Los Muertos are considered outstanding and have camping facilities. Nearby is an area of formidable cacti, the tallest species in the world.

> Continue northwest on **Mex 1** for 65km (42 miles) to Mulegé.

BACK TO NATURE

7 A visit to the breeding grounds of the gray whales around Guerrero Negro will certainly be a major attraction to naturalists, who travel to this area in the winter months. There are other areas of similar interest, however. About 70km (42 miles) southwest of San Ignacio is the Bahía de Ballenas (Bay of Whales), which is also a winter breeding ground for whales. It is accessible by a dirt road, and boat trips are available to observe the great creatures.

FOR HISTORY BUFFS

3 Loreto was founded in 1697 by a Jesuit priest of that name, and it became the first permanent Spanish settlement on the peninsula, forming a base for the colonization of the whole region. Of note is the **Misión de Nuestra Señora de Loreto** (Mission of Our Lady of Loreto). Built in 1752, it has been restored after suffering great damage from earthquakes. Take a look at the **Museo de las Misiones de Baja California** (Museum of Baja California Missions), which has many interesting displays relating to the establishing of the missions and the history of the peninsula.

SPECIAL TO ...

1 On 19 March San José del Cabo honors its patron saint, Joseph, with a lively festival of many events, including cockfights and horse races, rounded off by fireworks, regional music and dancing.

SCENIC ROUTES

From La Paz to San José del Cabo is an interesting stretch of dry, cactus-strewn terrain, with views of the distant Sierra de la Laguna. The drive between San José del Cabo and Cabo San Lucas is particularly lovely as you go past long beaches, rocks and boulders, set off by the exquisite emerald sea. The road from Cabo San Lucas to Todos los Santos passes magnificent beaches.

There is some outstanding scenery on the road from Loreto to San Javier, which runs for 33km (19 miles) southwest through marvelous mountain and canyon landscapes. You will need high-clearance vehicles for this journey, however.

Mulegé, Baja California Sur

5 Mulegé is a delightful little oasis lying on the banks of the Mulegé River, lined with date palms and olive groves. Compared to the somewhat harsh, arid landscapes of the surroundings, it is a real treat to come across this town. The old **Misión Santa Rosalía de Mulegé** (St Rosalie Mission) stands on a hill to the west; this was founded in 1705 by Jesuits. The local prison also warrants the tourist's attention. It is housed in an old hacienda-style building that stands on a hill overlooking the town. The prison has no bars and the inmates go out to work every day.

Mulegé offers freshwater fishing as well as sea fishing. Boats can be rented, and there are several good beaches for swimming. Nearby is **El Sombrerito** ('Little Hat'), a dramatic monolith shaped as its name suggests. Located at the mouth of the Mulegé River, it has a series of steps leading to the top.

*Continue on **Mex 1** northwest to Santa Rosalía.*

Santa Rosalía, Baja California Sur

6 Santa Rosalía was formerly a mining town, founded in the 1880s by the French, who owned the El Boleo copper company. This was active until there was a decline in the mid-1950s. French influences are evident. The **Misión de Santa Rosalía** was built of galvanized iron under the direction of Gustav Eiffel (of Eiffel Tower fame) for the 1898 International Fair in Paris. It was shipped in pieces to Mexico and reassembled. A number of houses show a French style of architecture. There are also some excellent beaches, and ferry services depart from here to Guaymas, on the mainland.

A couple of side trips may have appeal. The **caves of San Borjita**, located south of the town, are the oldest found so far on the peninsula. Another worthwhile trip is to the quaint village of San José de Magdalena, about 27km (16 miles) away. The village dates back to Colonial times and is set among lovely gardens and palm trees. The ruins of an old 18th-century **Dominican church** can be seen.

*Continue on **Mex 1** west for 64km (40 miles) to San Ignacio.*

San Ignacio, Baja California Sur

7 Situated in a valley, the little town of San Ignacio is another oasis of date palms, orange and fig trees which grow in profusion around a small lake. Its pretty pastel-colored houses have thatched roofs. The Jesuits founded a mission here in 1728 and planted date palms around the old Indian settlement. The most notable building is the imposing **Dominican church**, which was built in 1786 and is now well restored. There is good fishing in the freshwater lake, which is fed by an underground river.

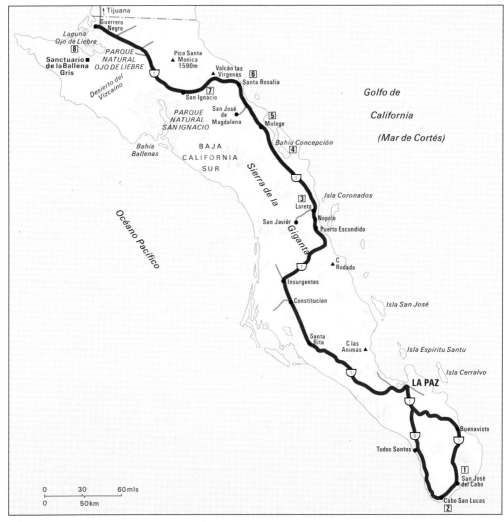

In the surrounding mountains there are a number of hidden caves with prehistoric Indian paintings. Trips can be arranged with a guide and by mule and these expeditions through the wilderness can take several days.

*Continue driving on **Mex 1** northwest for 143km (89 miles) to Guerrero Negro. Turn off to Laguna Ojo de Liebre, 12km (7 miles) further on.*

Laguna Ojo de Liebre, Baja California Sur

8 Laguna Ojo de Liebre is a protected breeding ground for the gray whale. It is also known as Scammon's Lagoon, after the American whaling captain, Scammon, who discovered the sanctuary in the 19th century. Every autumn a number of whales migrate here from the Bering Sea, a 9,677km (6,013-mile) trip. Between the end of November and March they stay to mate and bear their young, which are born after a gestation period of 13 months. The area has been turned into a national park as a way of protecting them. There are several places where you can observe the

The present cathedral in La Paz, built this century, rose from the foundation of the original Jesuit mission of 1720

huge mammals frolicking and cavorting (the biggest of them can weigh up to 25 tons). One good place is the observation tower in the San Juan estuary. This is a fascinating and unique experience for anyone visiting the area during those months.

A short side trip on a turnoff north of Guerrero Negro leads to a dramatic eagle monument which marks the border between Baja California Sur and Baja California Norte, north of the 28th parallel.

*Return south to La Paz on **Mex 1**.*

La Paz – San José del Cabo **164 (102)**
San José del Cabo – Cabo San Lucas **30 (19)**
Cabo San Lucas – Loreto **510 (316)**
Loreto – Bahía Concepción **79 (49)**
Bahía Concepción – Mulegé **65 (42)**
Mulegé – Santa Rosalía **57 (35)**
Santa Rosalía – San Ignacio **64 (40)**
San Ignacio – Laguna Ojo de Liebre **146 (91)**
Laguna Ojo de Liebre – La Paz **765 (474)**

RECOMMENDED WALKS

1 It can be an exhilarating experience walking along some of Baja California's fine beaches, with the great Pacific rollers pounding the shore against the dramatic background of wild cliffs and rock formations. One suggestion is a walk from the center of San José del Cabo to a tiny fishing settlement called Pueblo la Playa, 2.5km (1½ miles) east of town.

FOR CHILDREN

8 Children might enjoy the whales in Laguna Ojo de Liebre (if you arrive in the right season to see them) and some of the nature and wildlife. However, this area can be extremely hot in the long summer months and may not be very suitable for youngsters.

7 days – 2,136km (1,327 miles)

RESORTS & DESERT LANDS

Tijuana • Rosarito • Ensenada
Cabo Punta la Banda • Santo Tomás • San Vicente
Observatorio San Pedro Martir • San Quintin
El Rosario • Misión de San Fernando
Bahía de los Angeles • San Felipe • Mexicali
Tijuana

This tour starts from the border town of Tijuana and takes you on a southern route through the state of Baja California Norte. Popular beach resorts and extraordinary natural phenomena contrast with little missions, which played such an important role in the exploration of the area after the Spanish Conquest. Some of the driving is through parched desert regions, barren plains and wild mountain country studded with the ubiquitous cacti. You will also encounter fine views of the Pacific Ocean to the west and the Sea of Cortés to the east. Be prepared for intense heat in the interior for much of the year.

Sombreros by the stack: primitive but effective for keeping cool

[i] Avenida Revolución, Tijuana

*Take **Mex 1** southwest for 32km (20 miles) to Rosarito.*

Rosarito, Baja California Norte

1 The resort of Rosarito is renowned for its beautiful, long beaches. It has a pleasant seafront lined with bars and restaurants and offers good surfing and horseback riding. It makes a good place to stop off *en route*.

*Continue south on **Mex 1** for 79km (49 miles) to Ensenada.*

Ensenada, Baja California Norte

2 The beach resort of Ensenada is a long-time favorite, particularly with neighboring Californians. Situated on the Bahía Todos los Santos (Bay of All Saints), it has fine beaches on either side of the town: to the south there is good snorkeling and scuba diving, while to the north there are some excellent spots for surfing. Ensenada is an important fishing center and is often referred to as the yellowtail capital of the world; other fish include bonito, marlin and barracuda. Fishing trips can be arranged to suit your requirements. Surf fishing is also popular along the broad beaches and rocky inlets.

Ensenada boasts Mexico's largest winery, the **Bodegas Santo Tomás**, which has organized tours. You can enjoy some of the local wine with the seafood which is a specialty of many restaurants here. From the nearby Chapultepec Hills there are grand

Tijuana's Cultural Center, with its Omnitheater, presents Mexican history, archaeology and crafts

Hacienda del Pacifico, Ensenada. This popular resort and fishing port is on a protected natural harbor

views of the town and bay, which hosts regattas every July and the Ensenada–Newport Yacht Race in late April/early May. Other sporting events include November's famous Baja Mil (Baja 1000) car race down the peninsula to La Paz. Pre-Lenten festivities of Carnival are held on Shrove Tuesday.

If you would like to visit the installations at the Observatory of San Pedro Martir (further south along the itinerary), you can probably get a permit at the local tourist office.

*Continue south on **Mex 1** for 16km (10 miles). Turn right and continue for another 19km (12 miles) to Cabo Punta la Banda.*

Cabo Punta la Banda, Baja California Norte

3 Cabo Punta la Banda, located south of the Bahía Todos los Santos is a fascinating freak of nature. Here you will see the famous blowhole through which waves come hurtling with tremendous force, throwing the water up to a tremendous height. It is referred to as **La Bufadora** (the Snorting One) on account of the sounds it emits – sometimes more of a thunderous roar than a snort, especially at high tide. It is worth the short drive off the main road to witness this extraordinary spectacle.

*Return to **Mex 1** and continue southeast for 30km (19 miles) to Santo Tomás.*

Santo Tomás, Baja California Norte

4 The town of Santo Tomás lies in the valley of the same name, amidst the largest vineyards in Mexico. Take a look at the remains of the 18th-century church, located outside the

town on the road leading to the coast. This once was part of an old Dominican mission, later destroyed by the Indians. On the coast, about 31km (18 miles) west of Santo Tomás, is the **Ranch of La Bocana de Santo Tomás**. It offers water sports and tourist facilities.

*Continue south on **Mex 1** for 40km (25 miles) to San Vicente.*

San Vicente, Baja California Norte

5 Stop here to take a look at the old **Misión de San Vicente Ferrer** (Mission of St Vincent Ferrer), situated along the banks of the San Vicente River. You can see the ruins of the adobe buildings of the former town, founded by Dominicans in 1780 and abandoned in the mid-1800s. This mission, the third on the peninsula, became the administrative center of all the missions established by the Dominican Order in Baja California. Its fortifications are architecturally interesting.

If at this point you would like to relax at a beach, there is one at Playa San Isidro, about 20km (12 miles) west, which offers good surfing.

*Continue south on **Mex 1** from San Vicente. After 51km (32 miles) turn east to the Parque Nacional Sierra de San Pedro Martir. Drive to the Observatorio San Pedro (Observatory).*

Observatorio San Pedro Martir, Baja California Norte

6 The National Observatory of San Pedro Martir was set up in 1971 by the National Autonomous University of Mexico. It stands on the summit of the **Cerro de la Encantada** (Enchanted Hill) at an altitude of 3,078m (10,000 feet), the highest peak on the peninsula of Baja California. The environmental conditions (the air here is said to be the clearest in the world) make it ideal for research work of this nature.

FOR HISTORY BUFFS

2 Ensenada was discovered by the Portuguese explorer João Rodrigues Cabrilho in 1542. From 1888, when the northern and southern parts of the peninsula were divided, it served as capital of Baja California Norte until the capital was moved to Mexicali 22 years later. When gold was discovered in the late 1800s, there was a tremendous boom and the area prospered, but this was followed by a decline when the mines were exhausted. The town began to flourish again when agricultural programs were introduced and it gained importance as a seaport.

RECOMMENDED WALKS

6 The **Parque Nacional Sierra de San Pedro Martir** is a perfect area for an extended walk. The scenery is somewhat alpine in appearance, with delightful wooded areas of firs, pines and countless other varieties of trees and plants. In the middle of these beautiful forests you will find fresh green meadows, streams and hot springs.

The parched valleys near Mexicali are extremely hot in summer

Although the observatory itself is not open to the public, a permit obtained in Ensenada (see page 115) will allow you to visit the installations. A lookout post here offers a marvelous panoramic view of the Pico del Diablo mountain, the surrounding desert and the beautiful waters of the Sea of Cortés.

The **Parque Nacional Sierra de San Pedro Martir** (National Park of San Pedro) is a delightful area, with forests of fir and pine, fresh green meadows and streams, a welcome contrast to the arid terrain that surrounds it.

*Return to **Mex 1** and continue south to San Quintin.*

San Quintin, Baja California Norte

7 San Quintin is a little market town whose population relies mainly on farming and fishing. Set in a valley on the Bay of San Quintin, it enjoys a pleasant climate with cooling breezes from the Pacific. It is a popular resort with pleasant beaches and an attractive wharf, drawing large numbers of visitors with a special interest in fishing, aquatic sports and hunting. San Quintin is also renowned for its delicious shrimp and abalone. Further south a turnoff takes you to the beaches of Santa María and Pabellon, where the huge rollers attract surfers.

*Continue south on **Mex 1** for 64km (40 miles) to El Rosario.*

El Rosario, Baja California Norte

8 El Rosario is divided into two parts by a stream, known as Rosario de Arriba (Upper Rosario) and Rosario de Abajo (Lower Rosario). South of the little stream is a fine, sandy beach,

ideal for a few relaxing hours. The ruins of an old **Dominican mission** can also be seen here.

*Continue southeast on **Mex 1** for 64km (40 miles) to San Fernando.*

Misión de San Fernando, Baja California Norte

9 A little oasis, this old mission was founded in 1769 by Father Junipero Serra, best known for his missionary work that began in central Mexico and continued into Baja California and far up into the American state of California. San Fernando is the only one to have been built by Franciscan priests in northern Baja California during the Colonial era. Artifacts and the adobe ruins of the original mission can be seen.

*Continue southeast on **Mex 1** through Parque Nacional Desierto Central de Baja California. Beyond El Crucero turn left to Bahía de los Angeles.*

Bahía de los Angeles, Baja California Norte

10 This leg of the journey is quite long, but the reward you will get when you catch your first glimpse of the place is worth it. The small fishing port of Bahía de los Angeles lies on the Sea of Cortés, here forming a beautiful bay ringed by rugged mountain peaks and dotted with small islands – an ideal spot for fishing. Facing the town is the Isla Angel de la Guarda. Separated from the mainland only by a canal called Las Ballenas, this island provides a shelter for the bay and offers good fishing and water sports. The small island of Isla Smith is surrounded by a tremendous variety of fish. Another island, Isla Rosa, has a bird sanctuary open to visitors; excursions can be arranged. There are a number of other fishing villages along this part of the coast where pearl fishing is common.

*Return to **Mex 1** and continue back to Ensenada. Take **Mex 3** east, then at El Chinero branch off south to San Felipe, along **Mex 5**, a total of 938km (582 miles).*

San Felipe, Baja California Norte

11 The little town of San Felipe lies on the Sea of Cortés, protected from the sea by a tall headland. It offers good deep-sea fishing. Cabrilla, corbina, sawfish and sailfish are among the many varieties to be found in its waters. Several good beaches stretch along the coastline to the southeast of the town. The port is also the scene of various sporting events, which include regattas and cycling competitions.

*Take **Mex 5** northwest for 193km (120 miles) to Mexicali.*

Mexicali, Baja California Norte

12 Mexicali, the capital of the state of Baja California Norte, is a busy border town. Customs offices are open 24 hours a day and there is continuous activity. The town was founded in 1853 and owes its name to its location, being literally

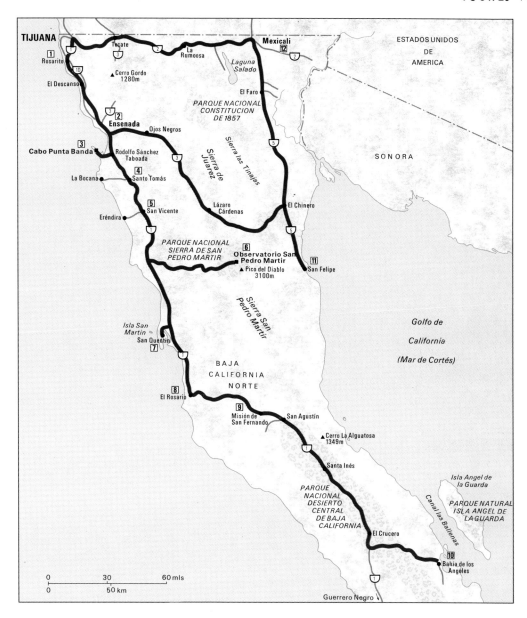

a combination of 'Mexico' and 'California'. (The US/Mexican border cuts right through the center of town, dividing Mexicali from its American sister, Calexico.)

Mexicali was a particularly popular spot for Americans during Prohibition, when not only drinking but gambling existed here. When gambling was later outlawed, the town turned to farming and developed into a prosperous commercial center.

Take time to pay a visit to the **Museo Regional** (Regional Museum of the University of Baja California), which has a display of material relating to the history of the city. The **Galeria de la Ciudad** (Art Gallery) has a collection of paintings by Mexican artists. Most of the shops, restaurants and nightclubs are near the international border. The **Centro Cívico y Comercial** (Civic Commercial Center) is an urban complex south of Mexicali, with restaurants and an attractive shopping area called the Zona Rosa (Pink Zone).

Mexican-type rodeos, called *charreadas*, usually take place on fiesta days and, during the winter, on one Sunday in each month. These present a colorful spectacle of equestrian skills, attractive costumes, and

lively singing and dancing. Winter is also the season for bullfights.

West of town a minor road leads to the Cañon de Guadalupe, a palm canyon with hot springs and camping facilities. Between the turnoffs to Cantú Palms and La Rumorosa, the same road leads up to a magnificent view of an important power station called Laguna Salada and stark, lunar-type landscapes below.

ⓘ Calle de Comercio 204

Return to Tijuana southwest on **Mex 2** *for 169km (105 miles).*

Tijuana – Rosarito **32 (20)**
Rosarito – Ensenada **79 (49)**
Ensenada – Cabo Punta la Banda **35 (22)**
Cabo Punta la Banda – Santo Tomás **43 (27)**
Santo Tomás – San Vicente **40 (25)**
San Vicente – Observatorio San Pedro Martir **122 (76)**
Observatorio San Pedro Martir – San Quintin **129 (80)**
San Quintin – El Rosario **64 (40)**
El Rosario – Misión de San Fernando **64 (40)**
Misión de San Fernando – Bahía de los Angeles **228 (141)**
Bahía de los Angeles – San Felipe **938 (582)**
San Felipe – Mexicali **193 (120)**
Mexicali – Tijuana **169 (105)**

SPECIAL TO...

2 Carnival is a very festive time in Ensenada, as with the rest of Mexico, and is celebrated with music, dancing, bands, floats, masked balls, fireworks, parades and much gaiety and color, the week before Lent.

FOR CHILDREN

12 The children will enjoy a visit to the **parque zoológico y lago** (zoological gardens and lake) located on the banks of the Río Nuevo (Nuevo River) in Mexicali.

INDEX

References to captions are in italic.

ACKNOWLEDGEMENTS

The Automobile Association would like to thank the following photographers and libraries for their help in the preparation of this book.

PETER WILSON took all the pictures in this book (AA PHOTO LIBRARY), except those listed below.

J ALLAN CASH PHOTOLIBRARY 22 Tlaxcala Cathedral.

JAMES DAVIS PHOTOGRAPHY Cover Oaxaca Cathedral.

MEXICAN MINISTRY OF TOURISM 92 Woman Sewing.

SPECTRUM COLOUR LIBRARY 4 Querétaro Plaza, 9 Mexico City, 39 Acapulco Beach, 79 Los Tules Condominiums, Puerto Vallarta, 114 Hats.

ZEFA PICTURE LIBRARY (UK) LTD 1 Round Pyramid, 3 Nr Oaxaca, 5 Sayil Palace, 6 Cancun sunset, 7 Sierra de Juarez, 12 Taxco, 24 Puebla, 34 Dancer, 36 Sierra Madre Occidental, 37 Mexico City, 38 Oaxaca, 40 Lace Maker, 50 Indian Church, Chamula, 52/3 Temple of Sun, Yucatán, 66/7 Guanajuato, 71 Theater Guadalajara, 78 Jalisco, Puerto Vallarta, 80/1 Sinaloa, 88 Sierra Madre Occidental, Rio Fuerte, 97 Veracruz, 108/9 Baja Bay.